מתנה זו נתונה לתלמידה היקרה והחשובה
לרגל סיום הלמודים
בבית שיינדל

ברכה והצלחה as you continue climbing
with great – סיעתא דשמיא -
the ladder that is
מוצב ארצה וראשו מגיעה השמימה
תלכי מחיל אל חיל

באהבה
ל.ר. מילר
בשם הנהלת בית שיינדל
כט' סיון תשפ"ג

# LIFE'S
# LADDER

# LIFE'S LADDER

## ספר עֲלֹה נַעֲלֶה

Reaching Up — Strengthening Basics in Our
*Bein Adam L'Makom*

Reaching Out — Enhancing Our Relationships
*Bein Adam L'chaveiro*

Reaching In — Developing Our Sense of
*Bein Adam L'atzmo*

## RABBI ZEV SMITH
### EDITED BY RABBI ZEV EPSTEIN

זכות לימוד התורה בספר זה
הוקדש לעילוי נשמת אבי
ר' ברוך חיים
בן אריה ליב ז"ל דיקמאן
שחל"ח ג' שבט תשע"ט

*FIRST EDITION JANUARY 2019*

*ALL RIGHTS RESERVED*

*Please send any*
*comments or questions*
*regarding this sefer to*
*asdickman1@gmail.com*
*or call 347.439.3294.*

*Transcription by Avi Noam Taub, info@transcriptionforeveryone.com*
*Editing by Mrs. L. Gruskin, 732.363.4997*
*Proofreading by Mrs. R. Gemal, 732.229.8712*
*Proofreading by Mrs. F. Badian, faigebadian@gmail.com*
*Cover design by Sruly Perl 845.694.7186*

*Printed by:*
*Machon Aleh Zayis*
*732.513.3466*

*Distributed by:*
*Israel Bookshop Publications*
*732.901.3009*

אשרי מי שגדל בתורה ועמלו בתורה
ועושה נחת רוח ליוצרו וגדל בשם טוב
ונפטר בשם טוב מן העולם (ברכות יז)

לזכר ולע"נ כבוד מו"ח הרה"ג
**רבי חיים ברוך וואלפין זצ"ל**
ראש ישיבת קארלין סטאלין

המית עצמו באהלה של תורה כל ימיו,
הרביץ תורה ויראה למעלה מיובל שנים
והעמיד תלמידים הרבה
בהנחילם תורת רבותיו גאוני קדם
ובראשם הרה"ג מו"ר רבי ראובן גראזאווסקי זצוק"ל,
וזכה להתקרב להם בקירבה יתירה,
עבד ה' מנעוריו, יראת ה' היתה אוצרו,
ובנועם מדותיו זכה שיתאהב שם שמים על ידו.

אוי מי יתן לנו תמורתו
שחל"ח ביום ט"ז מרחשון תשע"ט לפ"ק
תנצב"ה
**יעקב זאב סמיט וב"ב**

בשער הספר נבוא בזה
בברכה נאמנה למעלת כבוד הרב המחבר
**הרה"ג מוהר"ר זאב סמיט שליט"א**
יהא ה' בעזרו לעשות חיל ביתר שאת ועוז
במלאכת הקודש ובהרבצת תורתו והוראתו בישראל
ויפוצו מעיינות חכמתו חוצה,
למען דעת את הדרך ילכו בה ואת המעשה אשר יעשון,
מתוך בריות גופא ונהורא מעליא ואורך ימים ושנים טובות,
ונזכה בקרוב לחזות בשוב ה' את שיבת ציון.
המברכים מעומקא דליבא,
**ר' זכרי' סנטר וכל משפחת סנטר**

❦

Dedicated by
**Rabbi Zecharia Senter,**
**the Senter family,**
and the entire staff of
**KOF-K Kosher Supervision**

❦

מוקדש לעילוי נשמות
הגאון ר' **משה אהרן** בן ר' **ישראל פאלייעוו** ז"ל
ר' **דוד** בן ר' **יצחק משה רוזנבוים** ז"ל
ר' **אהרן דוב** בן ר' **דוד רוזנבוים** ז"ל
ר' **צבי אריה** בן ר' **אהרן דוב רוזנבוים** ז"ל
ר' **יעקב צבי** בן ר' **דוד רוזנבוים** ז"ל

# TABLE OF CONTENTS

# SECTION 2 – REACHING OUT

*Enhancing Our Relationships*
*Bein Adam L'chaveiro*

# SECTION 3 – REACHING IN

*DEVELOPING OUR SENSE OF
BEIN ADAM L'ATZMO*

# Acknowledgments

בס"ד

The completion of this *sefer* grants me the opportunity to express my *hakaras hatov* to some of the many to whom I am indebted.

My heart overflows with gratitude to the *Ribono Shel Olam* for granting me the privilege of learning His *Torah hakedoshah* and sharing it with His precious children. ‏אִילוּ פִינוּ מָלֵא שִׁירָה כַּיָם....

I am truly fortunate that this *sefer* was edited by Rabbi Zev Epstein. He did a masterful job in conveying the message, "‏עָלֹה נַעֲלֶה וכו' כִּי‏ ‏יָכוֹל נוּכַל לָהּ‏ — *Yes, you can and will do it!*" I am confident that the Torah world will reap much benefit from this rising star.

A special note of thanks to Camp Ohr Shraga, Yeshivas Novominsk, Mesivta Shalom Shachne, Irgun Shiurei Torah, Dirshu, and Project Chazak of the Chofetz Chaim Heritage Foundation for allowing me to be a part of their *avodas hakodesh*. The *shiurim* in this *sefer* were originally delivered under the auspices of these fine *mosdos haTorah*.

I never cease to be amazed by Rabbi Elozar Baruch Bald, *menahel* of Irgun Shiurei Torah, whose total devotion to *harbatzas Torah* is an inspiration. May he continue to merit the *brachah* of "‏הָעוֹבֵד ה' זוֹכֶה וְרוֹאֶה‏ ‏עוֹלָמוֹ בְּחַיָּיו, שֶׁיֵּשׁ לוֹ שִׂמְחָה גְדוֹלָה מֵמִצְוָה עַצְמָהּ עַצְמָהּ שֶׁזּוֹכֶה לַעֲשׂוֹתוֹ‏."

I owe an eternal debt of gratitude to Yeshiva Torah Vodaath for being my "home away from home" for so many years. Words cannot describe the profound impact that the beloved *rosh yeshivah*, Hagaon Harav Avroham Pam *zatzal* had on my life. He lovingly gave me so much of his precious time, and his imprint can be felt in every page of this *sefer*. I am forever grateful to his "*lieblings*," R' Berish and R' Moshe Fuchs, for all that they have done throughout the years. ‏יְשַׁלֵּם ד' שְׂכָרָם‏.

Some people personify ‏אַשְׁרֵי מִי שֶׁעֲמָלוֹ בַּתּוֹרָה‏. Others exemplify the words of Rav Chaim Volozhiner, ‏הָאָדָם לֹא לְעַצְמוֹ נִבְרָא רַק לְהוֹעִיל לַאֲחֵרִינִי‏. Somehow, Rabbi Shlomie Dickman is able to do both, simultaneously. His devotion to Torah and to Klal Yisrael is remarkable. May he and his *chashuve* family continue to see much *brachah* and *hatzlachah*.

I am forever grateful to my esteemed parents for their boundless love and devotion to our family. The credit for this *sefer* is truly theirs. With great devotion and wisdom, my esteemed mother-in-law continues to be the crown of her illustrious family. May they all enjoy many more years of good health and *nachas*.

No words can express my full appreciation to my wife for being the עֲקֶרֶת הַבַּיִת in every sense of the words. Her extraordinary devotion to Torah learning is what made this *sefer* possible. שֶׁלִּי וְשֶׁלָּכֶם שֶׁלָּה הוּא. May we continue to share much *nachas* from our precious children and grandchildren.

Yaakov Zev Smith
Chanukah 5779

# Editor's Foreword

On the porch of a bungalow at the edge of Camp Ohr Shraga, in the Catskill Mountain region of New York, Rav Zev Smith is hard at work. He "labors in the words of Torah," as he prepares *shmuessen* to be delivered to the hundreds of *bnei Torah* gathered together in this seasonal *makom Torah*. His formidable task is made somewhat easier by the idyllic setting, by the beauty of Hashem's world that surrounds him.

Rav Smith's *shiurim* deal with all aspects of *avodas Hashem*, and enlighten and enrich his *talmidim*. In each *shiur*, with great erudition and insight, Rav Smith brings together Torah sources and *ma'amarei Chazal* on the given topic, thus crafting each *shiur* into a veritable "*kol bo*" of information. Always focused on applying the Torah to daily life, these *shiurim* give his *talmidim* practical advice. And with his trademark warmth, wit, and storehouse of stories, his *shiurim* are always extremely popular.

At summer's end, Rav Smith brings his Torah teachings "מִן הָהָר אֶל הָעָם" — from the mountain to the people." Back home in New York City, Rav Smith delivers his *shiurim* to the *talmidim* of Yeshivas Novominsk and Mesivta Shalom Shachne, and to broader audiences during speaking engagements arranged under the auspices of the organizations of Irgun Shiurei Torah, Dirshu, Hakhel, and others.

Recently, Rav Smith recorded a distilled version of these *shiurim* for the Chofetz Chaim Heritage Foundation's Chazak Hotline. This book is a collection of edited transcripts of many of these wonderful audio *shiurim*. (If you wish to listen to the original *shiurim*, a chart following this foreword gives instructions as to how to access the audio files over the telephone through the Chazak Hotline.)

The messages contained in the following *shiurim* are the timeless messages of the Torah. It is hoped that these written renderings will allow Rav Smith to communicate his Torah teachings to an ever-widening audience.

While writing the book, Rav Smith's sensitivity to his fellow Jews was extended to his readership. Since each *shiur* is 30-40 minutes long, he instructed me to break down the *shiurim* with subheadings. Thus, in the book, each *shiur* can be "picked up and put down" and every individual can read and absorb the lessons at his own pace.

It was an immeasurably enriching experience to be able to consult with Rav Smith while writing this precious *sefer*, and, during the summer months, to "skip over" to Ohr Shraga to meet with him personally and discuss his teachings.

The *Mesilas Yesharim* (chapter 3) gives a classic *mashal* of a royal garden maze, fashioned from high walls of shrubbery. While in the maze the "players" cannot see the path to the building in the center, but one who has already arrived there can go up onto the roof and guide the others. Rav Smith is truly *"no'eh doresh, v'noeh mekayem"* — the living embodiment of his teachings — and the effect of his personal *avodas Hashem* is evident upon him. When speaking with him, one has a sense of assurance that he is listening to "the man on the roof" standing above the field, and directing those below as to how to successfully climb Life's Ladder. His message is always "Yes! You can do it." עָלֹה נַעֲלֶה וכו' כִּי יָכוֹל נוּכַל לָהּ (*Bamidbar* 13:30).

On a personal note, I found Rav Smith's scholarship to be matched only by his humility. He treated me with warmth and affection, and accorded me the honor of a colleague. But I was not fooled; I knew that I was being awarded the privilege to be counted among his *talmidim*.

My thanks to Artscroll/Mesorah Publications for granting permission for their *Shas* and other *sefarim* to be used as the source for many of the translations in this *sefer*.

I would be remiss not to mention Rabbi Shlomie Dickman — whose grace and good nature are matched only by his industriousness and persistence. I take the liberty of thanking him on behalf of today's English-speaking readership (a group in which I am also included) for producing another fine English *sefer* to help us better our *avodas Hashem*.

*Yeyasher kochacha!*

Zev Epstein
Fallsburg, NY
Erev Sukkos, 5779

*To access the audio recordings of the articles in this sefer, call the Chazak Hotline at 718.258.2008, press 4 for chizuk and emunah shiurim, and then press 2 for Rabbi Smith's shiurim.*

# REACHING UP

## STRENGTHENING BASICS IN OUR
## BEIN ADAM L'MAKOM

# שער
# בין אדם למקום


לזכר נשמות

אלימלך בן יוסף ז"ל

גיטל בת אשר אנשיל ע"ה

שמעון בן משה שמואל ז"ל


הונצח ע"י ר' יוסף אשר אנשיל

ורעיתו רלה וויינרעב נ"י

There is a well-known expression, "You are what you eat." However, it is more accurate to say, "You are what you *daven*."

We have the privilege to *daven* three times a day. The *sefer Kuzari* (3:5) comments that just as a person eats three meals a day for his physical sustenance, so too, he must *daven* three times a day for his spiritual sustenance. Shacharis gives us energy for the morning, Minchah keeps us going through the afternoon, and Ma'ariv nourishes us for the night. The three daily *tefillos* help us succeed throughout the day.

We are what we *daven*.

## ᏫᎡ Wherever You Go

The *Yerushalmi* (*Brachos* 9:1) relates the following story:

A boatload of people set sail across the sea. The seamen and the passengers were all non-Jews, except for one lone Jewish passenger, a young child. Out on the high seas, a raging storm developed and engulfed the boat, threatening the lives of all aboard.

The people began to cry out to their gods, but to no avail. The situation seemed hopeless, and it appeared that they would all drown. Just then the people noticed the Jewish child, sitting by himself.

"What are you doing?" they cried. "Get up and pray to your G-d! We heard that He listens to prayers!"

The boy *davened* a very sincere *tefillah* and miraculously the storm subsided.

The *Yerushalmi* continues:

The boat arrived at the next port and docked. All the people disembarked to go to the marketplaces, but the Jewish child remained in his place. The non-Jewish passengers approached him.

"Why do you remain behind? Why don't you get off like the rest of us?"

The child responded meekly, "What do you want from me? I am all alone, forsaken and forlorn. I don't know where to go or what to buy."

The reaction of the non-Jewish passengers is truly amazing. The boy's behavior struck a raw nerve after their harrowing ordeal on the ship. The passengers chastised the child.

"*You* are forsaken? *You* are forlorn? *We* are forsaken and forlorn! We cried out to our gods, but they couldn't help us. But you, a member of the Jewish People, how fortunate you are! You have a G-d that is so close and is listening to your prayers."

The non-Jews continued to reprimand the boy. "To say that you are alone is a disgrace to your G-d! כָּל אֲהֵיין דְּאַתְּ אָזֵיל אֱלָהָךְ עִמָּךְ — *Wherever you go, your G-d is with you.*"

What is the lesson of this story?

Of course, the story teaches us the power of a simple heartfelt prayer. Look how this boy's *davening* caused the storm to subside. But the real lesson of the story — the beauty of the story — is contained in the words of the non-Jewish passengers, which capture the essence of *tefillah*: "כָּל אֲהֵיין דְּאַתְּ אָזֵיל אֱלָהָךְ עִמָּךְ — *Wherever you go, your G-d is with you.*" A Yid is never alone.

As the *Yerushalmi* points out, the non-Jews' sentiment is actually found in a *pasuk* in *Parshas Va'eschanan* (*Devarim* 4:7): כִּי מִי גוֹי גָּדוֹל אֲשֶׁר לוֹ אֱלֹקִים קְרֹבִים אֵלָיו כַּה' אֱלֹקֵינוּ בְּכָל קָרְאֵנוּ אֵלָיו — *For which is a great nation that has a G-d Who is close to us, as is Hashem, our G-d, whenever we call Him?*

Wherever we are, in whatever situation we find ourselves, a Yid is never alone. A Yid is never helpless, and a Yid is never hopeless. Wherever we go, Hashem is there waiting for us, and for our *tefillos*.

## ❧ A Listening Ear

The *pasuk* in *Tehillim* (102:1), referring to *davening*, says: וְלִפְנֵי ה' יִשְׁפֹּךְ שִׂיחוֹ — *and pours forth his supplications before Hashem.*

When a simple Jew *davens* — when you or I *daven* — we are described as talking "before Hashem."

The *Yerushalmi* (ibid.) goes even further and gives the following description of how close Hashem is to us when we *daven*:

כְּאָדָם הַמֵּשִׂיחַ בְּאוֹזֶן חֲבֵירוֹ וְהוּא שׁוֹמֵעַ — *As a person who speaks into the ear of his friend who is listening,*

וְכִי יֵשׁ אֱלוֹהַּ קָרוֹב מִזֶּה — *is there a god closer than this,*

שֶׁהוּא קָרוֹב לַבְּרִיוֹת כְּפֶה לַאוֹזֶן — *that He is close to people like from the mouth to the ear.*

The *Mesillas Yesharim* (ch. 19) describes *tefillah* in a similar fashion: one *davens* the way one talks to a friend who is listening and wants to help. I would be afraid to describe it that way, but this is what the *Mesillas Yesharim* writes.

*Davening* is, simply, talking to Hashem.

The students of the Mirrer Yeshivah often marveled when they watched their illustrious *rosh yeshivah*, Rav Chaim Shmulevitz, learning. Occasionally, Rav Chaim encountered a difficulty; he couldn't understand something he was learning. He would rise from his seat, looking very disturbed, and pace back and forth. Finally, he would approach the *aron hakodesh* and he would *daven*. Using his own words, he would pray that Hashem enlighten him. Then he would sit down and continue learning. Suddenly he would smile; he understood the *pshat!* He would return to the *aron hakodesh* and say, "*Ah dahnk, Ribono Shel Olam!* Thank You, Ribono Shel Olam!"

Rav Chaim had a rapport with Hashem. He understood the unique gift of *davening*. He knew that if someone has a need, he can turn to Hashem at any time, not only during the three set *tefillos* of the day.

Once, Rav Chaim was *davening* at the Kosel and the students overheard him saying, "*Ich vil **du** Ribono Shel Olam, nisht a shaliach.* I want **You**, Hashem; I don't want a messenger." The *bachurim* did not know what their *rebbi* was referring to with these words, but they knew this: Rav Chaim had an ongoing relationship with Hashem. Whenever he had a need, whether it was big or small, he knew that he had Whom to turn to. That is the beauty of *davening*.

Similarly, the Brisker Rav was often heard mumbling under his breath to Hashem. While learning, or when making a difficult decision, or when he was advising others, the Rav would softly utter the words, לִישׁוּעָתְךָ קִוִּיתִי ה'. "Hashem, I need a *yeshuah*; I need help!"

*Davening* is not limited to Shacharis, Minchah, and Ma'ariv. Whenever we have needs, we can always turn to Hashem to solve our problems.

## To My Father in Heaven

Rav Yaakov Kamenetsky used to recount a remarkable story about an unusual *shidduch* that happened in prewar Europe.

There was an orphan girl who was noticeably short, named Shaina Miriam, living in the town of Mir. Although she was a special girl and had a good job as a librarian in the city, she could not find a *shidduch*. All her friends were already married with children, but being an orphan coupled with her physical disadvantage, Shaina Miriam received no suitable marriage offers.

One day, feeling desperate, Shaina Miriam had an idea — she would write a letter of *tefillah* to the Ribono Shel Olam. In the letter, she poured out her feelings, her desperation, and her hopelessness.

"Ribono Shel Olam! Please send me a *shidduch*! I want someone who is going to learn Your Torah, a boy who loves learning. I will help him with the money that I saved; it will only be for his learning. I know You, Hashem — only You — can help me!"

Shaina Miriam signed her name, put the letter in an envelope, and addressed it *"L'Avi she'ba'Shamayim* — to my Father in Heaven." It was a windy day, so she went outside and threw the letter into the air. As it fluttered away she quickly turned back before seeing where it would land. In this way, she made her *hishtadlus*, her effort, to find a *shidduch*.

A little while later, two Mirrer *bachurim* were walking near the yeshivah. One of the boys noticed the letter on the ground, and bent down to pick it up, intending to return it to its owner. But this was a very strange letter. It was addressed *"L'Avi she'ba'Shamayim."* Of course, one is not allowed to open a letter addressed to someone else, but does that include a letter addressed to Hashem? The *bachur's* curiosity got the better of him. He opened the letter and read it. He was very moved by the sincerity of the girl who wrote the letter. He was impressed with her simple *emunah*, her love for Torah, and her determination to support someone in learning Torah. The *bachur* wondered if the letter writer might be a suitable *shidduch* for him. He consulted Rav Elya Baruch Kamai, *rav* and *rosh yeshivah* of Mir, who advised him to pursue the *shidduch* and the rest, as they say, is history.

The *bachur's* name was Yitzchak Yechiel Davidowitz. Although six years younger than Shaina Miriam, Yitzchak Yechiel married the orphan girl and he became great in Torah and *yiras Shamayim*. Eventually, Rav Yitzchak Yechiel became the *mashgiach* in the Minsker yeshivah. It was there that he taught and guided many *gedolim*, among them Rav Yaakov Yitzchak Ruderman and Rav Yaakov Kamenetsky.

This beautiful story contains a penetrating lesson. A Yid is never alone. A Yid is never helpless, and a Yid is never hopeless. The young Shaina Miriam taught us that although she lacked a physical father, nevertheless she had a *Tatte* in *Himmel* Who was anxiously waiting for her *tefillos*.

This understanding is the essence of *davening*.

A young boy on a boat is faced with a dangerous and raging storm, but he is not alone. A young orphan girl has no one to care for her, but she has Whom to turn to. When Rav Chaim Shmulevitz did not understand the *pshat* in a Gemara, or when the Brisker Rav needed a good idea, or a *psak*, they knew the secret of לִישׁוּעָתְךָ קִוִּיתִי ה'. *Tefillah* is an opportunity for each of us to ask for all our needs — great and small.

## ⟳ The Little Things

An *adam gadol* was once *davening*, and those around him overheard him repeating the word "*ozeret*." Now that is a strange word. "*Ozer* — Helper" would be an understandable word to insert into *davening*; that word already appears many times in the *siddur*: "*melech ozer*," "*ozer dalim*," "*ki ein ozer*." But what does "*ozeret*" mean?

Someone had the courage to approach him and ask: "Why was the Rebbi repeatedly saying '*ozeret*'?"

The *rebbi* answered, "I will tell you. My wife has a cleaning lady (*ozeret*) that she is very happy with. The *ozeret* is also happy to work for us, but she recently mentioned that certain things have come up, and she may have to leave us. I know how important it is to my wife to have a good cleaning lady, so I *daven* that the *ozeret* should be able to continue working in our home."

I once told this story publicly and someone asked me, "Are you really allowed to *daven* for a cleaning lady?" I realized from that question why many of us are not really *davening* properly — we do not understand what *tefillah* is all about. We do not comprehend that *davening* is for each and every one of our needs — important or trivial (see Rabbeinu Yonah on *Mishlei* 3:6). After all, who else should we turn to when we need something? Isn't Hashem the *kol yachol*? Of course, we must perform our *hishtadlus* to attain our needs. That is why we invest our effort; that is why we make phone calls, and try to find the right person to help us. But ultimately it is all in the *yad Hashem*. That is what *davening* is all about.

Sometimes, of course, our *tefillos* are not answered in the way we hoped they would be. Our *emunah* dictates that Hashem knows what is best for us, and He has His reasons for not fulfilling any particular request. But that does not change the fact that Hashem listens to every *tefillah*, just sometimes the answer may be "No," or "Not right now."

## ❧ The *Ish Matzliach*

How does one achieve *hatzlachah* in his life? More important, how can one become an *ish matzliach*, so that everything he does is successful? Yosef Hatzaddik taught us the secret.

The Torah (*Bereishis* 39:2) refers to Yosef Hatzaddik as an *ish matzliach*. Whatever he touched was successful. What made Yosef the very embodiment of *hatzlachah*? The Torah provides the answer (ibid. 3):

וַיַּרְא אֲדֹנָיו כִּי ה' אִתּוֹ וְכֹל אֲשֶׁר הוּא עֹשֶׂה ה' מַצְלִיחַ בְּיָדוֹ — *His master perceived that Hashem was with him, and whatever he did Hashem made succeed in his hand.*

It was so apparent that Yosef and *hatzlachah* were one and the same that even his master Potiphar noticed this. In fact, Potiphar saw even more — he saw "*that Hashem was with him*" always. Evidently, the Midrash (*Tanchuma* 8) is bothered by this. How did a *rasha* like Potiphar see Hashem? Potiphar certainly did not have *gilui Shechinah*. What exactly did he see?

The *Tanchuma* offers an incredible explanation, which I believe teaches us the secret of the *ish matzliach*:

Potiphar noticed that whenever Yosef was working — when he was doing household chores, when he was preparing supper — he was mumbling under his breath. Potiphar was very concerned. He asked Yosef, "What are you doing? Are you bringing *kishuf*, witchcraft, into my house?" Yosef answered, "No, not at all. I am praying. When I prepare your supper, I want the supper to be tasty, so I pray that my cooking should be just right. When I take care of the household, I pray that things should run smoothly..."

Whatever Yosef did, he first prayed to Hashem for a positive outcome. Thus, when the *pasuk* says that Potiphar saw "*that Hashem was with him*," it means that he saw that: לֹא הָיָה שְׁמוֹ שֶׁל הַקָּדוֹשׁ בָּרוּךְ הוּא זָז מִפִּיו — *The Name of Heaven never left his mouth.*

Whatever Yosef did, he *davened* first. He was an *ish matzliach* because he was an *ish mispallel*.

Some of us might wonder, "Well, if I were in a life-threatening situation, of course I would *daven*. But should I *daven* before I make a business or *shidduch* decision?" The answer is — yes, absolutely. That is what *tefillah* is for. *Davening* is what gives us *hatzlachah* in all our endeavors, big or small. Of course, *davening* is a mitzvah, a privilege, and an expression of *emunah*. But *davening* is also a tool that grants us success in all that we do.

The *Sefer Hachinuch* (mitzvah 433) describes *davening* as follows: Hashem has everything that we need, and He gave us the key to access His storehouse of *brachah*. That key is the wonderful gift of *davening*.

In any endeavor, we must do our *hishtadlus*; we have to invest our best physical and intellectual effort to succeed. We also must do a spiritual act of *hishtadlus*, namely, *tefillah*. *Tefillah* is the most important part of our *hishtadlus*, and it is vital to internalize this idea (see *Niddah* 70b). People who do not realize this, fail to recognize the true meaning of *tefillah*. Many people work hard and strive for success, but are unaware that the most important ingredient of *hatzlachah* lies in *tefillah*. Hashem fulfills our needs based on our *davening*. *Hatzlachah* in what we do — in *anything and everything* we do — is sourced in our *davening*. Indeed, you are what you *daven*.

## ❧ Just Another *Meshulach*

I once heard a very insightful story:

A fundraiser was collecting money for a worthy organization. He contacted a potential donor who agreed to allow him to come to his office and explain the importance of the cause. When he arrived at the office, the secretary directed him, "Go down that hallway, turn right, and enter the second door on the left."

The fundraiser walked down the hallway, but became confused as to which room he was to enter. *I think she meant this room*, he thought, as he entered a tastefully appointed office. He found himself facing a bearded man in a black suit. The man gave the impression of being a rabbi, not a wealthy businessman, but the fundraiser nevertheless assumed that he was indeed the owner of the business.

He explained to the man the importance of the cause he was collecting for. "Please help me!" he tearfully concluded.

The man looked at him kindly and said, "*Antschuldig! Ich redt nisht kein English, ich kum fun Yerushalayim* — Excuse me, but I don't speak English; I am from Yerushalayim."

The fundraiser then realized that he had walked into the wrong room, and had just cried his heart out, and pleaded his case, to another *meshulach* who was also waiting to see the owner of the business!

This story is a beautiful parable for a serious mistake that people make. So much of our time is spent trying to meet our needs through all sorts of *hishtadlus* — calling people, meeting people… But actually we are just talking to another *meshulach*. The most truly effective *hishtadlus* is to talk to "the owner of the business Himself."

## ❧ A Flood of Mercy

Rav Pam used to say that people do not *daven* properly because they do not appreciate the true gift of *tefillah*. As he would put it: "*Davening iz nisht ah mabul fun verter* — Davening is not a flood of words; *davening iz ah mabul fun rachamim* — davening is a flood of mercy." Hashem is waiting to shower upon us a flood of compassion and goodness if we *daven* properly. One who views his *davening* as a *mabul* of *rachamim* that is the key to our needs, will *daven* differently.

\* \* \*

The *sefer Iyun Tefillah* is the written version of Rav Schwab's remarkable *shiurim* on *tefillah*. In the preface, his son Rav Moshe Schwab writes something that displays his father's rare and precious attitude toward *davening*.

For many years, Rav Schwab kept a diary. In one of his entries, he recorded the passing of a member of his community. He wrote about the *niftar*: "He was privileged to *daven* with tears. I was envious of him." Rav Schwab then writes that he was never jealous of any other individual except this man, because he *davened* with tears.

Rav Schwab was jealous of someone who *davened* with emotion, because he realized that that person carried the solution to all his needs. One who *davens* sincerely is addressing a listening Father, eager to help. This man was a true *ish matzliach*, worthy of being envied.

\* \* \*

I once spoke to a *ba'al teshuvah* who was very excited about the beauty of his newly discovered *Yiddishkeit*. He told me that for him the most amazing thing about Judaism is prayer.

"Can you imagine?" he said. "Little, old me — I can talk to G-d whenever I want!"

What a beautiful description of *davening*. Little, old me — you and I — can talk to Hashem whenever we so desire.

\* \* \*

Rav Chatzkel Levenstein wrote in a letter (*sefer Ohr Yechezkal* vol. 1 letter 286) that one attains success in his *avodas hatefillah* when he realizes that he is not *davening* merely to fulfill the mitzvah, but rather to fulfill his needs. He would interpret the Mishnah (*Avos* 2:13): אַל תַּעַשׂ תְּפִלָּתְךָ קֶבַע — *Do not make your davening something that you have to do;* do not *daven* because you must, אֶלָּא רַחֲמִים וְתַחֲנוּנִים — *rather, make your davening* a plea for mercy, *daven* because you understand that you are privileged to beseech Hashem for your needs.

* * *

Someone with problems once poured out his heart to Rav Shach. He confided that he was depressed because of his problems and he felt helpless. He asked Rav Shach what he should do.

Rav Shach opened a siddur and said, "Look!" as he pointed with great excitement and enthusiasm. "Look at the *Shemoneh Esrei*. We say, over and over, '*Baruch Atah Hashem.*' *Atah* means You. Do you hear that? We talk to Hashem directly, in the first person, 'You!' How can a person be depressed when he has the privilege to say "*Baruch Atah*," and to talk directly to Hashem?"

In one *Shemoneh Esrei*, we say *Atah* thirty-three times. That is what *davening* is all about. It is a *mabul* of *rachamim* which can help us with anything we might need.

## 🌀 Make Your List

Let us apply this practically. Here are some suggestions to help us improve our *tefillah*:

Make a mental list of your needs as they arise — a deal that you would like to see completed; a customer that you would like to attract; a cleaning lady that you need; success on a test that you are taking; *hatzlachah* in learning; a *shidduch* offer that you are seeking; something that one of your children needs — the list goes on and on. Then *daven* for those specific needs in the next *tefillah*. A *tefillah* for a personal need can be inserted into the *Shemoneh Esrei* in the corresponding *brachah* (e.g. *R'fa'einu* for a sick person) or in *Shema Koleinu*, or it can be recited at the end of the *Shemoneh Esrei*, in *Elokai Netzor*.

Aside from the fact that you will be *davening* for your needs, it will also train you to appreciate the value and function of *tefillah*. We all have many needs, and we must remember that there is nothing too big or too small for Hashem. Yosef was an *ish matzliach* because he was an *ish mispallel*. He realized that whatever he did he needed to *daven* for its success. Let us train ourselves to emulate him.

It is also a wonderful idea to educate our children to develop this attitude. When they have a request, tell them, "Let's take out a Tehillim — or let's have it in mind by the next *tefillah*." Before a big test, they should *daven* that they succeed. Of course, they must study for the test, but teach them to understand that *davening* is an integral part of their success.

## I Can't Wait

If *davening* appears to us like a *mabul* of *verter*, then it has little meaning. But if we train ourselves to appreciate *tefillah*, if we see the *mabul shel rachamim* in it, it will be a most gratifying experience. Let us cherish each of the thirty-three "*baruch Atah*s" that we say in every *Shemoneh Esrei*.

The following story illustrates this idea beautifully.

Rav Shlomo Wolbe, author of *sefer Alei Shur*, always *davened* Minchah at the earliest possible time. Since his yeshivah would *daven* Minchah later, Rav Wolbe would *daven* in a different yeshivah. This was a puzzling practice because on most days Rav Wolbe was in his yeshivah during Minchah time, and could have *davened* then, thereby avoiding the special trip to the early Minchah.

He was once asked why he did this and the answer he gave was amazing. "I *daven* Shacharis at 6:30 in the morning. Do you think that I can wait twelve hours to talk to my *Tatte* in *Himmel* again? I can't wait. I just have to *daven* as early as possible."

Rav Wolbe saw *davening* in all its beauty, with all the potential it contains.

We must strive to improve our *davening* — not necessarily by making longer or louder *tefillos*, but by nurturing our appreciation for *davening*. We must heighten our awareness of the essence of *tefillah*, and internalize the thought that "we are what we *daven*."

## We Are What We *Daven*

One final thought.

We all know the inspiring story of Chana. The prospect of her having a child seemed hopeless. In fact, her righteous husband, Elkana, comforted her by saying that he is to her like ten children — perhaps a subtle message to accept the situation as is.

But Chana believed a Yid is never hopeless. A Yid is never helpless; so she *davened*. Oh, did she *daven*! In fact, many important *halachos* of *tefillah* are gleaned from her supplication (see *Brachos* 31). As her reward, Chana was privileged to be the mother of Shmuel Hanavi who was equal to Moshe and Aharon (ibid.).

The story of Chana remains a wellspring of inspiration for those who feel hopeless and helpless. It is most fitting that it is read as the *haftorah* on Rosh Hashanah.

Consider this question: What would have happened if Chana would have accepted her prognosis and not *davened* for the seemingly impossible? I have no doubt that she would not be the paradigm of *tefillah* or the eternal *chizuk* in *tefillah*. And there would not have been a Shmuel Hanavi…

Indeed, we are what we *daven*!

# THE KING AND I
*Appreciating Shabbos*

The Gemara (*Kesubos* 103a) relates that after Rebbi Yehudah Hanasi was *niftar*, he would return home every Shabbos to be with his family.

Rav Pam made the following observation about this remarkable Gemara:

Who can imagine the *lichtigeh Gan Eden*, the exalted, glorious *Olam Haba*, of Rebbe Yehudah Hanasi? And yet every week he departed Gan Eden in order to spend Shabbos in this world. It seems that Rebbe Yehudah Hanasi enjoyed Shabbos more than Gan Eden.

In the Shabbos *zemiros*, we sing, מֵעֵין עוֹלָם הַבָּא, יוֹם שַׁבָּת מְנוּחָה. Shabbos is described as a taste, a semblance, of *Olam Haba*. But if Rebbe Yehudah Hanasi was willing to give up *Olam Haba* for Shabbos, then obviously Shabbos can be even greater than *Olam Haba*.

It is no wonder, then, that Hashem told Moshe Rabbeinu (*Beitzah* 16a):

מַתָּנָה טוֹבָה יֵשׁ לִי בְּבֵית גְּנָזַי וְשַׁבָּת שְׁמָהּ — *I have a wonderful gift in My storehouse of treasures whose name is Shabbos.*

Hashem describes Shabbos as a wonderful gift.

What is it that makes Shabbos so extraordinary? What is the nature of this wonderful gift that we have received from Hashem?

## ✺ Refresher Course

I once met a cousin of mine, a man in his fifties. He told me, "You are not going to believe this, but I am back in school!"

He was right; I did not believe it. Why was a fifty-year-old back in school? He explained: His company sent him for a refresher course, to update him on new developments in his field. Companies spend a significant amount of money for their employees to take these courses. They know that their employees will be more efficient and productive if they are up-to-date with the latest technology and advancements in their line of work. By investing in their employees' courses, they will be enhancing the quality of their work in the long run.

We *Yidden* also need refresher courses in areas of *Yiddishkeit*. Perhaps, we should have a refresher course reminding us of the true gift of Shabbos.

Shabbos comprises almost 20 percent of our lives. Between *hadlakas neiros* and Havdalah, Shabbos itself is close to twenty-six hours. When we factor in the Shabbos preparations, cleaning up after Shabbos, and *melaveh malkah*, we spend close to 20 percent of our week busy with Shabbos. Are we capitalizing on this wonderful gift?

We say in *Kabbalas Shabbos*: לִקְרַאת שַׁבָּת לְכוּ וְנֵלְכָה, כִּי הִיא מְקוֹר הַבְּרָכָה — *Toward Shabbos we shall go, for she is the source of our blessing.* Shabbos is the source, the wellspring, of blessing from which all of our weekday success is derived. As the *Zohar* (2:88) phrases it: כָּל בִּרְכָאן דִּלְעֵילָא וְתַתָּאָה בְּיוֹמָא שְׁבִיעָאָה תַּלְיִין — *All the brachos of the week are dependent on Shabbos.*

We must take advantage of this unique gift. Let us learn about Shabbos so we can make the most of it. There's so much *brachah* contained within it. To fully describe the greatness of Shabbos would indeed require a full-length book, authored by someone much greater than myself. Nevertheless, I would like to discuss a few important points that can enhance our *avodah* on this holy day.

## ❧ A Day Spent with Hashem

Rav Shimshon Pincus once asked a thought-provoking question. Every Yom Tov has its identity, with its own unique characteristics. Sukkos is *zman simchaseinu*; Pesach is *zman cheiruseinu*; and Shavuos is *zman Mattan Torahseinu*. If we would have to describe Shabbos, what would we say? Shabbos is *zman* what? What is the distinctiveness of Shabbos?

Suggested Rav Pincus: Shabbos is a *yom im Hakadosh Baruch Hu* — a day spent with Hashem. That is the essence of Shabbos.

Allow me explain: The Gemara (*Shabbos* 119b) says that whoever recites "וַיְכֻלּוּ" on Friday night, נַעֲשֶׂה שׁוּתָּף עִם הקב"ה בְּמַעֲשֵׂה בְּרֵאשִׁית — *becomes a partner with Hashem in creation.* That is one objective of Shabbos, to strengthen our *emunah* in Hashem's creation of the world.

Then, after we recite the passage of וַיְכֻלּוּ, we recite Kiddush that identifies Shabbos as *zecher l'Yetzias Mitzrayim*. Thus, Shabbos is also a restatement of our belief in the exodus from Mitzrayim, and this complements the aspect of *zecher l'Ma'aseh Bereishis*. *Ma'aseh Bereishis* and *Yetzias Mitzrayim* are the two cornerstones — the two wellsprings — of our *emunah*. Shabbos is a "double dose" of *emunah*; a day that is meant to re-energize our *emunah chushis* in Hashem and all His wonders.

The Ramban (*Shemos* 20:8), the *Chinuch* (mitzvah 32), and the Radak (*Yirmiyahu* 17:24) all say that Shabbos is a key ingredient of our *emunah*.

## ℘ Hilchos Shabbos

The more one learns about Shabbos, the more one comprehends how accurate it is that Shabbos is *yom im Hakadosh Baruch Hu*. Here are a few examples:

\* The Gemara teaches that a non-Jew may not keep Shabbos; in fact, a non-Jew who keeps Shabbos is liable to the death penalty. Why is that? A non-Jew, of course, is not *obligated* to keep Shabbos, but why is he *forbidden* to do so? One is allowed to perform a mitzvah that he is not required to do. For example, many mitzvos are not obligatory for women, but, nevertheless, women may perform these mitzvos.

The Midrash (*Shemos* 25:1, *Devarim* 1:21) answers: A non-Jew who keeps Shabbos is an interloper; he is compared to someone who intrudes on the king and queen in the middle of a private and intimate conversation. Shabbos is a day בֵּינִי וּבֵין בְּנֵי יִשְׂרָאֵל, a day that Hashem spends privately with Klal Yisrael. Non-Jews may not interrupt, and may not disturb that intimacy.

\* There are numerous *halachos* regarding proper speech on Shabbos. For example, on Shabbos it is forbidden to talk of mundane weekday matters. Why? The *Zohar* (*Beshalach* 47b) explains that when sitting with the king, we discuss only important topics. It is disrespectful to the king to focus on mundane, everyday matters.

\* The Brisker Rav (*Parshas Yisro*) points out numerous parallels between the *kabbalas Pnei HaShechinah* and *Kabbalas Shabbos*. Evidently, as we accept Shabbos we are preparing to spend a day with Hashem.

The Brisker Rav would usually *daven* Minchah early in the afternoon; therefore, on Fridays, he would not necessarily go to shul before Shabbos. Often, he would be at home when Shabbos began.

One Friday afternoon, the Brisker Rav was at home speaking in learning with a visitor. When Shabbos began, the Brisker Rav excused himself, stood up, put on his hat, and recited *Kabbalas Shabbos.*

His visitor asked, "Does *Kabbalas Shabbos* have the status of a *tefillah* such that one is required to wear a hat when he recites it?"

The Brisker Rav answered incredulously, "When one goes out to greet the king, doesn't he put on his hat?" (see *Shabbos* 119).

The point of the story is not that the Brisker Rav wore his hat, but *why* he wore his hat. His *Kabbalas Shabbos* was genuine; he was going to greet the King. We too can utilize *Kabbalas Shabbos* to draw Hashem into our lives in a more tangible way. The way to appreciate Shabbos is to experience and explore the greatness of spending one day a week with the King of all kings.

## ✒ A Shabbos Yid

The Gemara (*Shabbos* 119b) teaches us that when a person returns home from shul on Friday night, two *malachim* escort him. This is the source of our *minhag* to sing the *Shalom Aleichem.* We welcome the *malachim* into our home, "בּוֹאֲכֶם לְשָׁלוֹם — *Come in peace.*"

However, the Gemara (*Brachos* 60b) says that before a person enters the bathroom he should recite a specific phrase, because every person is constantly accompanied by *malachim*, and he must apologize and take leave of them before entering the bathroom. The *Shulchan Aruch* (3:1) rules that this phrase is no longer recited, because we are not on the level to merit being escorted by *malachim* and it would be presumptuous (יוּהֲרָא) to recite it (see *Beis Yosef* ibid.).

The question is obvious. If we no longer have the privilege of being escorted by *malachim*, why do we sing *Shalom Aleichem* to welcome the *malachim*?

The answer is simple: A Jew on Shabbos is on a unique level, one that he cannot attain during the week. A Jew on Shabbos is not a simple person, he is a different person altogether. He has a *neshamah yeseirah.*

He is experiencing a day with Hashem. He is a partner with Hashem Himself.

In fact, the Rambam (*Hilchos Ma'aser* 12:1) writes, *Even an ignoramus fears the Shabbos and doesn't sin on Shabbos.* Shabbos has that uplifting potential to change even an ignoramus. He becomes a Shabbos Yid.

The Shabbos Yid is able to have two *malachim* escort him. He is able to say, "I, simple, little, old me, have two *malachim* escorting me. Greetings! שָׁלוֹם עֲלֵיכֶם מַלְאֲכֵי הַשָּׁרֵת!"

## ༺ Experiencing Shabbos

The Shabbos Yid is different because he is spending a day with Hashem. What does this mean on a practical level?

During the week, we often find ourselves in a world that is so accurately described in *Koheles* (1:2) as: הֲבֵל הֲבָלִים הַכֹּל הָבֶל — *Futility of futilities, all is futile.* We are surrounded by the hustle and bustle of a world focused on *gashmiyus*, and so alien to *ruchniyus*.

But then Shabbos arrives; we take a vacation from the emptiness of this world and we devote ourselves to Hashem. A day spent with Hashem means, on a practical level, a day spent *davening*, learning Torah, and singing praises to Hashem.

An old European Yid once told me, "In Europe, *mir hoben nisht gemacht kein leben* — we couldn't make a living; *ober mir hoben gelebt* — but we lived!" On the other hand, in America, "*Mir macht a leben* — we make a living; *ober ver lebt* — but who is really living?"

During the week, we may not have the time or the focus for true "living." But on Shabbos, there is no excuse. Then the world stops, and we do what we are meant to be doing the entire week. On Shabbos we stop making a living and we start living.

The Ramban (*Shemos* 20:8) describes Shabbos as:

יוֹם קָדוֹשׁ לְהִתְפַּנּוֹת מֵעִסְקֵי הַמַּחֲשָׁבוֹת וְהַבְלֵי הַזְּמַנִּים, וְלָתֵת בּוֹ עוֹנֶג לְנַפְשֵׁנוּ בְּדַרְכֵי ה' — *A holy day when we disconnect from mundane activities and give our neshamos a treat in the ways of Hashem.*

Sometimes, during the week, our *neshamos* are starving. But Shabbos is a day of וַאֲנִי קִרְבַת אֱלֹקִים לִי טוֹב — *For me, being close to Hashem is goodness;*

a day of צָמְאָה לְךָ נַפְשִׁי — *My soul thirsts for You.* Throughout the week, we can barely squeeze in the minimum time needed for *davening*. But when Shabbos comes, we do not even notice the longer *Pesukei D'zimra*, *Birchos Krias Shema*, or the extra *tefillah* of *Mussaf*. On Shabbos we enjoy an unhurried, meaningful *davening*.

There's an incredible *lashon* of the *Zohar* (*Tikunei Zohar* 21): תְּפִילַת שַׁבָּת אֵינָה חוֹזֶרֶת רֵיקָם — *A Shabbos tefillah never goes unanswered,*

אֶלָא מִתְקַבֶּלֶת בְּרָצוֹן כְּמוֹ תְּפִילַת עֲשֶׂרֶת יְמֵי תְּשׁוּבָה — *rather it is accepted willingly just as a tefillah during the ten days between Rosh Hashanah and Yom Kippur.*

This is part of the gift of Shabbos: even our *davening* has a special power because Hashem is close to us, just as He is during the Aseres Yemei Teshuvah.

The *Shir Shel Yom* of Shabbos is מִזְמוֹר שִׁיר לְיוֹם הַשַׁבָּת (*Tehillim* 92). The next *pasuk* says: טוֹב לְהֹדוֹת לַה' וּלְזַמֵּר לְשִׁמְךָ עֶלְיוֹן — *It is good to thank Hashem and to sing praise to Your Name, O Exalted One.*

The Radak wonders, is it only on Shabbos that it is good to praise Hashem and to sing to His Name?

The Radak answers that Shabbos is more conducive for prayer and song: כִּי הָאָדָם פָּנוּי בּוֹ מֵעִסְקֵי הָעוֹלָם — *Because a person is not preoccupied with worldly activities,*

וְנִשְׁמָתוֹ זַכָּה מִטְרֶדֶת הַגּוּף — *and his neshamah is pure, more elevated,*

מִתְעַסֶּקֶת בְּחָכְמָה וּבַעֲבוֹדַת אֱלֹקִים — *and he is able to focus on wisdom and serving Hashem.*

On Shabbos our *neshamos* are not starving; they are bursting with feelings of love of Hashem. The *davening*, the *zemiros*, and everything else express our innermost desire of the theme of the day with Hashem — טוֹב לְהֹדוֹת לַה'.

Above all else, Shabbos is an opportunity to learn more Torah, both alone and with our children. It is a time to do what we don't have enough time for during the week.

The Gemara (*Gittin* 38b) provides three reasons why wealthy *ba'alei batim* lost their wealth. One of them is because they ate their Shabbos *seudah* during the time when the public Shabbos *drashah* was being said in the *beis midrash*. Instead of attending the *shiur*, they busied themselves with their *seudas Shabbos*.

The Chafetz Chaim in *Mishnah Berurah* (290:7) notes that these *ba'alei batim* weren't wasting time. They were not engaged in idleness or unbecoming activities. On the contrary, they were engaged in the mitzvah of enjoying the required Shabbos meal. Nevertheless, fault is to be found in their actions because by so doing they infringed upon the learning time of Shabbos. Shabbos is a day when we are meant to reconnect to our learning, and these *Yidden* compromised some of that time.

The Ben Ish Chai (*Shemos*, preface year II) quotes *mekubalim* who say that Torah learning on Shabbos is a thousand times more precious than weekday learning. Can such precious moments be squandered, albeit with *seudas Shabbos*?

## ⌘ Don't Waste a Minute

The Meiri (*Shabbos* 150a) writes:

הַיוֹם כּוּלוֹ קָדוֹשׁ לַה' — *Shabbos is a day that is entirely holy to Hashem,*

וְאֵיךְ יוֹצִיא קוֹדֶשׁ קָדָשִׁים לְחוּלִין — *so how can one take something that is the "holy of holies" and place it into the realm of the mundane?*

We must not take Shabbos, the ultimate *kedushah*, and waste it.

I recall Rav Pam repeating the following Midrash (*Bereishis* 22:13) with great emotion: Adam Harishon was created on the sixth day, and sinned that same day, toward evening. He was supposed to be punished for his sin immediately, but it was already Shabbos, and Shabbos pleaded to Hashem:

"Ribono Shel Olam! Today is Shabbos! Are You going to punish Adam Harishon on my day? זוֹ הִיא — זוֹ הִיא קְדוֹשָׁתִי — *Is that my kedushah?* בְּרְכָתִי — *Is that my brachah?* Is this what you make of me? That on my day the first punishment is given? Is that the *brachah* that you planted within me, the holy day of Shabbos?"

Rav Pam would say, "Sometimes a person has to stop and think when he is doing something — זוֹ הִיא קְדוּשָׁתִי? Is this what Shabbos is all about? Is this the *brachah* of Shabbos?"

The Midrash (*Eichah* 2:4) says that a city in Eretz Yisrael named Tor Shimon was destroyed because the people of the city played ball on Shabbos. I have no doubt that the people of Tor Shimon were not being *mechallel Shabbos*. I am certain that they played indoors, or within an *eruv*, and that the ball they used was not *muktzeh* (see *Rama* 308:45, and *Ketzos Hashulchan* 110:16). So what was their grave sin? They were *mechallel "kedushas" Shabbos*; they reduced the sanctity of Shabbos. They took the lofty day of Shabbos and used it to play ball. And Shabbos cried, "זוֹ הִיא קְדוּשָׁתִי?"

We must always remember the special potential of Shabbos *davening* and learning, on a day that even an ignoramus can't sin. Let us imagine Shabbos calling out with great joy and excitement, "זוֹ הִיא! זוֹ הִיא קְדוּשָׁתִי! בִּרְכָתִי!" Look at the potential of my day. Take advantage of this day of קוֹדֶשׁ קָדָשִׁים.

## ✺ Time with the King

Even before Shabbos actually begins, our preparation for the holy day of Shabbos should also reflect — in a practical way — our appreciation that Shabbos is our special day spent together with Hashem.

We know that we must complete all of our Shabbos preparations before the onset of Shabbos, because on Shabbos it is prohibited to cook food and do many of the other necessary preparations. This seems to be illogical. If Shabbos is such a special day, would it not be appropriate that we eat the freshest food possible? Why is Shabbos structured in such a way that we are not allowed to do so?

The following *mashal* will help us understand this, and the essence of Shabbos.

There was a poor man who struggled mightily to support himself and to meet his family's needs. The king of the land, who was righteous and benevolent, took a personal interest in all his subjects. He heard of this particular poor man's plight and wanted to help him.

One day, a uniformed messenger appeared at the poor man's door.

"His Royal Highness, the king himself, will be coming to visit you in your home on the following date, one week hence. Prepare yourself and your home for this royal visit."

But the poor man ignored the message. On the appointed day, the king arrived. He knocked on the door of the man's small home, and no one was home and nothing was prepared. Nothing was done to honor the king's visit. The king was a very kind person and was not angered by the man's lack of preparation. Actually, the king pitied him. "I came to help him; I came for his sake! I gave him time to prepare for my visit, but he ignored the opportunity!"

Just then the poor man opened the door. "My king!" he cried. "Please come in, come in…pardon my lateness, I was stuck in traffic…" The poor man ushered the king into his home and offered him a seat. "Please excuse me for a few moments…" he said, as he rushed out. In a frenzy, he ran to the store and bought ingredients to bake a cake. He rushed into his neighbor's kitchen. "Please let me bake a cake here!"

A short while later, with a freshly baked cake in hand, he rushed back to his home, huffing and puffing, stressed-out, and exhausted. "Your Majesty, here, if you please! I have made a special cake in your honor — please enjoy."

The king gave him a pitying look. "My dear subject, I did not come to your home to enjoy a piece of cake. I came to sit with you, to see you, and to help you. But this sort of union is not possible with a person who is stressed out and completely not himself. It is a pity, for you had so much to gain from my visit, but so much of that has been lost because you weren't prepared."

A sad, pitiful story. But tragically, all too often we are the *nimshal*. Doing things **on** Shabbos *l'kavod* Shabbos is a contradiction in terms. On Shabbos, by definition, everything has to stop. We have to prepare for the King **before** His arrival because once He comes, He comes as the *Mekor Habrachah*. It is not the time to be busy cooking and cleaning. What a pity to waste even one moment of the *brachah* of Shabbos.

## ⌒⌐ Erev Shabbos

The *pasuk* (*Shemos* 31:16) says: וְשָׁמְרוּ בְנֵי יִשְׂרָאֵל אֶת הַשַּׁבָּת, לַעֲשׂוֹת אֶת הַשַּׁבָּת — *The Children of Israel shall observe the Shabbos, to make the Shabbos.*

*Chazal* teach us that we must *make* Shabbos. There should be a definite, noticeable preparation for Shabbos so that we can realize and remind ourselves that the great day of Shabbos is coming. The Erev Shabbos is what makes the Shabbos. Shabbos doesn't need our potato kugel; the reason we prepare all the special Shabbos foods, the Radak (*Yeshayahu* 58:13) explains, is that when we make the festive, special *seudah*, it creates the atmosphere to improve in our *avodas Hashem* and to grow in our *emunah* and *ahavas Hashem*. The *gashmiyus* and *chitzoniyus* that we invest into Shabbos is meant to stimulate the *pnimiyus* of our relationship with Hashem.

I once enjoyed a very precious moment with Rav Pam. We were walking together and he was reminiscing. He asked me, "Do you know what I miss from prewar Europe where I grew up? Do you know what we don't have here in America?"

I did not know what Rav Pam was going to say. I imagined that he would say that he missed the intensity of the Torah learning, or the fiery *davening*.

"What I miss is the Erev Shabbos. In Europe, when *chatzos* Friday came, everything stopped. Eventually, the shul was filled with people preparing for Shabbos. Some were learning, some were saying *Shir Hashirim*, some were *ma'avir sedra*. You felt it. It was palpable. It was tangible that Shabbos was coming. And then, when Shabbos came, it was a Shabbos! In America we spend our Fridays in the regular hustle and bustle, engaged in our weekday pursuits, overwhelmed by the world around us. It is hard to feel Shabbos because Erev Shabbos is what makes a Shabbos and here we don't have the Erev Shabbos."

Rav Yaakov Kamenetsky expressed a similar sentiment. He said that in the early years in America when *chillul Shabbos* was so rampant, Shabbos was lost. But Klal Yisrael recovered from that time period. With the help of our *gedolim*, we recaptured the beauty and the splendor of Shabbos. But, he would add sadly, we have yet to recapture the Erev Shabbos.

Klal Yisrael needs an Erev Shabbos. The halachah places a great emphasis on preparing for Shabbos because that is what makes Shabbos real. Whether one is a *talmid chacham* or a simple person, he has to prepare for Shabbos. That is why even great *Amora'im* themselves would prepare for Shabbos (see *Kiddushin* 41a, *Shulchan Aruch* 250:1, and *Sefer Chassidim* 29). Additionally, many would go out to the fields to welcome the Shabbos as it arrived (see *Shabbos* 119). They made the Shabbos with the Erev Shabbos.

## ⟨∿⟩ Preparation Makes the Shabbos

There is so much that Shabbos has to offer. But we often just fall into Shabbos without making the necessary preparations. We waste the opportunity Shabbos presents, like that poor person in the *mashal* described above. The king arrives and we are not ready.

What a pity to enter Shabbos after a busy Friday, stressed-out and exhausted, about to collapse. Can't you hear Shabbos crying, "זוֹ הִיא קְדוּשָׁתִי?" Shabbos is not a day of gefilte fish — Shabbos is a day *im Hakadosh Baruch Hu*, when we can revel in our *neshamah yeseirah*, enjoy our celestial escort, and do nothing but spend the time with Hashem and His Torah.

Shabbos is the *mekor habrachah*, but it is so important to use Erev Shabbos to prepare for it. If a person comes into Shabbos after a hard day of work, worn out and stressed out, and the first child that steps out of line gets punished for the slightest thing done wrong — that is not the *brachah* of Shabbos. You can almost hear Shabbos cry out, "זוֹ הִיא זוֹ הִיא בִּרְכָתִי? קְדוּשָׁתִי?"

The Vilna Gaon (*Iyov* 1:2) writes: שַׁבָּת אֵין לָה מִגַּרְמֵיהּ כְּלוּם רַק מַה שֶׁמְּכִינִים בְּשֵׁשֶׁת יְמֵי הַמַּעֲשֶׂה — *Shabbos has nothing of its own; it only has what we prepare during the six days of the week.*

Shabbos has the awesome potential of *mei'ein Olam Haba* and, as we mentioned, Shabbos can be even greater than *Olam Haba*. But if we do not prepare for it, then it could be frittered away. I sometimes notice people falling asleep during *Kabbalas Shabbos*. I don't find fault with them, because they worked hard and they are tired. I don't blame them, but I pity them. Is this the *mekor* of the *brachah*? Is this the *chinuch* that they are transmitting to their children, to fall asleep by *davening*? The key to avoiding this type of situation is to be properly prepared and organized for Shabbos.

We should try to come home as early as possible in order to prepare for Shabbos. It is very important to rest on Erev Shabbos. This way, we can begin Shabbos in the right mood, and we will be better able to display extra *ahavah* to our spouses and children, as the halachah requires (see *Mishnah Berurah* 280:3). Without the necessary preparations on Erev Shabbos, we will not be able to access the full *brachah* of Shabbos.

Women work so hard preparing for Shabbos, but if they do not welcome Shabbos in the right mood, they too can lose the benefit of all of their hard work. As difficult as it may sound, women should try to come into Shabbos well rested. They will then be better prepared to create a true Shabbos atmosphere in their home.

## A New Heart

I want to close with a fascinating story. Rav Simcha Kaplan, the *rav* of Tzfas learned in the Mirrer Yeshivah before the war, and he heard this story firsthand from the person involved. (The story is printed in the *sefer L'Shichno Tidreshu,* vol. 1 p. 243.)

There was a couple living in Mir who were married for many years, but had no children. Finally, after many years of waiting, a son was born to them. But their great joy was short-lived. The child had a defective heart and was seriously ill. The local doctor could not help them, and he sent them to a heart specialist in Vilna.

The great specialist examined the baby once, and then again, and gave the parents his sad prognosis.

"There is no hope for this baby. His heart is terribly defective. Do not waste your energy running to other doctors. I can tell you with absolute certainty that there is nothing that can be done medically for your son. I suggest that you take him home and enjoy him for as long as he will live."

Naturally, the parents were devastated. Their first child — their only child — was deathly ill, beyond hope. In Vilna they met a fellow Jew and told him their situation. He advised them that on their way back from Vilna to Mir they should stop in Radin and see the *heilige* Chafetz Chaim to ask for his *brachah.*

Arriving in Radin, they went straight to the Chafetz Chaim's home, but they were not allowed to see him. The Chafetz Chaim was elderly and weak, and was not receiving people. They were devastated once again, but just then, a *yungerman*, a young scholar, walked by, and recognized them — he used to eat in their home when he was a *bachur* learning in the Mirrer Yeshivah. He was happy to see them, and asked, "What brings you here?"

They told him their sad story.

"As it happens," the *yungerman* told them, "I married the Chafetz Chaim's granddaughter. I am a *ben bayis* in the house. Come in with me; I will bring you to the Zeide."

The elderly Chafetz Chaim was sitting in his room, learning *sefer Ezra*. The *yungerman* escorted the couple inside, and told the tzaddik their story. The Chafetz Chaim looked up and said with his typical humility, "How can I help them? I have no money."

"Zeide, it is their only child…"

The Chafetz Chaim turned to the mother and told her, "*Tochterel*, my daughter, prepare for Shabbos early, and be *mekabel* Shabbos early, and you will see that the *zechus* of Shabbos will help you."

The couple walked out with a new sense of hope. They traveled home, followed the Chafetz Chaim's advice, and the baby had a remarkable recovery. In fact, the local doctor paid for their return visit to Vilna to enable the specialist there to re-examine him.

In Vilna the specialist looked at the baby again, and asked, "Is this a joke? This is not the same baby I saw initially. This is a very healthy baby!"

The mother beamed. "I have only one baby. This is the same child you saw earlier."

"What happened?" asked the incredulous doctor. "Where did you go? Did you go to another heart specialist?"

"No," replied the mother. "We went to a great sage in Radin, to the Chafetz Chaim."

The doctor said, "Ah! The Chafetz Chaim. We know of him. We doctors can only work with what we have. The Chafetz Chaim can create anew. The sage created a new heart for your child!"

I sincerely hope that nobody should ever need such a *brachah* like this sick child did. We are certainly unable to give such a lifesaving *brachah* and *havtachah* like the *heilige* Chafetz Chaim was able to give. We can only learn from and repeat the *havtachah* — if someone makes an effort to prepare properly for Shabbos, he will certainly receive the *brachah* of Shabbos, from the *mekor habrachah*.

Let us discover and appreciate the true beauty of Shabbos and the importance of the Erev Shabbos.

Make your own refresher course to learn about Shabbos. Choose any *sefer* that speaks to your *neshamah*, that touches your heart. Whether it is a *mussar sefer*, a *chassidishe sefer*, a *hashkafah* or halachah *sefer*, involve yourself, and focus on growing in your appreciation of Shabbos. Then the Shabbos will be proud of us, and proclaim — affirmatively — "זוּ הִיא בִּרְכָתִי! קְדוּשָׁתִי!"

# GOOD PR
## *Living al Kiddush Hashem*

The big day finally arrived. Klal Yisrael was encamped at Har Sinai, anxiously awaiting *Kabbalas HaTorah*. As a prelude to that great event, Hashem commanded Moshe Rabbeinu (*Shemos* 19:4–6) to deliver a message to Klal Yisrael, describing their new mission as the Chosen Nation:

The message ends with the words: וְאַתֶּם תִּהְיוּ לִי מַמְלֶכֶת כֹּהֲנִים וְגוֹי קָדוֹשׁ — *You shall be to Me a kingdom of priests and a holy nation.*

On a simple level, this concluding *pasuk* is transmitting the privilege of being a religious Jew. It is a statement of fact — through the Torah, you will be transformed into noble, special people.

However, we can understand this *pasuk* on a deeper, more practical level. It not only informs us of the heights we will reach when we accept the Torah, but it is a *precondition* that we must fulfill in order to be worthy to accept the Torah.

## Like Angels

In *Chazaras Hashatz* (*nusach Ashkenaz*), when we recite *Kedushah*, we say: נְקַדֵּשׁ אֶת שִׁמְךָ בָּעוֹלָם, כְּשֵׁם שֶׁמַּקְדִּישִׁים אוֹתוֹ בִּשְׁמֵי מָרוֹם — *Let us sanctify Your Name in the world, just as they sanctify You in the heavens on high.*

That seems to be a rather presumptuous statement. Can we truly sanctify Hashem's Name like the angels? Is it possible for us to attain that level of *kiddush Hashem*?

Let me tell you a story, retold by a well-known *rav*, who personally witnessed it (see preface to *sefer Divrei Chachamim*).

This *rav* was acquainted with a young Jewish man, whom we will call Michael. Michael came from an irreligious background, but at some point he began learning about *Yiddishkeit*. One day, he approached the *rav*.

"I am considering becoming religious, but I have some reservations. I have some philosophical questions that are really bothering me. If I would speak with someone who can solve my issues, I think I would make the commitment."

The *rav* answered, "I will take you to Rav Yaakov Kamenetsky. He will be able to answer your questions." The *rav* arranged for a meeting and when the day arrived, he accompanied Michael to Rav Yaakov's home. They arrived a few minutes early, and as they waited for their meeting, Michael had time to observe Rav Yaakov talking to a family with several children.

After a few moments of taking in this scene, Michael whispered to the *rav* who had escorted him, "We can leave — I am ready to become religious."

"But we didn't even speak to Rav Yaakov. You haven't asked him your questions!"

"That's true," replied Michael. "I didn't ask any questions, but I already got my answers. Just by watching this great man, I know the answers — by seeing the way he treats others, even the children. By witnessing his respect and love for people, I realize that if this is what our religion is all about, if this is what Torah is, then it is something that I want to be a part of."

Rav Yaakov not only learned Torah, he lived Torah. His every action bespoke the sweetness and the pleasantness of Torah — *derachehah darchei no'am*. What a remarkable *kiddush Hashem*. Imagine. Just by acting the way a religious Jew is supposed to act, Rav Yaakov brought another Jew back to *Yiddishkeit*.

I ask you — can a *malach* make such a *kiddush Hashem*?

Every day, each and every one of us has that opportunity to sanctify the Ribono Shel Olam's Name in this most incredible way.

## ❧ Bringing Out the Love

The ultimate *kiddush Hashem*, of course, is to die *al kiddush Hashem* — to sacrifice one's life for one's faith in Hashem. This was the *kiddush Hashem* offered by Rabbi Akiva, who was executed by the Romans. The Gemara (*Brachos* 61b) relates that at that final moment of his life, when he was being torn apart with the iron combs of the executioner, Rabbi Akiva was reciting the Shema.

"Rebbi!" cried his heartbroken *talmidim*. "Are you required to recite *Krias Shema* even now, under these circumstances?"

Rabbi Akiva responded, "Throughout my life, I waited to have the opportunity to fulfill the mitzvah recorded in the Shema of וְאָהַבְתָּ אֵת ה' אֱלֹקֶיךָ...וּבְכָל נַפְשְׁךָ — to show my love for Hashem with my very life. Now that I have the opportunity to do so, shall I not recite the Shema?"

Rabbi Akiva cited the *pasuk* (*Devarim* 6:5): וְאָהַבְתָּ אֵת ה' אֱלֹקֶיךָ בְּכָל לְבָבְךָ וּבְכָל נַפְשְׁךָ וּבְכָל מְאֹדֶךָ. This seems to be a mighty tall order; in its simple sense, the *pasuk* mandates a total, unconditional, and unlimited love for Hashem. It directs one to even give one's life for *ahavas Hashem*, as Rabbi Akiva did.

But the Gemara (*Yuma* 86a) expounds on this very same *pasuk* and derives a different teaching, which explains another method of showing one's unconditional love for Hashem on a constant basis: וְאָהַבְתָּ אֵת ה' אֱלֹקֶיךָ — *And you shall (cause) love (to) Hashem, your G-d,* שֶׁיְּהֵא שֵׁם שָׁמַיִם מִתְאַהֵב עַל יָדְךָ — *that the Name of Hashem should be loved because of you.*

The *pasuk* requires us to live our lives in such a way that we inspire those around us to love Hashem. By living the way a Jew is supposed to live, we will inspire others to love Him.

The Gemara explains: A Jew must study Torah, he must be honest and act with integrity, and his interaction with others should be very pleasant. If he does so, what is the result?

מַה הַבְּרִיּוֹת אוֹמְרוֹת עָלָיו — *What do others say of him?*

אַשְׁרֵי אָבִיו שֶׁלִּמְּדוֹ תוֹרָה — *How fortunate is his father, who taught him Torah.*

אוֹי לָהֶם לַבְּרִיּוֹת שֶׁלֹּא לִמְדוּ תוֹרָה — *Woe unto those who have never learned Torah.*

פְּלוֹנִי שֶׁלָּמַד תוֹרָה רְאוּ כַּמָּה נָאִים דְּרָכָיו, כַּמָּה מְתוּקָנִים מְעֲשָׂיו — *This person who learned Torah, see how pleasant are his ways. How good and proper are his actions.*

Dying *al kiddush Hashem* is one form of *kiddush Hashem*. But there is another way to fulfill the mitzvah — namely, **living** *al kiddush Hashem*: to live one's life as an eloquent testimony of the privilege to be an *ehrliche* Yid. אָשִׁירָה לַה' בְּחַיָּי — *With my* **life***, I will praise Hashem* (*Tehillim* 104:33). That is a living *kiddush Hashem*.

A *gadol* once noted that there are two exceptional mountains in our history: Har Hamoriyah, the site of the *Akeidah*, where Avraham was willing to slaughter his son; and Har Sinai, where we received the Torah. Har Hamoriyah teaches us how to die *al kiddush Hashem*, but Har Sinai teaches us how to live *al kiddush Hashem*. And such a *kiddush Hashem* has the great power to inspire those around us as they observe the way we live our lives.

## ❧ The Chosen People

The Novominsker Rebbe told a story that he heard from the person involved.

A Yid entered a taxi in Manhattan and the non-Jewish driver told him, "You Jews are the Chosen People."

The Yid responded, "Well, *I* certainly agree. But why do *you* say so?"

The taxi driver answered, "I'll tell you what just happened. I picked up a religious Jew and was driving him to his destination. But a block and a half before we got there he told me, 'Stop, let me out here. Don't worry, I will pay you the entire fare.'

"'But we're a block and a half away from where you have to go,' I said.

"'Yes, I know,' he answered. 'But look, we are right outside a subway station. Many people are coming up to the street. If I get out now you will be able to quickly get another fare, which you may lose otherwise. I can walk the rest of the way.'

"That man was willing to walk a block and a half just so that I should have another customer. In my mind, people who think of the other guy are from the Chosen Nation!"

Again, I ask you. Can a *malach* make such a *kiddush Hashem*, to inspire a non-Jew to say that we are the Chosen Nation?

Rabbi Manis Mandel, the legendary *menahel* of Yeshivah of Brooklyn, told me the following story:

One day, a nonreligious Jew came into his office in yeshivah and asked him if a particular family had their boys enrolled in his school.

"Yes," answered Rabbi Mandel.

"If so, I want to register my sons as well," said the irreligious man.

Rabbi Mandel was somewhat shocked. This nonreligious man was obviously aware that he was in a yeshivah — a religious school where the boys were all observant, and where they learned Torah. And yet he wanted to enroll his sons.

"I see you are surprised, Rabbi," said the man. "But let me explain. This family lives right next door to us, and we see their boys all the time. We have never seen such refined young men. They always talk respectfully. They are so well behaved and so well mannered. And what's more, they are so nice and pleasant; it is simply a pleasure to be in their company. My wife and I decided that we want our children to be like them. We decided to find out which school they attend and to enroll our boys there as well."

Rabbi Mandel was quick to add the story's postscript. Decades later, this once nonreligious family is an outstanding family of *bnei Torah* and *marbitzei Torah*.

Just think, your son's *rebbi*, or your daughter's *morah*, might be a member of this family. Today, a member of this family might be one of *your* neighbors — or even one of your *mechutanim*. All because of a few yeshivah boys who lived *al kiddush Hashem*, and who were a living testimony to the *darchei no'am* of the Torah.

This is exactly as the Gemara predicted. The natural reaction to a living *kiddush Hashem* is, "Fortunate is one who learns Torah, woe to the person that doesn't learn Torah!" This man and his wife felt that their children must have a Torah education.

The *Tanna D'vei Eliyahu* (28) explains this idea as well. When people observe the pleasantness of a religious Jew, they swear: אֲנַחְנוּ נִלְמוֹד גַּם כֵּן תּוֹרָה וּנְלַמֵּד לְבָנֵינוּ תּוֹרָה — *We will also learn Torah and we will teach our children Torah.* If this is what Torah does to a person, then we want to embrace Torah as well.

It is known that after concluding the formal *Shemoneh Esrei*, the Chafetz Chaim would often *daven* to Hashem in his own words. On several occasions, he was overheard imploring, *"Ribono Shel Olam, kach es nafshi al kedushas Shemecha* — take my soul *al kiddush Hashem."* The Chafetz Chaim longed for the day when he would be able to have the privilege to die *al kiddush Hashem.*

As we know, those *tefillos* were not accepted. But the *ko'ach hatefillah* of the Chafetz Chaim was renowned; his far-reaching *tefillos* always bore fruit. If so, asked Rav Pam, why wasn't this particular *tefillah* accepted?

Evidently, Rav Pam explained, the Chafetz Chaim created a far greater *kiddush Hashem* by living *al kiddush Hashem* than he would have by dying *al kiddush Hashem.* His mission was to be a living *kiddush Hashem.*

And it is not only the Chafetz Chaim. Every Jew's mission — indeed, every Jew's privilege — is to create a *kiddush Hashem* and to fulfill the *pasuk* (*Vayikra* 22:32): וְנִקְדַּשְׁתִּי בְּתוֹךְ בְּנֵי יִשְׂרָאֵל — *And I shall be sanctified within the Children of Israel.*

The *Sifri* (*Vayikra* 22) takes note of the Torah's juxtaposition of the above *pasuk* with the following *pasuk*, which mentions Hashem taking us out of Mitzrayim: וְנִקְדַּשְׁתִּי בְּתוֹךְ בְּנֵי יִשְׂרָאֵל אֲנִי ה' מְקַדִּשְׁכֶם...הַמּוֹצִיא אֶתְכֶם מֵאֶרֶץ מִצְרַיִם לִהְיוֹת לָכֶם לֵאלֹקִים — *And I shall be sanctified within the Children of Israel, I am Hashem Who sanctified you, Israel...Who took you out of the land of Mitzrayim to be a G-d unto you.*

The *Sifri* comments: עַל תְּנַאי הוֹצֵאתִי אֶתְכֶם מֵאֶרֶץ מִצְרַיִם שֶׁתִּמְסְרוּ עַצְמְכֶם לְקַדֵּשׁ אֶת שְׁמִי — *I took you out of Mitzrayim on the condition that you devote your lives to sanctifying My Name.*

The *Sifri* is difficult to understand. There were, of course, many periods in our history when our nation was called upon to die *al kiddush Hashem* — most recently, we know of victims of the Nazis who marched into the gas chambers with *Shema Yisrael* on their lips. There was Communist Russia, the Crusades, the Spanish Inquisition, the *dor hashmad* in Roman times, and unfortunately many, many more. Throughout Jewish history, so many members of our nation made the ultimate sacrifice and gave their lives *al kiddush Hashem.*

But there have also been periods in our history when Jews lived in relative peace and security among their non-Jewish neighbors. During those times, Jews have lived their lives without being challenged with this ultimate sacrifice. Today in America we are living in a blessed era of peace. This leads us to a question: In such eras of relative stability *baruch Hashem*, how do we fulfill the condition that we sacrifice our lives *al kiddush Hashem*?

The answer is simple. There are two forms of *kiddush Hashem* — dying *al kiddush Hashem*, and living *al kiddush Hashem*. Hashem took us out of Mitzrayim and gave us the status of the *Am Hanivchar*, the Chosen Nation. That was given along with the commandment to sacrifice our lives for Hashem when circumstances warrant doing so, as Rabbi Akiva did. But in addition to the ultimate sacrifice, *Yetzias Mitzrayim* also came together with the privilege and the unique mission of Har Sinai, to live *al kiddush Hashem*, thereby fulfilling וְאָהַבְתָּ — שֶׁיְּהֵא שֵׁם שָׁמַיִם מִתְאַהֵב עַל יָדֶיךָ.

## ⌒ Chaveirim and Hatzolah

A friend of mine related to me a conversation that he had with a Jamaican delivery boy who works in the Flatbush area.

"Rabbi, I have to ask you something. At a previous delivery, I accidently locked my keys in my van, and I couldn't get in. Jewish people on the street tried to help, but without the tools and know-how, there was nothing that anybody could do. So someone scribbled down a phone number and told me, 'Here, call this number — they will come and help you.' Well, I didn't want to have to pay for a lock-out service, but I had no choice, I had to do my job. So I called the number. In a few minutes, these guys came and they got the door open right away.

"'Great!' I said. 'How much do I owe you?'

"'Nothing,' they answered.

"'What?' I couldn't believe it. 'Nothing?'

"'Well, that's what we do. We're Chaveirim, friends who help others.'

"'No charge?'

"'No charge,' they said, and they drove off!

"Rabbi, were those guys for real? Is there really this Chaveirim group? Do they really just drive around helping other people?"

"Absolutely," answered my friend.

The delivery boy went on, "I have another question, Rabbi. I work in Flatbush, and I see those Hatzolah cars and ambulances driving back and forth. Do they also work for free?"

"Definitely," said my friend.

That is when this delivery boy, truly impressed, asked his final question: "If G-d has you guys, why does He need the rest of us?"

Again, I ask, can angels make such a magnificent *kiddush Hashem*?

Living *al kiddush Hashem* is also a fulfillment of וְנִקְדַּשְׁתִּי בְּתוֹךְ בְּנֵי יִשְׂרָאֵל. Note that the *pasuk* does not say "תְּקַדְּשׁוּ — *go and sanctify*" as a verb, rather it says "וְנִקְדַּשְׁתִּי — *and I will be sanctified*" which is a reflexive term. What is the message?

There are many wonderful people engaged in *kiruv rechokim* on a professional level, who "*go and sanctify*" — they go out to teach others and draw people closer to an appreciation of the beauty of the Torah. But there is another effective method of *kiruv rechokim*, which each of us can engage in. This *kiruv rechokim* happens by itself — "*and I will be sanctified*," by being a living *kiddush Hashem*.

Every person has a different profession: some people are in the rabbinate, others are in the field of education; some are professionals, others are businessmen; some are retailers, some are service providers; and some are professional homemakers. However, every single Yid has one important *mission* that really should be the center of his existence. The mission is וְנִקְדַּשְׁתִּי בְּתוֹךְ בְּנֵי יִשְׂרָאֵל. In the office, on the train or plane, on the street, or in a store — the way we act, drive, and shop, the way we deal with people — every interaction — is an opportunity שֶׁיְּהֵא שֵׁם שָׁמַיִם מִתְאַהֵב עַל יָדֶיךָ.

Imagine a secret garden full of beautiful flowers and visual delights, surrounded by a high impenetrable wall, completely blocking it from view. But there's a door in the wall, of course, and the door has an old-fashioned keyhole, the type that one can peek through and see a small glimpse of the other side.

Sadly, for so many people, Torah is an inaccessible treasure. They do not know the beauty of a *blatt Gemara*, of a Shabbos, or of a yeshivah. But there is the keyhole through which they can catch sight of all the beauty. We are the keyhole. Those estranged from Torah get a glimpse of the Torah by observing our actions, and the way we live our lives. The ultimate *kiruv rechokim* is when they see us and say, "I want to be like him. If that's what Torah did to him, I want the Torah to do that to me as well."

One can learn the entire Torah, but the crucial question is: What impact did it have on him and on his character? In Yiddish the question is phrased thus: *Du host gelernt gantz Shas* — you may have learned *Shas*; *ubber vos hut Shas **dir** gelernt* — but what has *Shas* taught you? How did *Shas* affect you?

## ᏇᎧ *Gedolim* **Pictures**

*Megillas Rus* is the inspiring and sometimes heart-wrenching story of Rus and the incredible *mesirus nefesh* that she exhibited as she left a life of royalty and was reduced to abject poverty. Rus was persistent in her drive to connect herself to Hakadosh Baruch Hu and to His Torah. After the loss of her husband and father-in-law, and without any means of support, Rus joins her mother-in-law, Naomi, on her journey back to Eretz Yisrael.

Naomi herself discourages Rus, telling her to return to her father's land: "Do not join me, you will only suffer deprivation. I have nothing to offer you…" But the *pasuk* (*Rus* 1:14) tells us, וְרוּת דָּבְקָה בָּהּ — *Rus clung to her*. She clung so dearly to the *derech Hashem* even in a most difficult and challenging situation. What gave her the strength and courage to do so? How was Rus able to overcome the fear of an uncertain future, a future that seemed destined for misfortune?

Rav Pam once suggested an answer based on a few words in the Midrash.

The Midrash (*Rus* 2:5) explains why Naomi was given that name. "Naomi" is a contraction of the words, מַעֲשֶׂיהָ נָאִים וּנְעִימִים — *Her deeds were beautiful and sweet.*

Naomi was a very pleasant person. Naomi was a living *kiddush Hashem*, someone whose life was an eloquent expression of the *ne'imus*, the sweetness, of Torah. This is what had such an impact on Rus. וְרוּת דָּבְקָה בָּהּ — *Rus clung so dearly to **her***, to Naomi, to her living example of what Torah can do to a person.

This *vort* is a fitting tribute to Rav Pam, who in his own life had this very same effect on so many people — even non-Jews.

A number of years ago, Yeshivah Torah Vodaath wrote and dedicated a *sefer Torah* in Rav Pam's honor. In order to publicize the *hachnasas sefer Torah*, the yeshivah printed posters to be hung around the neighborhood. Naturally, the advertisements featured a nice picture of Rav Pam.

One poster was hung up on East 7th Street in the Kensington neighborhood, where Rav Pam himself lived. Rebbetzin Pam was unhappy about it. East 7th Street was a quiet residential block, not a busy avenue with stores and businesses. The Rebbetzin felt that the poster marred the quiet character of the street and was concerned that it violated the rights of the neighbors. The Rebbetzin decided that she was going to remove the poster. But when she went out the next morning to take it down, it was no longer there.

A short time later, the Rebbetzin met her neighbor, an Italian woman, and she wanted to apologize for this "misdeed." She wanted to let her neighbor know that she herself was unhappy about it.

"In fact," said the Rebbetzin, "I actually went out to take it down myself. But by the time I got there, someone had already taken it down."

The Italian neighbor smiled.

"Do you know who took it down?" the neighbor asked. "I did!" And she explained:

"We have lived next door to you for so many years. We have always been so impressed and so inspired by Rabbi Pam's greatness. And we always wanted to have a picture of him in our house. Here was our opportunity! When we saw that advertisement, we took it down and it is now hanging in our home."

Can you imagine walking into an Italian home and seeing *gedolim* pictures? Again I ask — can an angel make such a *kiddush Hashem*?

## 🌊 Your Report

Before a person can merit wearing the crown of Torah, there is an important prerequisite — he must realize what he represents. He must understand that he is a spokesman, an ambassador, for the Torah. This is the meaning of the *pasuk*, וְאַתֶּם תִּהְיוּ לִי מַמְלֶכֶת כֹּהֲנִים וְגוֹי קָדוֹשׁ. Before *Kabbalas HaTorah*, one must be aware that he represents the Torah. Let us be careful not, *chas v'shalom*, to *mis*represent the Torah. People are watching. We are constantly in the spotlight of the public eye. We must always be cognizant of others' reactions: מַה הַבְּרִיּוֹת אוֹמְרוֹת — *What will people say?* For every action, there's a reaction.

Many years ago, a secular reporter in Eretz Yisrael wanted to interview the Chazon Ish. The Chazon Ish agreed, and they decided to take a walk together. They began walking briskly, but suddenly the Chazon Ish slowed down.

"Why has the Rav slowed down? Is everything all right?"

The Chazon Ish replied, "Do you not see? There is an elderly man walking in front of us. It would be insensitive to walk briskly past an older person who is frail and walks slowly."

This response made a tremendous impression on the reporter. He wrote that he believed that the Chazon Ish became such a great man because of his deep sensitivity for others.

People are constantly watching us and they are "writing a report" about us. What will our "reporters" say? Will they say כַּמָּה מְתוּקָנִים מֵעֲשָׂיו! כַּמָּה נָאִים דְּרָכָיו! Or will they say, *chalilah*, the opposite?

## 🌊 The Opposite Effect

The abovementioned Gemara in *Yuma* begins by relating the glowing praise showered upon the Jew who conducts himself properly. Then the Gemara goes on to caution us to avoid an opposite scenario:

אֲבָל מִי שֶׁקָּרָא וְשָׁנָה — *On the other hand, one who learns Torah*... but does not conduct himself with integrity, and does not act pleasantly toward others,

מַה הַבְּרִיּוֹת אוֹמְרוֹת עָלָיו — *what do people say of him?*

אוֹי לוֹ לִפְלוֹנִי שֶׁלָּמַד תּוֹרָה — *"Woe to this one, who learned Torah.*

פְּלוֹנִי שֶׁלָּמַד תּוֹרָה רְאוּ כַּמָה מְקוּלְקָלִים מַעֲשָׂיו וְכַמָּה מְכוֹעָרִין דְּרָכָיו — *This man who was taught Torah, see how corrupted are his acts, how unbecoming are his ways."*

Instead of a *kiddush Hashem*, one can be making a horrific *chillul Hashem, chas v'shalom*, as people will say, "Look at the way a Torah Jew acts!" Instead of *kavod haTorah*, and *kiruv rechokim*, such a person is the cause of *bizayon haTorah* and *richuk kerovim*.

Unfortunately, I learned the truth of this idea firsthand many years ago.

Growing up, we lived next door to a wonderful couple, devoted *ba'alei teshuvah* who showed tremendous *mesirus nefesh* for Torah. Among other things, they had uprooted and relocated themselves to Brooklyn from their native community to live among *frum* Jews. But after a few years, we noticed that their commitment to *Yiddishkeit* seemed to be diminishing, and their observance was becoming shallow. Eventually, they left the neighborhood. We later found out that the family, who was originally so devoted to *Yiddishkeit*, had unfortunately embraced a Hindu religion. We were devastated.

What brought about this tragedy? The wife was once telling our family how upset and disillusioned she was with her new job. She had begun teaching in a religious school. She gave up a well-paying teaching career in the public school system in order to work in a more religious environment. However, the way the religious students treated her, their disrespectful attitude and behavior, gave her real misgivings about *Yiddishkeit*.

"If this is what being religious is all about, I must have made a wrong decision," she said.

She left her job and eventually left the neighborhood. The girls at her religious school thought that she had found a new job. They did not realize that she found a new religion. This is what the Gemara is referring to: *chillul Hashem, bizayon haTorah*, and even *richuk kerovim*.

This incident clarified a statement of *Chazal* (*Yuma* 86a) that there is no atonement for the sin of *chillul Hashem*. So too we find (*Avos* 4:4) that a person is held accountable even for a *chillul Hashem* done *b'shogeg* —

unintentionally. Why is this true? Because you cannot turn back the clock; the damage done through *chillul Hashem* is irreversible. Can you bring back a family that left *Yiddishkeit* and embraced Hinduism? What *kapparah* can there be for such a serious sin? What kind of *teshuvah* can one do? This is why living *al kiddush Hashem* is of such paramount importance. This is why we were reminded of it right before *Kabbalas HaTorah*.

Let us remember our responsibility. We must always keep in mind that we are wearing the crown of the Torah, that we are the ambassadors for the Torah. וְנִקְדַּשְׁתִּי בְּתוֹךְ בְּנֵי יִשְׂרָאֵל is our lifelong mission. Let us be sure to always be the catalyst for a *kiddush Hashem*, and not *chas v'shalom* the opposite.

The Gemara (*Shabbos* 114) says that a *talmid chacham* who walks around with a stain on his clothing makes a *chillul Hashem* because he causes people to despise the Torah. "Look," they will say, "he learns Torah, but he is sloppy and unkempt."

And what if the one who learns Torah has a stain on his character? What if he is too busy to notice other people, or if he is not courteous? What if he is rude or impolite? The way we treat others can make a *kiddush Hashem*, or *chas v'shalom* a *chillul Hashem*.

Rav Mattisyahu Salomon once made the following statement: "We are 'building another Hitler' with the way we drive!" When we drive aggressively, and are not courteous or patient with the other drivers on the road, we create a horrible *chillul Hashem*. This fosters hatred toward Jews similar to that generated by Hitler, *yemach shemo*.

This comes across as a very harsh statement, but we see it to be true. Non-Jews do not see our Torah learning, or the *chessed* that we do, or the *tzedakah* that we give. They see how we drive and park. They see the way we interact with others. We have to represent Hashem and His Torah properly, even when we drive.

## ✿ Protecting Our Beauty

We must strive to create the type of reaction described by the *navi* (*Yeshayahu* 61:9): כָּל רֹאֵיהֶם יַכִּירוּם כִּי הֵם זֶרַע בֵּרַךְ ה' — *All who see them will recognize them, that they are the seed that Hashem has blessed.*

Everybody, Jews and non-Jews alike, will say, "Ah, there goes a religious Jew. How wonderful, how lucky they are to have the Torah."

When that reaction is heard in this world, Hashem looks down lovingly and proclaims (*Yeshayahu* 49:3): יִשְׂרָאֵל אֲשֶׁר בְּךָ אֶתְפָּאָר — *Israel, in whom I take glory.*

Many years ago, a friend of mine learned in Yeshivas Bais Shraga in Monsey. Near the yeshivah there was an old non-Jewish cemetery that dated back to the Civil War era. Late one evening, my friend went out for a stroll. Passing by the cemetery, he saw someone moving among the headstones. His curiosity overcame his fear, and he went to investigate the "ghost." It was none other than the legendary *mashgiach* of Bais Shraga, Rav Mordechai Schwab.

"It certainly is uncomfortable to meet your *mashgiach* in a cemetery at two in the morning!" recalled my friend. "But I don't know who was more embarrassed, me or the Mashgiach."

Rav Schwab felt compelled to explain to his *talmid* why he was there.

"Monsey has only recently become a predominantly Jewish neighborhood. Before we arrived, many non-Jews lived here, and this cemetery is theirs. Since this cemetery is located off of a busy intersection, debris and clutter fly in on a regular basis. I am always worried — what will the non-Jews think when they see garbage and dirt in their cemetery? They will think that Jews do not have proper respect for the deceased, which would be a terrible *chillul Hashem*. Therefore, often, late at night, when no one is around, I come out and I clean up."

Rav Schwab was a person who was a living *kavod Shamayim*, who understood that we have to maintain our exalted status of *mamleches kohanim v'goy kadosh*.

We have to protect the inherent beauty of the Torah way of life. We do so by watching the way we interact with people, the way we travel, the way we drive, the way we shop. We project the correct Torah image by being well mannered; by acting properly, such as saying "Good morning," and "Excuse me"; and by holding the door open for people.

This awareness is especially important during the summer months, when many people move up to the Catskill Mountains to spend their vacation. The Catskill region is a quiet and serene area during the winter months. We must be sensitive to the year-round residents and to how they will react to the annual "invasion" of thousands of Orthodox Jews.

## ᏬᎩᏬ Good PR

I will conclude with a beautiful story about Rav Moshe Schisgal (*Reb Moshe* p. 219, ArtScroll, 1986), son-in-law of Rav Moshe Feinstein, who Rav Pam once described as "the essence of Torah." I believe this story helps us understand Rav Pam's description.

After Rav Schisgal's passing, his *rebbetzin* received a letter from someone in the neighborhood whom she did not know at all.

*With tears flowing down my face, I must relate how your husband saved my family from much pain... We have a store on the Lower East Side. We are not religious, and neither is our son. But we were not prepared for the news when he came home one day and informed us that he is marrying a non-Jewish girl.*

*We were devastated. Marrying out of the faith was inconceivable to us. But what could we do? We weren't religious, so what could we tell him? How could we explain that he mustn't throw away something that we had never attached importance to?*

*Right after we received the news, we were in the store and your husband walked in. I told him the story. He said, "Let me speak to your son." We had nothing to lose, of course, and I arranged a meeting. Luckily, our son agreed to meet him. And he took a fifteen-minute walk with Rav Schisgal.*

*When our son came home he told us: "If we have such a man as part of our people, I cannot marry this girl." He broke off all ties with her! A short while later, he met and married a fine Jewish girl. They have actually become more religious over the years, and I am happy to tell you that they recently enrolled our little granddaughter in a religious school!*

They concluded the letter with the following words:

*Let me say that with the rabbi's passing, we have lost a good public relations man for Judaism.*

That's *kulo Torah*. His every action expressed the beauty of Torah. Rav Schisgal was the ultimate *kiddush Hashem*. The wayward son did not see the Torah knowledge that Rav Schisgal possessed, but he saw his incredible *ne'imus* of Torah — פְּלוֹנִי שֶׁלָּמַד תּוֹרָה רְאוּ כַּמָּה נָאִים דְּרָכָיו, כַּמָּה מְתוּקָנִים מְעֲשָׂיו!

We all have to be good public relations spokespeople for *Yiddishkeit*.

נְקַדֵּשׁ אֶת שִׁמְךָ בָּעוֹלָם, כְּשֵׁם שֶׁמַּקְדִּישִׁים אוֹתוֹ בִּשְׁמֵי מָרוֹם.

# GLATT YOSHER
## Living Honestly

---

After the passing of Rav Moshe Feinstein, many stories about this great tzaddik came to light. I remember hearing something at that time which left an indelible impression on me.

As a young *rav* in Russia, Rav Moshe suffered terribly under the wicked Communist regime. In addition to continual harassment and persecution, the Communists actually tried to kill him several times. Incredibly, Rav Moshe once commented that he was able to forgive the Communists for everything that they had done to him except for one thing — once, while escaping, Rav Moshe was forced to lie to save his life.

"For *that* I will never forgive them," said Rav Moshe.

This is an amazing statement considering the following: The situation under the Communists was one of perpetual *pikuach nefesh*; the Chafetz Chaim had ruled that one is allowed to be *mechallel Shabbos* in order to escape the Communists. Rav Moshe was certainly justified in deviating from the truth — even obligated to do so. But nevertheless, he never forgave those who caused him to lie. A shining example of the *pasuk* (*Tehillim* 119:143) שֶׁקֶר שָׂנֵאתִי וַאֲתַעֵבָה — *I have hated falsehood and abhorred it*.

Rav Yaakov Kamenetsky once expressed the following thought: Both Avraham Avinu and Yitzchak Avinu exhibited their greatness at *Akeidas Yitzchak* — Avraham was prepared to slaughter his child and Yitzchak was prepared to sacrifice himself. What was the "*akeidah*" of Yaakov Avinu? Yaakov's ultimate sacrifice was when he had to deviate from the truth in his dealings with Lavan, because falsehood was the antithesis of Yaakov's very being.

תִּתֵּן אֱמֶת לְיַעֲקֹב — *grant truth to Yaakov* (*Michah* 7:20), Yaakov was the paragon of truth.

This was Rav Moshe's pain as well. Even though he was saving his life, deviating from the truth was a terrible trauma for him.

There are many Torah sources that underscore the primacy of honesty in all areas of a person's life:

* The *pasuk* in *Tehillim* (101:7) says: דֹּבֵר שְׁקָרִים לֹא יִכּוֹן לְנֶגֶד עֵינָי — *One who tells lies shall not be established before My eyes.* Hashem cannot tolerate a person who speaks false words.

* The Gemara in *Pesachim* (113b) says a similarly harsh and forceful statement: הַקָּדוֹשׁ בָּרוּךְ הוּא שׂוֹנֵא הַמְדַבֵּר אֶחָד בְּפֶה וְאֶחָד בְּלֵב — *Hashem hates one who is dishonest.*

* The Gemara in *Shabbos* (55a) states: חוֹתָמוֹ שֶׁל הַקָּדוֹשׁ בָּרוּךְ הוּא אֱמֶת — Hashem's "seal" — His very essence — *is truth.*

* The Gemara in *Sanhedrin* (92a) teaches: כָּל הַמְחַלֵּל דִּבּוּרוֹ כְּאִילוּ עוֹבֵד עֲבוֹדָה זָרָה — *Someone who lies is as if he served avodah zarah.*

* And of course, the Gemara in *Shabbos* (31a) lists the questions that we will be asked on that awesome day — the Day of Judgment. One of the first questions will be: נָשָׂאתָ וְנָתַתָּ בֶּאֱמוּנָה — *Were you faithful in business dealings?*

These are just a few of the many sources that discuss this topic. But let us focus on the Gemara in *Sanhedrin*, and on one point in the Gemara on *Shabbos* 31a:

Why does the Gemara say "נָשָׂאתָ וְנָתַתָּ בֶּאֱמוּנָה" with faith, as opposed to "בֶּאֱמֶת" — with truth and honesty — which is what the Gemara actually means? The Gemara is teaching us that being dishonest stems from a lack of *emunah.* Indeed, Rav Chaim Vital (*Sha'arei Kedushah* 2:5) puts it drastically: הַמְדַבֵּר שְׁקָרִים כּוֹפֵר בֵּאלֹקֵי הָאֱמֶת וּמוֹדֶה בְּאֵל אַחֵר שֶׁהוּא שֶׁקֶר — *One who speaks falsehoods denies the true G-d, and accepts a new god which is sheker.* Lying is a form of blasphemy, in which one serves the god of *sheker.*

We see this in other sources as well, including the *Zohar* (*Bamidbar* pp. 198b, 226b): לֵית אֱמוּנָה בְּלָא אֱמֶת — *there is no faith without the truth;* אִיהוּ אֱמֶת, וְאִיהִי אֱמוּנָה — *He is truth, He is faithfulness.* Emes and *emunah* are one and the same.

We say in *Birkas Krias Shema* of Shacharis: אֱמֶת וֶאֱמוּנָה חוק וְלֹא יַעֲבוֹר — *True and faithful, it is an unbreachable decree.* This can be homiletically translated, that the pair — *"emes and emunah"* are a *"chok v'lo ya'avor"* — is inseparable.

We know how terrible falsehood is, but what is the relationship between *emes* and *emunah*? And what message does that teach us that we can apply to our daily lives? The lesson here is a key one that reveals a very vital attitude for daily living.

## ᗆᕽᗆ Hashem's World

I once gave a *shiur* on the importance of honesty, particularly in business. After the *shiur*, I was approached by someone who told me the following:

"Everything that you said is true in theory, but when I first started working I was told that you cannot make it in today's business world if you're too honest. And I see that as the reality. So the *shiur* was nice and all, but not relevant for today's day and age."

I told this person, "My dear friend, you and I live in Hashem's world. It is Hashem Who controls it. And Hashem's essence is truth. Hashem doesn't tolerate any deviation from truth; He abhors and despises *sheker*. How can you believe that you cannot be successful in business by living with *emes*? Quite the contrary, you cannot be successful by cheating! Can somebody really gain by doing something that Hashem hates with such a passion?"

I must say, it was terribly disappointing to hear a believing Jew speak that way. Don't we all know that one of the basic principles of our *emunah* is the fact that a person's *parnassah* is predestined (see *Beitzah* 16a)? And don't we all know and believe what the Gemara teaches us (*Yuma* 38b): אֵין אָדָם נוֹגֵעַ בַּמּוּכָן לַחֲבֵירוֹ אֲפִילוּ כִּמְלֹא נִימָא — *A man cannot touch something that has been set aside for his friend — even a hairsbreadth of it.* A person cannot take what is not rightfully his.

And of course, every Jew certainly believes what the Gemara in *Ta'anis* (2a) teaches, that the key of *parnassah* is in the hand of the *Eibishter*.

Being dishonest not only shows a lack of *emes*, it also bespeaks a terrible lack of *emunah*. It is also a serious violation of basic *emunah* to think that one can gain from doing something that Hashem cannot tolerate.

Beyond that, we must also internalize the crucial understanding that dishonesty cannot bring gain. There used to be a popular saying, "Crime doesn't pay." Today, with all of the cheating that takes place in this world, the saying has lost its popularity. But it has not lost its truth…and practicality.

## ⟨℘⟩ The Eternal *Shidduch*

The Midrash (*Shocher Tov Tehillim* 7:11) tells an incredible story: When Noach entered the *teivah*, all creatures came to him in pairs. *Sheker* wanted to enter the *teivah*, but came alone. Noach said, "I'm sorry, we only take couples, שְׁנַיִם שְׁנַיִם וכו' זָכָר וּנְקֵבָה. There are no singles in this *teivah*. לֵךְ הָבִיא לְךָ בֶּן זוּג — [Sheker], go find a shidduch.

This incredible Midrash continues: הָלַךְ וּמָצָא אֶת פַּחְתָא — *Sheker went out and found [a perfect shidduch]: P'chas.*

What is "*P'chas*"? Losses and damages. A few contemporary examples would be: repair costs, fines, a ticket, bounced checks, lost items. In business these are all called "normal losses."

*Sheker* now had a mate — Dishonesty was paired with Loss. Noach allowed the two into the *teivah*.

The Midrash continues: After surviving the *mabul*, *Sheker* left the *teivah* and made his way in the world, plying his "trade." He worked hard for days and weeks and years. One day, he attempted to gather his fortune, to see how much wealth he had amassed. To his dismay, he realized that he had no meaningful amount saved.

"I worked so hard! I cheated here, and lied there; I fooled that person, and pulled off so many '*shticklach*'! Where's all my money that I earned all of these years?"

Says the Midrash, *P'chas* took it all. *Sheker* forgot that he had a *shidduch*. Losses absorbed all of *Sheker's* gains.

This is the *pshat* in the *pasuk* in *Tehillim* (7:15): הֵנֵּה יְחַבֶּל־אָוֶן וְהָרָה עָמָל וְיָלַד שָׁקֶר —
*And he is pregnant with evil schemes but gives birth to failure.* Rashi explains
that all of the money that a person gains dishonestly will be lost in
different ways. Rashi, in fact, alludes to the above Midrash. A person
will never benefit from, and will never enjoy anything that he takes
dishonestly. Medical expenses, car repairs, bad investments — these are
some of the countless ways that a person's ill-gained money disappears.

In Hashem's world, no one gains from dishonesty. Can it be
otherwise? If Hashem runs and controls the world, and Hashem hates
falsehood, is it possible that a person will gain by being dishonest?

Certainly, in our world of *sheker*, people do lie and people do cheat.
We all have *bechirah*, we all have free choice. It may look like your
competition is getting an unfair advantage because he is doing things
that are dishonest. But will those people really gain? Will they ever
benefit from even one penny of money that was taken dishonestly? Will
they enjoy it in the long-term? The *shidduch* that was made thousands of
years ago between *Sheker* and *P'chas* is an eternal bond. It may look like
a person gains from dishonesty, but it is not so. It may take a few weeks,
or a few years, but ultimately, *sheker* turns into *p'chas* — and sometimes
into very painful forms of losses. Cheating is not only terribly wrong, it
is terribly foolish.

No one gains from doing the wrong thing. This is a basic part of our
*emunah*, and this has to be our attitude, even when faced with temptation
that can be difficult to resist.

The Rambam, in his *tzava'ah* (ethical will) to his children, pleads
with them to love the truth, live the truth, and to be *moser nefesh* for
the truth. The Rambam compares a life built on truth to a building
constructed on a secure foundation. On the other hand, the Rambam
enjoins his children to hate dishonesty, and compares anything based on
falsehood to a structure built on a very faulty foundation.

## ✺ Our Troubled Times

*Chazal* foresaw the ugly signs of the *Ikvesa d'Meshicha*, the era
immediately preceding the arrival of Mashiach (see *Sotah* 49b). One of
these signs is: הָאֱמֶת תְּהֵא נֶעְדֶּרֶת — *honesty will be missing.* We see this all
around us; there is so much *sheker* in the world.

Someone once came running to his *rebbi*. "Rebbi! I have to fill out a form and it asks for my age. I am forty years old, but what should I write? If I write that I am fifty, I can get a senior discount earlier. But if I write that I am thirty, I will receive a different benefit — reserved for younger people — for longer. What should I do?"

The rabbi, genuinely confused, replied, "Why not write the truth?"

"You know," said the man, "I never even thought of that!"

Often, in our world, people are not the least bit concerned with honesty, and are only preoccupied with the thought, "How can I benefit most?" Unfortunately, they have forgotten the ancient truth, that one won't, one can't, ever gain from dishonesty. Let us never forget the inseparable *shidduch* of *sheker* and *p'chas*.

I once had a problem with an appliance that I had bought months earlier. The appliance had a six-month manufacturer's warranty, and I was past the six months. I had purchased the item at a Jewish store, and I brought it back to see if it could be repaired.

The salesman told me, "It's no problem. I'll scan the item again, and print up another receipt showing that you purchased it less than six months ago. Then I can get you a new one."

I was shocked. I couldn't believe it. This was a "religious" person. He was going to lie for money? And, worse yet, he expected that I would unflinchingly agree. Such behavior is not only lacking in *emes*, it is lacking in *emunah*. In Hashem's world of *emes*, is it conceivable to change the date and take something that is not rightfully ours?

The Chazon Ish (*Igros* 1:94), in a very emotional letter, writes to an individual who apparently did something wrong in an attempt to earn money: "How could you have done that? Don't you know the lesson of the *mann*? A person will only receive what is destined for him, no more and no less. Do you think that by deviating from the halachah, the ultimate truth, you will gain?"

The Chazon Ish adds a powerful *mashal*: Someone who turns to improper means to earn *parnassah* is compared to a man who sees that his house is burning and wishes to douse the flames with any available liquid. Grabbing the first jug that he sees, he begins to pour from it —

but it is full of gasoline! Obviously, the man's efforts will only aggravate the situation. If you are struggling with your *parnassah*, adding *sheker* to the situation will only make it worse.

Do you want to have *parnassah*? Hashem has your *parnassah*. Do you really believe that you can secure it through dishonest means?

It is very challenging to live honestly in a world that is so unscrupulous. How do we maintain our devotion to truth? The key is the carefully chosen words of the Gemara: נְשָׂאתָ וְנָתַתָּ בֶּאֱמוּנָה, let us live with *emunah* and make sure that all of our dealings are with *emunah*. Remember Rav Chaim Vital's priceless words: If someone lives dishonestly he is embracing a new god called *sheker*. The world we live in, for all of the *sheker* within it, is still Hashem's world. Hashem's essence is truth, and we have to make sure that it is ours as well. I was told that almost 20 percent of certain types of insurance claims are false. As believing Jews, we must abhor these types of practices.

The Chazon Ish writes in his classic work *Emunah U'bitachon* (4:13) that we have to devote more time to talking about honesty. As true as it was then, it is all the more so in our times. It is over sixty years since the Chazon Ish passed away, and we see how the world has fallen even lower into the clutches of *sheker*. Today, unfortunately, lying has become an accepted way of life. Someone once showed me a quote from a prominent newspaper: "Lying has become an integral part of American culture, a trait of the American character. We lie and we don't even think about it; we lie for no reason and the people we lie to are those closest to us."

## To Jew

Rav Shimon Schwab once spoke at an Agudah Convention. Anybody who heard that address will never forget the pain that his words engendered. He reported that he had seen in a dictionary that the word "Jew" can also be used as a verb, as in "to Jew." What does it mean? To cheat, to be engaged in sharp practices. What a horrific *chillul Hashem*. The non-Jews, searching for a word that is synonymous with dishonesty, arrived at the word "Jew"!

Of course, this is laced with anti-Semitism. And, perhaps, people naturally expect a higher level of conduct from the Jewish nation, and when we fall short of it, they criticize us. But this is a wake-up call for us. It implies that the outside world has the impression that Jews are less than honest. That is a terrible *chillul Hashem*, because Hashem is *emes*, His Torah is *emes* and His people have to be the epitome, the very embodiment, of *emes*. What a gruesome *chillul Hashem* to have lived to see a day that "to Jew" is synonymous with dishonesty.

We have a mission: We must talk about *emes*. We must demonstrate the importance of *emes* to our children and to the world. We have to act in a manner that is fully consistent with *emes*, until we will be privileged to see the day when there will be a revision in those dictionaries: **Jew** (verb, as in "to Jew") — to be scrupulously honest in business; to be extra careful that everything done and every word spoken is the pure truth.

We have to live in a way that our actions proclaim, "Honesty is an integral part of the Jewish character; we are honest in every situation because we are privileged to serve Hashem, Whose very essence is *emes*, and we are privileged to learn the Torah that is *emes*."

## ❧ Do as I Do

\* A person goes on a Chol Hamoed trip with his children, to an attraction where the entrance fee is based on age. He tells his seven-year-old child, "Tell the man that you are six years old, so we will pay less."

\* A father is busy at home when the phone rings. Covering the phone, the child tells the father, "Tatty, it is for you!" "Tell them I am not at home now," says the father.

\* A child innocently asks his parent, "Can I use my friend's bus pass even though I'm not entitled to the free ride?" The parent responds, "You can use if it won't cause a *chillul Hashem*."

The *pasuk* (*Yirmiyahu* 9:4) says: לִמְּדוּ לְשׁוֹנָם דַּבֶּר שֶׁקֶר — *They train their tongues to speak falsehoods.* In the above examples, that is exactly what the parent is doing. He is training himself and his children to lie and cheat.

We have to live *emunah*, we have to live *emes*, and we have to make sure our children see our devotion to *emes*. They should see that we believe *b'emunah sheleimah* that we won't ever gain from deviating from the truth. We have to be *mechanech* our children and our grandchildren — and, maybe more important, ourselves — in the absolute importance of truth.

The Shelah Hakadosh (*Sha'ar Oisios, Derech Eretz 21*) writes with great admiration that he once met a pious Sephardic Jew, who, as the Shelah describes, "could not lie for all the money in the world." The Shelah asked him how he developed his tremendous devotion and sensitivity to *emes*. The Yid answered, very proudly, that he received it from his father.

"My father trained us and ingrained within us the importance of *emes*. When one of his children did something wrong, and admitted his guilt, he was rewarded! He paid us to say the truth. My father lived the principle of the *pasuk* (*Mishlei* 23:23): אֱמֶת קְנֵה וְאַל תִּמְכֹּר — *Purchase truth, do not sell it*. My father actually 'bought' truth. He paid money so that we should learn the value of truth."

The Shelah goes on to discuss how important it is to train children in this matter. One must teach children to have sensitivity to *emes* and an aversion to *sheker*. As Dovid Hamelech writes (*Tehillim* 119:163): שֶׁקֶר שָׂנֵאתִי וַאֲתַעֵבָה — *I have hated falsehood and abhorred it*. We must hate a mistruth. We must develop an inability to tolerate any deviation from truth.

The most effective, and the most long-lasting *chinuch habanim* is a "do as I do" *chinuch*. Rav Shraga Feivel Mendlowitz would say it succinctly — there are some things that can't be taught, they have to be "caught." It has to be contagious. If we desire to see our children becoming honest people, we must show them our own commitment and passion to honesty. A child who sees a parent's love for truth will develop sensitivity to truth.

One of the regular attendees of my *shiurim* often asks me questions which deal with monetary issues. There are things that many people in business assume are permissible, yet he will often ask if he indeed may do them. These types of questions, and this type of questioner, are a rarity in our times. I once asked him, "You seem to be so devoted to every nuance of *Choshen Mishpat*; did you have a special *chinuch* about it?" He became teary-eyed. "My *chinuch* was from my father. He was such an *ish emes*, and he made such an impression on me." The greatest *chinuch* is when our children are inspired by our devotion to absolute truth.

## ❧ Everlasting Impressions

On Shevi'i shel Pesach 5761, I visited Rav Pam and he shared with me some personal recollections from his youth. That time I spent with my *rebbi* was very precious to me.

Rav Pam told me that lately he had been thinking about his mother, one incident in particular. (According to my calculations, this was something that had happened eighty years earlier.) He related:

My father, who was the *rav* of a town in Europe, once had occasion to travel to America. One of the townswomen came to visit my mother to make a request.

"We are having a terribly difficult time financially. We simply have no money. I heard that the Rav is in America. Could you please contact him? Maybe the Rav could approach my Uncle Yankel, and tell him of our situation. Hopefully he will send us money."

My mother thought that this was a very silly request. The woman was not sure exactly where her uncle lived. Find "Uncle Yankel" in America? How, exactly? So my mother listened to the woman and then basically ignored her request. There was no point in mentioning it to the Rav.

A few weeks later, this woman was sitting *shivah* for a relative. My mother went to be *menachem avel*. As soon as she walked through the door, the woman told her, "Rebbetzin, Rebbetzin! You saved us! We received money from my Uncle Yankel from America."

My mother was in a quandary. She had done nothing. It was a coincidence; the uncle sent them money on his own. But what should she do? It was inappropriate to discuss the matter now, in a *beis aveil*. She felt that perhaps she should just nod and remain quiet, and set the record straight at a later time. But my mother felt that she simply could not do that.

It would not have been honest to hear an untrue statement and not correct it. She couldn't tolerate a falsehood — even only temporarily, and despite the fact that she didn't prompt it, and it was the woman's mistake. My mother told her, "I'm so happy that you received the help, but I must tell you that it had nothing to do with me. I don't deserve this credit."

Rav Pam related that the incident weighed heavily on his mother's mind even years later. She felt that perhaps it was wrong to respond to the woman's remark; it was not the right time or place for such talk. But she could not help it; she could not tolerate to hear an untruthful statement.

I thought to myself, *The story is amazing, but what is even more inspiring is that now, eighty years later, Rav Pam is still thinking about it.*

That is *chinuch.* That is why she was *zocheh* to have a child like Rav Pam who was the essence of truth. A mother who is passionate about truth, and devoted and committed to absolute truth, will convey these feelings to her children.

Today this is more necessary than ever. Our children must hear and see that although we live in this world of *sheker,* we will not even contemplate deviating from the *emes.* Our children desperately need this *chinuch* in our turbulent times.

## Apologies and Commitments

I would like to suggest a wonderful *segulah* for successful interpersonal relationships, specifically *shalom bayis.* Every so often, practice repeating the words, "I was wrong. I am sorry. I made a mistake."

An important aspect of *emes* is being *modeh al ha'emes* — admitting to one's mistakes. Very often, in a close relationship — especially in a marriage — something may begin as a small misunderstanding, but develops and evolves into something much bigger. Why? Because we cannot bring ourselves to admit that we were wrong, or that we made a mistake. As a result, we become more ensnared in the issue or problem, and the tension and hurt feelings continue to grow. Not admitting to the truth is really a deviation from the truth. And often, a "small" untruth will snowball into something much larger.

Ours is a world that is not willing to admit and that is always playing the blame game. But the *middas ha'emes* trains us to say those important words: "I was wrong. I am sorry. I made a mistake."

The Midrash (*Vayikra* 13:1) says that when Aharon corrected Moshe about a certain halachah, Moshe sent out a proclamation: "I made a mistake. Aharon is correct." That admission is the sign of greatness. And that idea of admitting when we are wrong is an important facet of *emes*.

Another practical example of honesty in our daily lives is keeping one's word and meeting one's commitments. If you tell someone, "I'll do it..." or "I'll be there..." or "I'll meet you in a half hour..." be true to your word. If you said that you will do something, do it. A word is sacred. In Yiddish there is an expression, *ah vort is ah vort*. How much aggravation and how much disappointment arises from people who say they will do something, but don't keep to it? How often does this strain, or even break, friendships? When people rely on things they were assured would be done, and then it is not done, they resent it, and it causes friction between people.

Rav Nosson Tzvi Finkel, the late Mirrer Rosh Yeshivah, in his address to the yeshivah on Rosh Hashanah, pleaded: "At this time, people are looking for *kabbalos*, for something to accept upon themselves to do in the new year. I have a very good suggestion. Accept that if you say that you will do something, do it. If you say 'I'm coming in an hour,' be there in an hour. Believe me, this will prevent much aggravation."

## ☙ Small Claims Court

Perhaps the most important practical example of honesty in daily living is truthfulness in our financial dealings.

In our very challenging world, a person could so very easily write, or type into a computer, a few words, or a different date, or a changed fact — and it can make a difference of hundreds or even thousands of dollars for him. And in the world around us, everybody is doing this. But we have to remember what we will be asked: נָשָׂאתָ וְנָתַתָּ בֶּאֱמוּנָה?

*Chazal* tell us (*Sanhedrin* 8a): דִּין שֶׁל פְּרוּטָה כְּדִין שֶׁל מֵאָה — *The judging of a perutah (a small coin) is equal to the judging of a hundred (coins).* Even a very small amount of money must be treated like a very large amount.

The Gemara (*Baba Kama* 119a) furthermore says, and the *Shulchan Aruch* (359:4) records it: הַגּוֹזֵל אֶת חֲבֵרוֹ בְּשָׁוֶה פְּרוּטָה כְּאִילוּ נוֹטֵל נִשְׁמָתוֹ מִמֶּנּוּ — *One who steals a perutah from another person is as if he took his life.*

There is no *kleinikeit*, there is no "small money," and no "small claims court" in our *Shulchan Aruch*.

How often does it happen that we call a car service, and just then someone offers us a ride? If we called a car service, and the driver began the job, we have to pay for that. One may not just cancel a car service because he found a ride. It is also important to remember that it is unfair to keep the driver waiting for an unreasonable amount of time.

How often do children — or maybe even adults — borrow small change (e.g. for a soda) without really thinking of it as a proper loan? Will we remember to repay it? נָשָׂאתָ וְנָתַתָּ בֶּאֱמוּנָה applies even to a *perutah*.

The wife of the Chazon Ish owned a small store. Once, she had a minor dispute with a customer, and they agreed to abide to what the Chazon Ish would decide. The Chazon Ish listened to both sides of the story, and ruled against his *rebbetzin* — the customer does not have to pay.

After the customer had left, the Chazon Ish's wife who felt that she was clearly correct asked her husband why he ruled as he did. The Chazon Ish responded, "I also think that you were probably right, but I have a small doubt that maybe the costumer was right. *Uhn oib m'nemt yenem's perutah, vos is vert der gantze leben* — if we take someone else's *perutah*, of what value is our lives?"

## ⁜ Please Don't Forget!

Rav Segal, the Manchester Rosh Yeshivah, would relate the following amazing story. It is printed in his *sefer* (*Yireh Vada'as* 1:78) where he records a *kabbalah*, a tradition, about this story going back to Rav Chaim Volozhiner.

Rav Chaim Volozhiner had a *talmid* who became very ill and had to return home. Rav Chaim sent another *bachur* to accompany the ill *bachur* on his trip.

On their way, the boys stayed overnight at an inn. The next morning, while settling their bill, they realized that they were seven small coins short. The healthy *bachur* told the innkeeper that he would pay him the missing amount on his return journey. However, he forgot and never repaid the seven coins.

Rav Chaim Volozhiner had instituted that learning would never cease in the *beis midrash* of Yeshivas Volozhin. Twenty-four hours a day, there were shifts that constantly learned Torah. Rav Chaim himself would often take a shift as well. Late one night, Rav Chaim was learning in the *beis midrash* when an image of that sick *talmid* who had recently been *niftar* appeared before him.

"Why have you come back?" asked Rav Chaim.

"I will tell you, Rebbi," said the boy. "*Baruch Hashem*, my judgment in *Shamayim* was very favorable. But there was one thing that marred my record. I was told that I still owe seven coins to that innkeeper, and one cannot enter Gan Eden if he owes money. I pleaded that it was not my fault. I had died, and my friend simply forgot to repay the money. Because of my pleas I was granted permission to come back to this world to resolve the matter. Please, Rebbi! Please arrange that the money should be repaid."

A child comes home from the store and tells his parent, "I was short a few cents; the storekeeper said that I should pay him next time…" When that happens in my house, I give the child the money and send him back to the store at once. "Don't wait until next time. What will be if you forget?"

Every loan must be repaid, even the "small" ones.

## ❦ A Bag of Quarters

Whenever we take something that is not due to us, we unknowingly pay a heavy price for it.

The story is told of a farmer delivering sacks of his produce to a storekeeper.

The storekeeper says, "Please bring the sacks into my storeroom. For every sack that is brought, I will put a small coin in this little box."

The storekeeper's idea, of course, was to keep track of the amount of sacks that the farmer hauls. When the farmer finishes, the storekeeper will count the coins, and pay the farmer a few coins for each coin in the box. But the foolish farmer didn't understand the system, and every time he passed the little box on his way in or out, he stole a glance at the storekeeper. If the storekeeper's attention was elsewhere, the farmer grabbed a coin or two.

"What are a few small coins to the storekeeper? I am going to take them for myself."

Foolish farmer! Every small coin in the box means a much larger payment to you.

It is the oldest truth; the inseparable pair of *sheker* and loss. When we take even a little bit untruthfully, we lose in the long run. There is no end to the ways that we can lose the money. We must live our lives as eloquent testimony that "to Jew" means to be outstanding in our honesty. We must not only be concerned with being "*glatt kosher*"; we must be sure to be "*glatt yosher*," as well. We must be careful with what goes *into* our mouths, and we must be careful with what leaves it as well.

The Smag (*sefer Mitzvos Hagadol* 74) wrote something incredible: I often implore others to be honest because Mashiach will not come if Jews are not honest. Why? When Mashiach comes Hashem will make clear to the world that we are His beloved nation, worthy of His favor and worthy of redemption. But if Jews are not honest, the very arrival of Mashiach will cause a *chillul Hashem*, because the *goyim* will say, "*These* are Your Chosen People? *These* are the people that You redeemed? They lie and they cheat."

When will we be worthy of the *Geulah*? When we will have a reputation for being honest. Then Hashem will be proud to say, "These are My children. This is My Chosen People. They are *glatt yosher*."

## Scuffed Shoes

Let me conclude with the following story:

Yankele, a young orphan worked in the home of the local *rav*. Due to his poverty, Yankele wore a very old, tattered pair of shoes. He very much wanted a new pair, and, in fact, he went to the shoe store and "picked out a pair" that he would like. Of course, it was wishful thinking; the shoes cost twenty rubles and he could not afford them. But some kind townsfolk were aware of his situation and decided to donate the money, so that Yankele could purchase them. Unbeknown to Yankele, they brought twenty rubles to the *rav* and explained what the money was intended for. Just then the *rav* had to step out, so he put the money in a drawer in his study.

Moments later, Yankele was cleaning the study, and chanced upon the money in the drawer. Did the *rav* put it there? Would he miss it if it was taken? Look, it was just the amount for the shoes that he had "chosen"! But how could he take money that wasn't his? But he really did need shoes. Yankele fought with himself, back and forth, until, in a moment of weakness, he took the money. He quickly ran to the store and bought the shoes. A beautiful shiny pair of shoes, all his own!

But his happiness was short-lived. "What are people going to say? Where did I get twenty rubles for a new pair of shoes? Everyone will realize that I stole the money from the *rav*. I have new shoes, but I can't wear them in public."

Yankele had an idea. He took the shoes, scratched off all of the shiny coating, and made scuff marks all over them. That way no one would realize that the shoes were new.

When the *rav* returned home, he went to his study to give the money to Yankele. But the money was not there. Then he noticed that Yankele was no longer wearing tattered shoes. He was wearing new shoes that were terribly scuffed and scratched. The *rav* understood the whole story.

"Oy, Yankele! Yankele! Had you overcome your desire to take something that was not yours, you would have had those beautiful new shoes without a single scratch or scuff mark!"

We can all learn a penetrating lesson from this story. Hashem gave each of us a *neshamah* that sparkles and shines with His *kedushah*: נְשָׁמָה שֶׁנָּתַתָּ בִּי טְהוֹרָה הִיא — *The soul that You placed in me is pure.* Hashem gives us instructions: keep this beautiful *neshamah* clean; keep it pure and holy and pristine; keep it sparkling.

"And don't worry," says Hashem, "I will give you what you need; I will see to it that you have *parnassah*. But live with *emunah*! Do not deviate from *emes*, because by doing so, you will unnecessarily mar the beauty and dull the shine of your *neshamah*."

Every *perutah* that we are destined to have, we will have: בְּהֶתֵּר וְלֹא בְּאִסוּר, בְּנַחַת וְלֹא בְּצַעַר — *through permitted means and not forbidden means, with ease and not with suffering.* We do not have to deviate from the truth in any way to get what is destined for us. We should not want what is not ours; such "gains" are only destined for *p'chas.*

Let us cherish the truth. Then we will see the fulfillment of the Smag's promise — our well-deserved redemption.

Rav Chatzkel Levenstein made the following astonishing statement in a *shmuess* that he delivered: "I realize that I really don't have *emunah*. But it's never too late…"

And he went on to present a new *emunah* initiative that he wanted to set in place — for himself and for the *talmidim*.

At the time, Rav Chatzkel was over eighty years old. And of all of his *middos tovos*, Rav Chatzkel was particularly renowned for his *emunah*. The Chazon Ish once commented, "Some people have *emunah* in their hearts and some have *emunah* in their minds. But Rav Chatzkel has *emunah* in his hands!" Rav Chatzkel was the very embodiment of *emunah*.

Rav Chatzkel's statement teaches us a crucial lesson. The *avodah* of attaining *emunah* entails a lifetime of involvement in *emunah*; it is a process of continual growth. This is the meaning of the *pasuk* (*Chavakuk* 2:4): וְצַדִּיק בֶּאֱמוּנָתוֹ יִחְיֶה — *and the righteous person will live through his faith*. One must *live* with *emunah*. *Emunah* is not only a mitzvah, it is a way of life.

There is a very important aspect of *emunah* that although it is a vital part of a Jew's lifelong mission of וְצַדִּיק בֶּאֱמוּנָתוֹ יִחְיֶה — living with *emunah*, it is not spoken about enough. I am referring to *emunas chachamim*, placing our faith and trust in our *gedolim*.

## ᴗ Torah and Politics

Rabbi Moshe Sherer would often recount a story that occurred in the summer of 1962. At that time, the United States voted in the United Nations against Israel on a certain issue. Shortly thereafter, Rabbi Sherer received an invitation to the White House to meet with President Kennedy. The president wanted to explain to him — and to the other invited Jewish leaders — why he had taken such a tough stance against Israel. Rabbi Sherer was very interested in attending this meeting, but to his chagrin, it was scheduled for ten o'clock on Tishah

B'Av morning. How would he go to the White House on Tishah B'Av? What would he do about sitting on a chair? Should he shave or not? Should he wear his shoes or his sneakers? Immediately he called Rav Aharon Kotler, his guide in all aspects of his *klal* work.

Rav Aharon told him that for the halachic dilemmas involved, he should consult with Rav Moshe, the *posek hador*. "But then," said Rabbi Sherer, "Rav Aharon stayed on the phone with me for *over an hour*, telling me what to say to the president. With amazing perception and clarity, he said, 'The president will say this, and you will counter with this… The president will ask you this, and you are to respond with this.'

"I was shocked. Rav Aharon was an *ish kadosh*, a man who was *kulo Torah*! He never looked at a *New York Times*; he certainly never listened to a radio. Where did he get all of this information from?"

But Rabbi Sherer's amazement only grew during the meeting when he saw how accurate and on target Rav Aharon was. Rav Aharon's guidance carried the day. The clear directions and the preparation that Rabbi Sherer had received yielded tremendously successful results on that Tishah B'Av morning.

When relating the story, Rabbi Sherer would marvel aloud, "How amazing! Someone so completely immersed in Torah was able to advise me about politics that would seem to have no connection to him."

It certainly is amazing, but it is not unbelievable. The truth is that Rav Aharon was able to advise Rabbi Sherer not *despite* his status as an *ish kadosh* and someone who was *kulo Torah*, but precisely *because* of it.

## ᐤᔕᐤ Privy to the Unknown

The *Avos D'Rabi Nosson* (4:1) teaches that: תַּלְמוּד תּוֹרָה חֲבִיבָה לִפְנֵי הַמָּקוֹם — *Learning Torah is extremely beloved before Hashem*, and if someone learns Torah, יוֹדֵעַ דַּעְתּוֹ שֶׁל מָקוֹם — *he will know the knowledge of Hashem*. Someone who learns Torah understands the world because he recognizes what the Ribono Shel Olam wants. יוֹדֵעַ דַּעְתּוֹ שֶׁל מָקוֹם, he is privy to a deeper understanding of how the Ribono Shel Olam directs this world.

Whether you call it *siyata d'Shmaya*, a *mofes*, or *ruach hakodesh*, a *gadol b'Torah* is blessed with incredible insight and understanding of the world. A *talmid chacham* who spends his days and his nights, his weekdays, his *Shabbosos*, and his Yamim Tovim, learning and toiling to understand the Torah becomes a יוֹדֵעַ דַּעְתּוֹ שֶׁל מָקוֹם. If we don't understand that, perhaps it is because we underestimate how beloved *talmud Torah* is in Hashem's eyes.

In *sefer Nefesh Hachaim* (*sha'ar daled*, ch. 1), Rav Chaim Volozhiner describes what he refers to as גְּדוּלַת יְקַר תִּפְאַרְתָּהּ וּמַעֲלָתָהּ שֶׁל הַתּוֹרָה. He explains the greatness, the glory, and the power of the Torah, and what the Torah means to the world and to Hashem. Further (ch. 20), he writes that a *talmid chacham* is the *ben yakir* — the precious child, who comes and goes as he pleases in the palace of the King and is privy to all of the secrets of the King. The *talmid chacham* is a dearly beloved child of Hashem due to his great diligence in learning Torah and because he lives a life devoted to the goal of doing Hashem's bidding. With his Torah and *yiras Shamayim*, he is able to know what is hidden from everyone else. All the doors are open for him, and he becomes a יוֹדֵעַ דַּעְתּוֹ שֶׁל מָקוֹם.

## ᠍᠍᠍ Together with Hashem

The Chazon Ish (*Emunah U'bitachon* 3:22) writes that from a Torah perspective, the אִישִׁיּוֹת הַיוֹתֵר חֲמוּדָה — *the most beloved personage*, is the *talmid chacham*.

If we understand this above concept, explains the Chazon Ish, we can understand a well-known, but seemingly perplexing Gemara.

The Torah requires a person to have *yiras Shamayim*. This mitzvah is found in the *pasuk* (*Devarim* 6:13) אֶת ה' אֱלֹקֶיךָ תִּירָא — *You should fear Hashem, your G-d.* Now, every time a *pasuk* says the word "אֶת," something unwritten is understood to be included in that *pasuk*. But what could be included in the mitzvah of *yiras Shamayim*? Rabbi Akiva (*Bava Kama* 41b) taught that in this *pasuk*, the word "אֶת" is meant to include *talmidei chachamim*. Not only must we fear Hashem, we must also revere and respect *talmidei chachamim*.

It is incredible that a human being can be included in the same category as Hashem Himself! This shows us the great level that a *talmid chacham* has attained. Since the *talmid chacham* is so close to Hashem and so beloved in His eyes, he is included — together with Hashem! — in the same category of those whom we must revere.

In addition, given the fact that the beloved *talmid chacham* is privy to the יוֹדֵעַ דַּעְתּוֹ שֶׁל מָקוֹם, a further equation is formulated: *emunas chachamim* is one and the same with *emunah b'Hashem*. Thus, we must not only revere a *talmid chacham*, we must also have faith in him and accept what he says as the absolute truth.

## He Rules…

And the concept of *emunas chachamim* goes even further.

The *pasuk* says (*II Shmuel* 23:3): צוּר יִשְׂרָאֵל מוֹשֵׁל בָּאָדָם צַדִּיק — *the Rock of Israel, ruler over men, a righteous one.*

*Chazal* (*Tanna D'vei Eliyahu*, ch. 2) say something incredible on this *pasuk*:

Hashem says: "אֲנִי מוֹשֵׁל בָּאָדָם — *I rule people,*

וּמִי מוֹשֵׁל בִּי — *and who rules Me?*"

An astounding question: Who rules Hashem?

And *Chazal* give an equally astonishing answer: צַדִּיק — *a tzaddik!*

A tzaddik rules Hashem. How so? שֶׁאֲנִי גּוֹזֵר גְּזֵירָה וְהוּא מְבַטְּלָהּ — *for I make decrees and he annuls them.*

This *Chazal* is the source for the familiar quote: צַדִּיק גּוֹזֵר, וְהַקָּדוֹשׁ בָּרוּךְ הוּא מְקַיֵּם — *A tzaddik makes a decree, and Hashem fulfills it.*

It is unbelievable; it would be impossible for us to say this, if not for the fact that it is sourced in *Chazal*. But when a tzaddik says something, it happens. It is, *kaviyachol*, as if the tzaddik rules and dictates what will take place in Hashem's world. When you ask a *talmid chacham* for advice, you know you will receive sound and true guidance. The tzaddik is privy to the דַּעְתּוֹ שֶׁל מָקוֹם, to classified information, and more amazing, he dictates דַּעְתּוֹ שֶׁל מָקוֹם.

This is an incredible thought, and it gives us new insight into the *ko'ach* of our *gedolim*.

The following *mashal* crystalizes this concept: The boys in a class do not know what their *rebbi* is going to do at any given time. When will the test be? What day will *rebbi's* Chanukah party be? Why was *rebbi* absent today? Will he come tomorrow? No one knows.

But sometimes there is one boy in the class who *does* know. He can answer with certainty all of the above questions. Who is that boy? The *rebbi's* son! Given his intimate relationship, and the fact that he lives in the same house as the *rebbi*, he is privy to information that the others are not.

This is the first step in the tzaddik's relationship with Hashem. When you ask a true *talmid chacham* for advice, you can't go wrong because he knows better. With his *da'as Torah*, he is aware of יוֹדֵעַ דַּעְתּוֹ שֶׁל מָקוֹם. A tzaddik knows what the Ribono Shel Olam wants.

But the relationship goes even deeper. Going back to the *mashal*, imagine that the *rebbi* has decided that he would like to host his class for a Chanukah party on the first night of Chanukah. But before making his announcement, his son comes over to him with a surprise. He has finished the *masechta* that he was learning and would like to make a private family *siyum* at their home on the first night of Chanukah. The *rebbi*, of course, will postpone the class party to the next night.

This is the second part of the relationship. Beyond the tzaddik's status as the יוֹדֵעַ דַּעְתּוֹ שֶׁל מָקוֹם, the tzaddik also has the *ko'ach* of צַדִּיק מוֹשֵׁל בִּי. Beyond being privy to information, the tzaddik, *kaveyachol*, is in the unique position of being able to sway, and almost dictate, the will of Hashem.

## ⸾ Rav Chatzkel — The *Mofes Hador*

I was privileged to learn from *rebbeim* who learned in the prewar Europe era in the Mirrer Yeshivah. Having fled the Nazis, they escaped with the yeshivah to Shanghai, China. Although I was not there, I was powerfully affected by their experiences, just from hearing their firsthand accounts of the incredible miracles that they experienced on a constant basis during that period.

(As an amazing aside, it is worthwhile to retell the following: When the yeshivah escaped to Shanghai, they "found" a large *beis midrash* — unused for many years — in which they were able to learn. And when they counted the seats in the *beis midrash*, the number of seats equaled the number of their group. There was exactly one seat for each *talmid* and each *rosh yeshivah*. How did a *beis midrash* appear in the middle of China? A Jew had emigrated to Shanghai years before. He was an assimilated Jew; he married a local non-Jewish woman, and lived out his life in his adopted city. After his death, his wife wanted to perpetuate his memory. Ironic as it may seem, the non-Jewish wife was apparently more interested in religion than her departed husband, and she built a large shul in his memory. For many years, no one could fathom the purpose of this shul. Eventually, the yeshivah came and studied Torah there, with incredible diligence, for a number of years. Hashem prepared the *beis midrash* for them years in advance.)

Rav Chatzkel Levenstein was known as the *mofes hador* — the wonder of the generation. It was he who guided the yeshivah during the escape from Europe to China. He instructed them when and where to go. At times he would say, "We cannot leave now." The *talmidim* often thought he was making a grave error, but they listened to him and were always saved. Once he said, "We must move on immediately." The next day, the building that his group was staying in was bombed. Throughout these difficult times, Rav Chatzkel constantly guided the yeshivah and kept them safe.

How did he always know what they should do? No one knew the answer to this question. Finally, his *talmidim* confronted him. They told him that his advice did not seem to make sense and that he was endangering the entire yeshivah. Rav Chatzkel listened compassionately and responded, "What should I do? Every time I have a decision to make, one of my great *rebbeim* — Rav Nachum Velvel (the son of the Alter of Kelm), or Rav Daniel (Movshovitz), or Rav Yeruchem (Levovitz) — appears to me in a dream and tells me exactly what to do. I know it doesn't make sense, but I know that this is the right thing to do."

A tzaddik, a *talmid chacham*, is יוֹדֵעַ דַּעְתּוֹ שֶׁל מָקוֹם; he knows what will be. From danger to danger, Rav Chatzkel guided them; no one could fathom his instructions, but that is what *emunas chachamim* is all about. When you follow the advice of a *gadol*, you cannot go wrong because Hashem Himself says, "צַדִּיק מוֹשֵׁל בִּי" — the tzaddik decrees and I listen," *kaviyachol*.

## ◦◦ The Chazon Ish — The Mystery of the Generation

We know that in his generation, the Chazon Ish was the *tzaddik hador*, the *masmid hador*, and the *posek hador*. But what is incredible is that in the secular Israeli world, the Chazon Ish was referred to as the "*chidas hador* — the mystery of the generation."

It is well known that the Chazon Ish possessed incredible medical knowledge that astounded even the greatest doctors. There are people who have in their possession diagrams that the Chazon Ish drew to help surgeons perform very delicate surgeries. In fact, one doctor is quoted as having exclaimed, "The *rav* in Bnei Brak knows more than I do with my thirty-three years of studying and practicing medicine!" The Chazon Ish's *rebbetzin* once said in jest, "When I married him, I thought I was marrying a *rav*…and he became a doctor!"

Where did the Chazon Ish acquire this astonishing knowledge of medicine?

The Chazon Ish was not only the *chidas hador* regarding medicine; he was also one of the greatest *mechanchim* of his era. He was the leader who dealt with the trauma of the youth who lived through the horrors of World War II. The Chazon Ish was the father to hundreds of refugees struggling to regain their devotion to *Yiddishkeit* after the war.

Again one wonders, where did the Chazon Ish attain this knowledge from?

Needless to say, the Chazon Ish never went to medical school, and he never studied psychology. What he studied, *l'havdil*, was the *heilige* Torah. He was the *ben yakir*, he was אִישִׁיוּת הַיּוֹתֵר חֲמוּדָה, and he gleaned vast expanses of knowledge from the Torah (See *Shu"t Shevet Halevi* 10:13). From the blueprint of the world, he understood the makings of the world; he became a יוֹדֵעַ דַעְתּוֹ שֶׁל מָקוֹם. The Chazon Ish's medical knowledge and his brilliance in *chinuch* were sourced in the *kedushas haTorah* in which he toiled.

If we appreciate what the Torah is, and the love that Hashem has for the Torah, we can appreciate and truly internalize the *emunah* we must have in the *talmidei chachamim*. *Emunas chachamim* is really *emunas Hashem* and *emunah* in *Toras Hashem*.

This brings us to the basis of the concept of *emunas chachamim*. This is why we turn to *gedolim* not only when it comes to a question in halachah, but for guidance in every aspect in our lives. The Chazon Ish (*Igros* 3:92) observed that the Haskalah movement began with the premise that there are two parts of a person's life. *Gedolim* are here to answer our questions in halachah, but as far as how we live our lives, we must be in tune with "other realities." That philosophy is the ruination of Klal Yisrael.

I know a very successful businessman who, for many years, would ask the Satmar Rebbe, Rav Yoel, whenever he had a question in business matters. After the Satmar Rebbe passed away, he started going to Rav Moshe Feinstein. One of his business associates once chided him, "You go to Rav Moshe Feinstein for business advice? What does Rav Moshe know about business?" The man chuckled and replied, "I don't go to Rav Moshe for business advice per se. I go to Rav Moshe to ask him what Hashem wants from me in my business." That is a Yid with a firm understanding of the importance of עֲשֵׂה לְךָ רַב (*Avos* 1:6). He understood that the business advice that he received from Rav Moshe was coming to him from the *ko'ach haTorah*.

## ❧ When Right Becomes Left

The *pasuk* in *Parshas Shoftim* (*Devarim* 17:11) establishes the Torah's requirement to follow *da'as Torah*: לֹא תָסוּר מִן הַדָּבָר אֲשֶׁר יַגִּידוּ לְךָ יָמִין וּשְׂמֹאל — *Do not turn from what they tell you, to the right or to the left.*

Rashi here says something puzzling: Even if they tell you עַל יָמִין שֶׁהוּא שְׂמֹאל — *that the right is the left,* listen to them.

This sounds irrational; if a *gadol* tells you that this is the left and then points to the right, why should you listen? He is clearly making a mistake!

The Ramban explains: It may appear to *you* that left is right and that right is left, but the *gadol* has a *ruach Hashem* within him. The Ramban continues: לְעוֹלָם נִשְׁמָרוּ מִן הַטָּעוּת וּמִן הַמִּכְשׁוֹל — *They are forever protected from the mistake and the stumbling.*

In your perception, you think that he is wrong, but you do not realize that he is יוֹדֵעַ דַּעְתּוֹ שֶׁל מָקוֹם, you do not realize that he knows better. And by listening to him, you will never be led astray.

The Midrash (*Shemos* 3:8) says the same idea: כָּל מִי שֶׁנּוֹטֵל עֵצָה מִן הַזְּקֵנִים אֵינוֹ נִכְשָׁל — *Anyone who takes counsel from the elders will not stumble.*

I can personally attest that countless times in my life I have received advice from *gedolim* that I couldn't understand. But there was one thing that I *did* understand — I understood that they knew better. *Baruch Hashem*, I listened to them all the time, and I have never regretted it. Sometimes it seems to us that they are wrong, but we cannot forget לְעוֹלָם וְשָׁמְרוּ מִן הַטָּעוּת. *Gedolim* have that *siyata d'Shmaya*, the יוֹדֵעַ דַּעְתּוֹ שֶׁל מָקוֹם guiding them when they offer advice.

The Gemara in *Pesachim* (42a) relates an almost comical incident. Rav Masna ruled that matzah must be baked using *mayim shelanu*. *Mayim shelanu* means "water that stayed overnight." The next morning, the women lined up in front of Rav Masna's house with their pitchers in order to buy water from him. They thought *mayim shelanu* means "our water" and that Rav Masna had ruled that only *his* water may be used for matzah.

Why does the Gemara relate this story? The women made a silly mistake! It is amusing, but what is the lesson to be learned from it?

Rav Yisrael Salanter (quoted in *sefer Orchos Yosher siman* 15) says that this Gemara is teaching us the level of *emunas chachamim* of a simple housewife. "The *rav* said *mayim shelanu*, so I may only use his water. I don't understand why. To me it doesn't make sense. But if that's what the *rav* said, that is what I will do."

Imagine if this would happen nowadays, if a *rav* would *pasken* that only his water may be used for baking matzah. It would be a major scandal. People would protest, "He is trying to make money! He is abusing his authority!" But look at the *emunas chachamim* of these women. They misunderstood, but they are to be admired and emulated.

## ✺ *Bayamim Haheim* — In Your Days

Unfortunately, people are apt to say, "Well, if we would have a Rav Aharon Kotler in our days, if we would have a Chazon Ish or a Rav Chatzkel, I would surely listen to them. But there's a *yeridas hadoros*, a weakening of the generations. Our *rabbanim* are not like the *gedolim* of yesteryear."

I once spoke about this topic of *emunas chachamim*, and someone told me afterward, "I can't bring myself to blindly follow today's *rabbanim*. I knew Rav Aharon Belzer! He was a *malach*, a *kadosh*. Today we don't have anyone who can compare to him."

This attitude borders on *kefirah* (heresy). The man's respect for a *gadol* of yesterday is certainly admirable, but he is missing the basics of *emunah*. He does not realize that *emunas chachamim* is not *emunah* in the *chacham* himself. Rather, it is *emunah* that someone who spends his days and nights learning Torah is connected to Hashem. He is the intermediary of **his** times, the one who is privy to *ratzon Hashem*.

There is a Gemara in *Rosh Hashanah* (25b) that says this explicitly. The Gemara interprets the *pasuk* (*Devarim* 17:9): וּבָאתָ אֶל הַכֹּהֲנִים הַלְוִיִם וְאֶל הַשֹּׁפֵט אֲשֶׁר יִהְיֶה בַּיָּמִים הָהֵם — *And you should come to the kohen and the judge that will be in your days.*

The Gemara wonders, of course one must go to the judge of his days; is it possible to go to the judge of the last generation? Answers the Gemara, the *pasuk* is teaching us a very crucial lesson. The *gadol* of your times has the same qualifications and has the same powers as the *gadol* of a previous generation.

The Gemara (ibid.) teaches: יִפְתָּח בְּדוֹרוֹ כִּשְׁמוּאֵל בְּדוֹרוֹ — *Yiftach in his generation is as Shmuel in his generation.*

Shmuel was the great *navi* who, the Gemara says, was equal to Moshe and Aharon. Yiftach was not nearly as great as Shmuel; they were worlds apart. But the Gemara is teaching us that the *gadol* in your times — whether he's a Shmuel or a Yiftach — is the conduit to *ratzon Hashem*. He is the *gadol* who will channel Hashem's *ratzon* to his generation.

The *Chinuch* (mitzvah 496) explains the mitzvah of heeding the words of *gedolei Torah*. We must listen to our *gedolim* because: *They toiled days and nights to understand the depths of the words (of the Torah) and the wonders of knowledge.*

The *talmid chacham* is the one in his generation who is outstanding in his devotion to Torah. True, we do not have a Vilna Gaon; we do not even have a Rav Aharon Kotler. But the *gadol* in our generation has the same qualifications. He is the *ben yakir*, he is the Shmuel of our

generation. He has the same unusual, unlimited powers of the יוֹדֵעַ דַּעְתּוֹ
שֶׁל מָקוֹם and of צַדִּיק מוֹשֵׁל בִּי.

## ᐴ Links in a Chain

The Rambam (introduction to *Yad Hachazakah*) lists the forty generations from Rav Ashi going back to Moshe Rabbeinu. The Rambam concludes: נִמְצָא שֶׁכּוּלָם מִן ה' אֱלֹקֵי יִשְׂרָאֵל — *all of the gedolim are receptors of the word of Hashem Himself.*

That is a concept that warms our hearts. Of course the earlier *gedolim* are greater than our *gedolim*. But the *gadol* that we have is a link in the chain that goes all the way back to Moshe Rabbeinu, directly to the Ribono Shel Olam. In Yiddish there's a beautiful expression: "*Voil zenen de oigen vos haben gezein de oigen* — how fortunate are the eyes that were able to see the eyes (that saw previous generations)." That's the uniqueness of a *mesorah*. We have eyes that are *zocheh* to see our *gedolim*, and our *gedolim* saw their *gedolim*, and their *gedolim* saw their *gedolim* — until Rav Ashi, going back to Moshe Rabbeinu.

Today, at many *chasunos*, the one-man band consists of one musician playing a single keyboard. These sophisticated machines cost thousands of dollars, and they produce extraordinary, beautiful music. Imagine if the wedding's musician sets up in the hall, but cannot play his machine. What's wrong? The outlet is too far from the bandstand and the keyboard's cord is not long enough. A quick foray to the local convenience store provides the solution. For $1.99 he buys an extension cord, and the keyboard can play once again.

Does it make sense? The sophisticated machine that cost thousands of dollars doesn't work, but with a simple $1.99 cord it works?

It's not the cord. The cord just connects him to the power — and then everything works.

That is *mesorah*. The *gadol* of our generation connects to the power that goes all the way back to Moshe Rabbeinu who received the Torah from Hashem. If a person doesn't respect the wisdom of our *gedolim* it is because he does not understand that our *gedolim* have the same qualifications as the previous *gedolim* — they are all people who give their lives for the *dvar Hashem*. For such people, Hashem reciprocates and gives them *da'as Elyon*.

Rav Dessler has a beautiful *shmuess* in *sefer Michtav M'Eliyahu* (vol. 1 p. 75) entitled *Michtav B'dvar Emunas Chachamim*. He points out so beautifully that the concept of *emunas chachamim* is at the very heart of the miracle of Purim, and the story of *Megillas Esther*.

The events in the Megillah did not take place in quick succession. A full nine years elapsed between Achashverosh's banquet and the Jewish victories against their enemies, including Haman's execution. At the beginning of the story, it seemed obvious to the people that their leader, Mordechai, was making wrong decisions for them. And for nine long years, the people seemed to be correct. Only at the end of the story, did the truth of Mordechai's actions come to light.

When Achashverosh invited the Jews to his royal banquet, many of them said: "This king is a madman. Who knows what he will do if provoked? It's dangerous not to go." But Mordechai Hatzaddik gave forth his ruling: "We are not permitted to go. Going to the party may not entail any specific *issur*, but it is nevertheless forbidden." The people felt that Mordechai was being unwise, and that his ruling was reckless. So they went to the banquet, and all was well. Or so it seemed…

The scene repeated itself when Haman rose to power and everyone was commanded to bow to him. Everyone did — except for Mordechai. Again, the people told Mordechai, "You are being rash, you are inciting Haman's wrath! He's going to take revenge for what you're doing." But, as the *pasuk* (*Esther* 3:2) says: וּמָרְדֳּכַי לֹא יִכְרַע וְלֹא יִשְׁתַּחֲוֶה — *Mordechai would not bow and would not prostrate himself.*

And what happened? Exactly what the people had predicted, Haman was enraged. He planned his murderous revenge to wipe out the Jewish nation. And the people must have thought, "Mordechai is a *talmid chacham* and a tzaddik, but he's not politically correct. He doesn't know how to live in this world. *Oy*, why didn't we force him to bow to Haman?"

When the Jews of Shushan attended Achashverosh's banquet, no immediate repercussions were evident. But the sin of נֶהֱנוּ מִסְּעוּדָתוֹ שֶׁל אֲחַשְׁוֵרוֹשׁ, of partaking in Achashverosh's wanton feast, was actually the catalyst of Haman's terrible decree of annihilation. Mordechai's refusal to bow and the public opposition to his action were a classic example of עַל יָמִין שֶׁהוּא שְׂמֹאל. The people were convinced that they knew what was "right," and indeed, to all outward appearances, it seemed that they had an accurate perception of the events. Mordechai's refusal incited Haman just as they had predicted.

But, as we read in the Megillah (*Esther* 4:1): וּמָרְדֳּכַי יָדַע אֶת כָּל אֲשֶׁר נַעֲשָׂה — *And Mordechai knew all that had occurred.*

Mordechai knew the truth. *Chazal* refer to *gedolim* as *einei ha'eidah* — the eyes of the people. They have a certain vision that allows them to see what others don't see. And, Rav Dessler suggests, it was Mordechai's *mesirus nefesh* not to bow to Haman that repaired the damage done when the Jews were **not** *moser nefesh* to stay away from the feast.

Throughout the nine years, the people thought, "Mordechai is a great tzaddik, a wonderful person, but he doesn't know how to live in the real world. We can't follow his advice." Suddenly, at the end, they realized that what they thought was the problem was, in fact, the solution. What they thought caused the *churban*, וּמָרְדֳּכַי לֹא יִכְרַע, brought the *geulah*. What they understood to have caused the *tzarah* was really the *hatzalah* that saved them.

What was the end of the story?

Rav Dessler explains: The terror of Haman's decree brought the Jews to *teshuvah*, and they re-evaluated their loyalty to their *gadol*, Mordechai. When Mordechai accepted Esther's plan of action, which entailed a national three-day period of fasting and prayer, the Jews followed his lead wholeheartedly. It was this *teshuvah* and loyalty which brought about the awesome *hatzalah* and the eternal day of לַיְּהוּדִים הָיְתָה אוֹרָה וְשִׂמְחָה וְשָׂשֹׂן וִיקָר.

The *nes* of Purim teaches us that when we listen to *gedolim*, we will not be misled. That's the greatest strength of a Yid. When we discuss *emunah*, we need to internalize that *emunas chachamim* is an integral part of *emunah*.

## ༠࿇ *Asei Lecha Rav*

A precursor to *emunas chachamim* is, of course, understanding the importance of עֲשֵׂה לְךָ רַב — *make for yourself a rebbi.*

Rav Pam once told me that the author of the *Kitzur Shulchan Aruch*, Rav Shlomo Gantzfried, *iz gevehn a kluger mentsch* — was a very wise person. Why? Because very often when discussing thorny situations that arise in halachah, he will set forth basic guidelines, but will conclude: יַעֲשֶׂה שְׁאֵילַת חָכָם — *ask a rav's advice*. Sometimes the answer is not black and white. What, then, is the best *eitzah*? Ask your *rav*. That is a practical application of *emunas chachamim*.

For boys learning in yeshivah, the importance of עֲשֵׂה לְךָ רַב cannot be stressed enough. Rav Chaim Shmulevitz (*Sichos Mussar* p. 61) would say that he had often seen two boys arrive at the yeshivah with equal capabilities and with equal potential, but after several years, they are on completely different levels; one is tremendously accomplished, and one never really developed. What is the difference? One listened to his *rebbi*, and one didn't. One fulfilled עֲשֵׂה לְךָ רַב, and one decided that he could manage on his own.

Success in yeshivah is not dependent on how much of a *lamdan* one is, but on how much of a *talmid* one is. One must realize that an integral part of a becoming a *talmid chacham* is being a *talmid*. The true *talmid* lives and breathes עֲשֵׂה לְךָ רַב.

Certainly, maybe more important, after someone leaves the yeshivah, it is vital that he continue to observe עֲשֵׂה לְךָ רַב.

The Chazon Ish (*Igros* 1:53) writes: A person in this world is like someone lost in a dense forest. He has no map. There is no path. But there is an *eitzah*. There are people who have previously traveled through the forest; they have already found their way out. If one follows them, then he, too, will successfully make it through. The *gedolei Torah*, the *einei ha'eidah*, have the wisdom of the Torah. They are the ones who can guide a person through the maze that we call *Olam Hazeh*.

## ৽ Stay Connected

Once people leave the yeshivah or Bais Yaakov, whether they succeed in life or fail, depends on whether or not they have a *rav*. I know someone who did wonderfully in yeshivah. But as soon as he left the environment of the yeshivah, he had a terrible *yeridah*; he experienced a massive decline in his life. I asked him frankly, "Who is your *rav*? Where do you *daven*?"

He chuckled and answered, "What do you mean? I have five shuls where I *daven*! During the week, one shul; Friday night, another shul; Shabbos morning, a third shul; Shabbos Minchah and Motza'ei Shabbos, two more shuls…"

Five shuls and no *rav*. That young man was missing עֲשֵׂה לְךָ רַב, and that explained his problem.

It is also very important for women to have a *rav* whom they can turn to, not only for questions on kashrus, Shabbos, or Yom Tov, but for questions of *chachmas hachaim*, as well. Since women do not go to yeshivah, and may not have *rebbeim* from their student days, their need to establish a relationship with a *rav* or *rebbetzin* is perhaps even more pressing.

I once heard from an expert in *shalom bayis* issues, that many couples experience much tension and anxiety in their marriage when one spouse desires to move their *frumkeit* level beyond the comfort level of the other partner. This can shake the core of a marriage. Being *frum* is wonderful, but a person has to make an intelligent decision: Is this a *frumkeit* or a *krumkeit*? In these matters, one must consult not with the "*daled chelkei Shulchan Aruch*" but with the timeless advice of עֲשֵׂה לְךָ רַב.

This scenario occurs all too often with *bachurim* as well. They really want to do the right thing, but they don't have proper guidance. They decide to accept a certain *chumrah* upon themselves, and their parents object. But they feel it is important, and *nebach*, they give their parents tremendous aggravation. By doing so, they violate *kibbud av va'eim*, trampling on the mitzvah *Chazal* refer to as *chamurah she'b'echamuros* — the most important of the important [mitzvos]. They should have asked a *rebbi* if their *chumrah* is worthwhile, given the fact that their parents object to it. All good intentions notwithstanding, sometimes people can do more damage than good. At every stage of life, a Yid must seek direction from his *rav*.

עֲשֵׂה לְךָ רַב and *emunas chachamim* are not only obligations, they are privileges. Asking *she'eilos* and receiving advice gives us an insight into what is the right thing. Especially regarding questions of *shalom bayis*, *chinuch habanim*, or what should be brought into the Jewish home. The privilege of עֲשֵׂה לְךָ רַב is immeasurable.

## ⟐ Respecting a *Gadol's* Time

It must be mentioned that while we should always avail ourselves of the advice of our *gedolim*, we must nevertheless take care not to waste their time. That is also part of *emunas chachamim*. It is hard to understand how people trouble *gedolim* and *rabbanim* to come to every *vort*, bar mitzvah, dinner, and parlor meeting — as if the *gedolim* are props to be set out at our *simchos*. An invitation may be an expression of our love and esteem for them, but our *gedolim* are our most valuable resource; they are the national security of Klal Yisrael. As such, we must protect them — we have to protect their health and protect their time. They are so, so busy. We should make it clear to them that although we would love to have them come, we know the value of their time, and we do not want to impose upon it.

I remember once hearing someone say, "*Mir darf oisnutzen gedolim* — we have to use our *gedolim* well." The wording didn't sit right with me. I actually asked Rav Yaakov Kamenetsky what he thought about that expression.

Rav Yaakov smiled and, with his typical wisdom, he told me, "*Mir darf oisnutzen, nisht oismutchen* — you have to use them, but not wear them out." What he meant was just this. We should use them, and ask them our questions when we have them, but we must not waste their precious time.

## ⟐ Success in Life

A person in his life has his own partiality. Sometimes, parents make decisions regarding the future of their children based on unimportant considerations. For example, a child is having trouble in a particular yeshivah; he is not thriving, and he needs help. It would be best if he would be transferred to a different yeshivah. But the parents are worried about what people will say. They claim that they have to protect the child's good name; it is in his best interest. They think they are acting for the benefit of the child, but they are really thinking of their own benefit. Had they consulted with a *gadol* who does not have a bias, he would see the answer so clearly — חֲנֹךְ לַנַּעַר עַל פִּי דַרְכּוֹ — and he would advise them to place the child where he belongs.

How often are people afraid to consider a *shidduch* even though it is a very good *shidduch* for their child, because they are worried about the family's prestige? The other family may not be on par with them; they could really find more prominent *mechutanim*. If they would ask a *she'eilah* it would be so clear to the *gadol* what direction should be taken.

If only people would be quicker to ask about what technology and media they should, or should not, bring into their homes. Even if they think they need it, if they would listen to the *gedolim* who guide us they would understand that these things are inflicting terrible *nisyonos* on ourselves and our families.

*Emunas Hashem* and *emunas chachamim* are one and the same. Part of our *emunah* in Hashem is our *emunah* in Moshe Rabbeinu, and in the *gedolei Torah* of every generation. And our success in this world is dependent upon it.

## ᏯᏞ For in You I Trust

I would like to conclude with a homiletical interpretation of the *brachah* of עַל הַצַּדִּיקִים, which we say every day in the *Shemoneh Esrei*. In *nusach Sefard*, this *brachah* concludes: וְשִׂים חֶלְקֵנוּ עִמָּהֶם, וּלְעוֹלָם לֹא נֵבוֹשׁ כִּי בְךָ בָּטָחְנוּ.

Three times a day, a Yid implores Hashem: וְשִׂים חֶלְקֵנוּ עִמָּהֶם — *let my lot be with the gedolim.* Let me live with *gedolei Torah.* Let me enjoy their wisdom and their guidance: וּלְעוֹלָם לֹא נֵבוֹשׁ — *so that I never go wrong.*

Why is that so? What is the secret of listening to a *gadol*?

כִּי בְךָ בָּטָחְנוּ — *for in You I trust.* My belief in *chachamim* is based on my belief in You, the *Borei Olam.*

וַיַּאֲמִינוּ בַּה' וּבְמֹשֶׁה עַבְדּוֹ — *They believed in Hashem and Moshe His servant* (*Shemos* 14:31). Living with *emunas Hashem* means living with *emunas chachamim.*

May the Ribono Shel Olam give the *einei ha'eidah* — the *gedolim,* our *rabbanim* — the strength and long life to continue to guide us. May He give us the wisdom to internalize that yearning of וְשִׂים חֶלְקֵנוּ עִמָּהֶם — the desire to live with our *gedolim,* to follow their advice and realize the *brachah* of אַשְׁרֵי אָדָם בֹּטֵחַ בָּךְ.

# BUILDING WITH TEARS

*Feeling the Churban —*
*Yearning for the Geulah throughout the Year*

A tragedy, indeed! A Yid was *bentching*, and as he said the words, "בּוֹנֶה בְרַחֲמָיו יְרוּשָׁלָיִם — *Who builds Yerushalayim with mercy*," he was so overtaken with anguish and feelings of loss over the destruction of the Beis Hamikdash that he took a knife from the table and stabbed himself. As a result of this terrible incident, *Chazal* instituted a halachah, which is codified in the *Shulchan Aruch* (180:5) that before *bentching* all knives must be removed from the table, or covered.

## Living with Yerushalayim

The question is obvious. What are the chances that such a tragedy will happen again? Probably zero. If so, why did *Chazal* institute this halachah? I once heard a wonderful explanation: True, it won't happen again. But *Chazal* wanted to demonstrate how deeply a Jew can feel the pain of the *Churban*. Look at how this Yid lived with Yerushalayim in his heart, and how he suffered so greatly from its loss that he actually killed himself from the pain.

The Gemara (*Bava Basra* 60b) says that after the Beis Hamikdash was destroyed, there were people who declared that they would never again eat meat or drink wine. Who can eat meat, if meat was used for the *korbanos*? Who can drink wine, if wine was used for the *nesachim*? Imagine! When we, today, see a piece of meat, we see a tantalizing taste of this world. But when they saw meat, they saw the *Churban*. When they saw wine, they saw the destruction.

## What about Me?

If we have the courage, we should ask ourselves, "What about me? Am I fulfilling the halachah that appears in the first *siman* of the *Shulchan Aruch* which states that a person must be *meitzar* (suffer) and *do'eig* (worry) over the *Churban*?" We have an obligation to mourn the Beis Hamikdash. This obligation actually applies throughout the year. Of course, the obligation is stronger during the Three Weeks, and even more so during the Nine Days, but it applies all year round, too. Are we successfully fulfilling this *chiyuv* to feel the loss of the real Yerushalayim and the Beis Hamikdash? I am the first to plead guilty. I, too, find it difficult. How is one supposed to feel the loss of something he never experienced and can't even imagine? The Beis Hamikdash is so distant from our hearts and minds.

## ☙ Why Are We Suffering?

I would like to suggest a practical, and hopefully workable, idea that can help us fulfill our obligation. The Gemara (*Sanhedrin* 104b) tells a very moving story about a woman who lost a child and cried day and night. Rabban Gamliel, who lived close by, heard her crying, and he, too, began to cry. He, however, cried over the *Churban*. He cried and cried until he literally cried his eyelashes out. Why was Rabban Gamliel crying so intensely? And what was it about hearing this woman cry over her loss that caused Rabban Gamliel to cry over the *Churban*?

I believe that Rabban Gamliel was pained by very troubling questions: Why is a Jew suffering? Why is a Jew crying? Why are there *Yiddishe tzaros*? Why is there a *Yiddishe krechtz*? Why do we hear of tragedies? Why do we hear of young children fighting for their lives and succumbing to illness? Why do we hear a mother crying for the loss of a child, if life is supposed to be אֵם הַבָּנִים שְׂמֵחָה — *the mother of children rejoices* (*Tehillim* 113:9)?

The Midrash says that when Mashiach comes, *davening* will be very different. There will no longer be the *brachah* of *R'fa'einu*, where one *davens* for a *refuah*, and there will no longer be a *brachah* for *parnassah*. *Davening* will consist of *tehillah* — praise, and *hoda'ah* — thanks. אָז יִמָּלֵא שְׂחוֹק פִּינוּ וּלְשׁוֹנֵנוּ רִנָּה — *Then our mouths will be full with happiness, our tongues with song.* That is the way the world is supposed to be. So why is a Yid crying? Why do so many people have problems with health and *chinuch habanim*? Why is there so much to cry about?

The answer to all these very painful questions is one word: *Churban*. Each tragedy is another expression, another manifestation of the *Churban*. The Gemara (*Sotah* 49a) says that from the day the Beis Hamikdash was destroyed, every day's curse is worse than the previous day's. Each day is more difficult, more painful than the preceding one. We constantly see new expressions of the *Churban*. Rabban Gamliel understood that the child's passing away and the mother's crying are not the way life is supposed to be. He cried because he recognized another *eichah* to cry about.

## ❧ The Bottomless Pit

The Gemara (*Chagigah* 5b), in describing the *Churban Habayis*, says that we were thrown from the highest rooftop down into the deepest pit. That's what the *Churban* did to us.

I have a good friend whose child was born with the dreaded illness. The doctors said it's very uncommon for a child to be born with it. Why do we have such pain? Why do we have such suffering? מַה זֹּאת עָשָׂה אֱלֹקִים לָנוּ — *What has Hashem done to us?* (*Bereishis* 42:28). There is a one-word answer to this question: *Churban*. Each *tzarah* is another manifestation of each day's curse getting worse than the last. It's our falling deeper and deeper into the seemingly bottomless pit.

Why is the situation in Eretz Yisrael so dangerous? Why do our brothers living in Eretz Yisrael have to fear for their lives? It's supposed to be כְּלִילַת יֹפִי — *the perfection of beauty* (*Eichah* 2:15). It's supposed to be מְשׂוֹשׂ לְכָל הָאָרֶץ — *the joy of all the earth* (ibid.). Again, this is another manifestation of the *Churban*. Every year, we have to cry *eichah* for so many *more* reasons. The *eichah* that Yirmiyahu cried two thousand years ago is constantly gaining new meaning and new painful expressions. We live comfortably in America; we are no longer persecuted. How can we feel and mourn what we are missing? Look at all the pain and suffering of our brothers in Eretz Yisrael. Look at the unfortunate among us, who suffer from terrible *tzaros*.

## ❧ Mourning — The Big "But"

Rav Hirsch points out that the word "אֵבֶל — *eivel*" (mourning) is the same letters as the word "אֲבָל — *aval*" (but). I think he means to say the following: Imagine a person who lost a child *R"l*, is sitting *shivah*, and someone says to him, "Why are you crying? You have so many other wonderful children." The mourning father would look at him strangely and say, "Of course I have wonderful sons and daughters, **but** I lost this child." *Eivel*, mourning, is all about feeling the "*aval*." When a person experiences the "*aval*," it overshadows all the good that he has in his life.

Yes, we have security and we feel comfortable in America, in a *medinah shel chessed*, but how big and painful is the "*aval*," the "but." Look at what we are missing; look at how many Jews are suffering. Look at all the tears, all the suffering, and look at the pit that keeps getting deeper and deeper.

## ✑ It Is Our Problem

A number of years ago, I had to be *menachem avel* a family who suffered the tragic loss of a young child. It was so painful; I simply didn't know what to tell the mourners. Then the Ribono Shel Olam gave me a thought. The standard *nusach* we tell mourners is, הַמָּקוֹם יְנַחֵם אֶתְכֶם בְּתוֹךְ שְׁאָר אֲבֵלֵי צִיּוֹן וִירוּשָׁלַיִם — *Hashem should comfort you among the rest of the mourners of Tzion and Yerushalayim*. This line seems so insensitive. Here these people are overtaken with grief from their own tragedy, and the bulk of our statement is about Yerushalayim. It's very nice to mourn Yerushalayim, but this does not seem to be the proper time to mention it, while this family is struggling with their loss.

I think we say this because this is actually the greatest source of comfort and consolation for them. Often you see *tzaros* happen to wonderful people, who surely cannot deserve such a punishment. And when a young child is *niftar*, he is often too young to even think about sinning. So when we mention Yerushalayim, we are telling the mourners, "Why are there *tzaros*? It's not your fault; it's part of the *Churban*. It is part of the '*aval*.' It is part of the deep pit we are in." So this becomes the most meaningful *nechamah* — comfort, that we can give a person. הַמָּקוֹם יְנַחֵם אֶתְכֶם בְּתוֹךְ שְׁאָר אֲבֵלֵי צִיּוֹן וִירוּשָׁלַיִם. This is another painful expression of *our* problem — the *Churban*, because they too, are part of the *Churban*.

We find it hard to be *meitzar v'do'ieg* on the *Churban Beis Hamikdash* that we can't visualize. And we can't cry about the *eichah* of Yirmiyahu of two thousand years ago. But we can cry about our *Churban*, about our "*aval*," about how much we are missing, how much Klal Yisrael is affected by this terrible *Churban*. The Gemara is teaching us, perhaps, that we can learn from Rabban Gamliel's action that an acceptable way of mourning the Beis Hamikdash is by incorporating our own tragic experiences into the mourning of the *Churban*.

## Our Spiritual *Churban*

Of course, it's not only the physical tragedies we are mourning, but the spiritual as well. *Baruch Hashem*, Torah is blossoming. *Yeshivos* are growing; *ba'alei batim* are learning. But we also know that there is a painful other side to the story. The "*aval*," the "but." Why are there so many *bachurim* today who have no interest in learning? Why are so many people more addicted to a cigarette than to a *blatt Gemara*? Why are so many people attached to their computers and not to the Ribono Shel Olam? Why are there so many "children-at-risk"? Why are so many wonderful families sitting at their Shabbos table singing הַשּׁוֹמֵר שַׁבָּת הַבֵּן עִם הַבַּת — *Who keeps the Shabbos, the son and the daughter*, while one of their own children, their own siblings, is roaming the streets, being *mechallel Shabbos*, drifting aimlessly, wandering without a purpose in life?

Life is not supposed to be this way. Life is supposed to be a long expression of חוֹלַת אַהֲבָה אָנִי — *I am sick with love for You* (*Shir Hashirim* 5:8). A person should be full of love for Hakadosh Baruch Hu. Why do people have questions in *emunah*? Why do we have all these difficult situations in *chinuch habanim*? The list of questions goes on and on.

The answer to all these questions is one word: *Churban*. What we are missing in *ruchniyus* is also an expression of the deep pit that keeps getting deeper and deeper. It's also part of the awesome "*aval*" in our lives. It's also a painful expression of אֲבֵלֵי צִיּוֹן וִירוּשָׁלָיִם. Every time we see a child who doesn't want to learn, we should cry, "*Eichah?* How can this happen?" It's not supposed to be like this.

## A Transformative Place

*Chazal* describe what it was like in the Beis Hamikdash. The *gilui Shechinah* there was so apparent. The Mishnah (*Avos* 5:4) lists ten miracles that took place in the Beis Hamikdash, some on a daily basis. Imagine a place that defied nature, that represented the clear manifestation of *Hashem echad u'shemo echad*.

כִּי מִצִּיּוֹן תֵּצֵא תוֹרָה — *From Tzion will come forth Torah* (*Yeshayahu* 2:3). *Tosafos* (*Bava Basra* 21a) says that when people came to Yerushalayim and saw the *avodah*, they were inspired, transformed. When they saw the *kavod haShechinah* that permeated throughout the Beis Hamikdash, it transformed them. The Gemara (*Megillah* 14a) says that the amount of *nevi'im* that Klal Yisrael had was twice the amount of people who left Mitzrayim. That is the effect of living with the Beis Hamikdash. The Beis Hamikdash was a power plant, a generator of *yiras Shamayim*. When a person came to Yerushalayim, he was overtaken with such remorse for any sins he might have committed that he would do *teshuvah* immediately (*Midrash Rabbah, Shemos* 36). The Beis Hamikdash was an embassy of *hashra'as haShechinah* that inspired and transformed so many people.

Seeing the splendor of the Beis Hamikdash was enough to melt even the coldest heart. The Midrash (*Bereishis* 65:22) describes an incredible incident that took place with a terrible *rasha*, a Yid named Yosef Mishisa. When the Romans conquered the Beis Hamikdash, they were afraid to enter it. Yosef Mishisa volunteered to do what even the Romans dared not do. He went into the Beis Hamikdash and came out carrying the Menorah. The Romans were shocked at this impropriety. They said he could take anything else, but not the Menorah. But Yosef Mishisa refused to re-enter. They threatened to kill him, but he was adamant; he would not go back into the Beis Hamikdash. So they gave him a most painful death, and he died *al kiddush Hashem*. As he was dying, he cried out, "Woe to me that I angered my Master." He had sinned once, but he would not do it again.

The story is puzzling. He was such a terrible *rasha*, yet he suddenly had a change of heart. What caused this sudden transformation? It was a moment in the Beis Hamikdash, explained the Ponevezher Rav. That was all that was necessary to change him. He had walked into that embassy of *kedushah* and *taharah*, and he was a changed person. Think about it: a moment in the Beis Hamikdash was enough to transform even such a terrible person.

## A Simple Jew in the Times of the Beis Hamikdash

Can we imagine what a Yid living in the times of the Beis Hamikdash looked like, the *emunah* that he had and the excitement for Torah and mitzvos that he lived with? The Vilna Gaon once said, "I can imagine what a *Rishon* was like, but I can't fathom what a simple Yid was like in the times of the Beis Hamikdash." Imagine! A simple Yid in the times of the Beis Hamikdash was beyond the comprehension of the Vilna Gaon. That's what it was like living during the times of the Beis Hamikdash, constantly seeing, כִּי ה' הוּא הָאֱלֹקִים אֵין עוֹד מִלְּבַדּוֹ — *Hashem is the Master, there is nothing but Him* (*Devarim* 4:35).

## The "Death" of Klal Yisrael?

Rav Wolbe related that Rav Chatzkel Levenstein once asked him how many Jews perished in the Holocaust. Rav Wolbe answered, "People say six million." Rav Chatzkel replied, "That's what people say, but I say that all of Klal Yisrael perished in the Holocaust. So many survived, but is this a Klal Yisrael? The Holocaust affected the entire Klal Yisrael."

When I heard this, I began thinking. How many Jews perished in the *Churban Habayis*? All the *Yidden*. All of Klal Yisrael was affected by the *Churban Habayis*; we were all victims of the *Churban*. The physical problems — the health problems, the *parnassah* problems; and the spiritual problems — the *chinuch habanim* problems, the lack of desire for learning or *davening* — they are all part of the *Churban*.

Maybe this is the solution. If we can't be *meitzar* and *do'eig* on the *Churban* that took place two thousand years ago, let's mourn over our *Churban*, about our inadequacy in Torah and mitzvos. Let us cry that instead of living life with a deep connection to Hashem, we live life feeling so distant from Him. Let's cry about our "*aval*," every tear and every struggle of it.

## "Don't Leave Me"

Let me close with a thought I had in camp on Motza'ei Tishah B'Av a number of years ago. That year, Tishah B'Av was on Thursday, and the *rabbanim* allowed the *bachurim* to do laundry and get haircuts Thursday night in honor of Shabbos, because there were too many *bachurim* to be able to do it on Friday. I had gone out a little late to be *mekadesh* the *levanah*. There was a beautiful *levanah*, and it was very moving, especially since the Gemara (*Sanhedrin* 42a) connects *Kiddush Levanah* to being *mekabel p'nei haShechinah*. In the background, I could hear people already doing laundry and taking haircuts. The contrast struck me. On one side, I saw the *Shechinah, kaviyachol,* and the Nine Days; and on the other, I saw people going back to their regular, normal lives.

This reminded me of what I once heard from an *avel* who had suffered a devastating loss. He told me that the most painful moment was immediately after the *shivah* ended. Throughout the week of *shivah,* people came and were supportive, but when the last person left, he realized that he was now left to deal with his problems on his own.

Seeing the *levanah* while hearing the background noise of "business as usual," it occurred to me that on Motza'ei Tishah B'Av, the *Shechinah* must feel like an *avel* ending *shivah.* During the Three Weeks, hopefully, we are focused on feeling the pain of the *Shechinah* — we are *menachem* the *avel,* the *Shechinah, kaviyachol,* that is in exile. Motza'ei Tishah B'Av, we can't go back to business as usual. The *Shechinah* is surely crying out, "*Yidden,* please don't leave Me!"

## Make It Last

Rav Shraga Feivel Mendlowitz used to say at the *Ne'ilas Hachag* at the end of Yom Tov, "We don't leave Yom Tov; we take Yom Tov with us." The lessons we have internalized throughout the Yom Tov should be eternalized as part of us forever. The same can be said regarding Tishah B'Av and Bein Hameitzarim. After three weeks of feeling the loss, of mourning, and living *tzipisa l'yeshuah,* we must hold on to this feeling of *meitzar u'do'eig* all year. Let us try in these days of the Three Weeks to increase our feelings of loss, our "*aval,*" so that it can last through the year, long beyond Tishah B'Av, and hopefully, we will soon see the fulfillment of the words of *Chazal* (*Ta'anis* 30b): "Anyone who mourns the Beis Hamikdash will merit witnessing its rejoicing."

# REACHING OUT

*Enhancing Our Relationships*
*Bein Adam L'chaveiro*

שער
בין אדם לחבירו

לזכר ולעילוי נשמת
האדם היקר באנשים
ר' אברהם בן ר' חיים זאב שאהנבערגער ז"ל
נפטר בשם טוב
י"ז שבט תשנ"ז

# BATTLING TERRORISM
## *The Primacy of Bein Adam L'chaveiro*

Lately, we are witnessing a global rise in terrorism. In Eretz Yisrael, France, and in other countries, Arab terrorists are inflicting destructive and murderous violence on innocent populations. Someone recently asked me, "How is a believing Jew supposed to process and understand this? Why is Hashem allowing this to happen?"

I told him that I am not privy to Hashem's Master Plan, but I can reference a Ramban that may help us understand it.

The Torah (*Bereishis* 16:6) relates that Sarah oppressed Hagar, וַתְּעַנֶּהָ שָׂרַי וַתִּבְרַח מִפָּנֶיהָ — *and Sarah dealt harshly with her, so she fled from her.*

The Ramban comments that Sarah sinned in her treatment of Hagar, and Avraham sinned as well, by allowing her to act in that manner. And then the Ramban writes the following incredible words:

וְשָׁמַע ה' אֶל עָנְיָה — *Hashem heard Hagar's pain,*

וְנָתַן לָהּ בֵּן שֶׁיְּהֵא פֶּרֶא אָדָם — *and gave her a son who would grow up to be a pereh adam, a wild man,*

לַעֲנוֹת זֶרַע אַבְרָהָם וְשָׂרָה בְּכָל מִינֵי הָעִנּוּי — *who would afflict the offspring of Avraham and Sarah with all manner of afflictions.*

Hashem allows the Arabs to afflict Klal Yisrael because Sarah pained Hagar, and because Avraham allowed it.

Rav Shach would often cite this passage with great emotion, and express his amazement at the far-seeing *da'as Torah* of the Ramban that allowed him to make such an astonishing statement.

What is the depth of the Ramban's statement? What is the message for us?

### ❧ Bein Adam L'chaveiro

Let us ponder a bigger question.

After the destruction of the First Beis Hamikdash, Klal Yisrael went into *galus* for a mere seventy years. And yet our current *galus* has stretched into an interminable two thousand years of darkness. We sometimes wonder, מַה נִּשְׁתַּנָּה הַלַּיְלָה הַזֶּה — *Why is this "night" [of this galus] different [from the other galuyos]?*

The Gemara (*Yuma* 9b) provides the answer. During the First Beis Hamikdash, the people were guilty of terrible sins — they committed the three cardinal sins. But in the era of the Second Beis Hamikdash, their sins were just as bad — they were guilty of *sinas chinam*, baseless hatred. Even though they were עוֹסְקִים בַּתּוֹרָה וּבְמִצְוֹת וּגְמִילוּת חֲסָדִים — *involved in Torah and mitzvos and doing kind deeds*, since they harbored feelings of *sinas chinam* toward one another, their merits could not protect them from *churban* and *galus*. The Gemara concludes with its famous teaching: We learn from here that the sin of *sinas chinam* is equal to the three cardinal sins. This is why our *galus* is so much longer.

It is noteworthy that the Gemara describes the Jews during the time of the Second Beis Hamikdash as being *oseik* in Torah, mitzvos, and *chessed*. "*Eisek*" connotes an intense involvement (see *Taz O.C.* 47:1). These were great people. Unlike the people of the First Beis Hamikdash who wallowed in the three cardinal sins, these people excelled in the three foundations of the world — Torah, mitzvos, and *chessed*! In light of their apparent righteousness, how was this problem of *sinas chinam* so overwhelming, so destructive, and so long lasting? How do we understand what happened at that time?

The answer is contained in a small phrase that I would like to coin, a pithy adage that we should live with:

כַּמָּה גְּדוֹלָה בֵּין אָדָם לַחֲבֵירוֹ — *How great and how important is bein adam l'chaveiro, our interpersonal relationships.*

The *churban* that we are experiencing to this very day — this almost two-thousand-year-long *eichah* — teaches us the absolute importance of *bein adam l'chaveiro*. And this is the depth of the Ramban's statement as well. We are suffering at the hands of the Arabs today because there was something amiss in the *bein adam l'chaveiro* of Avraham Avinu and Sarah Imeinu, on their great level.

## ❧ True Beauty

Rav Shalom Eisen was a *rav* and a *posek* in Yerushalayim, who was famous for his expertise regarding the *daled minim*. From all over

Yerushalayim, people would bring their *lulavim* and *esrogim* for him to examine.

Once, before Sukkos, a newly married young man conducted an exhaustive search, and found a most beautiful *esrog*. He spent a small fortune to buy it, but knew that it was worth the money. He decided to show it to Rav Shalom, not to ask if it was kosher — this *esrog* was clearly one of a kind — a real beauty! — but simply because he knew that the *rav*, of all people, would appreciate its uniqueness.

When the young man handed Rav Shalom the *esrog*, his opinion about the *esrog* was validated; Rav Shalom's eyes widened in admiration and wonder at its perfect beauty.

But after looking at the *esrog*, Rav Shalom looked at the young man and said, "For you, this *esrog* is *pasul*!"

The young man was shocked. How could this *esrog* possibly be *pasul*? And what did Rav Shalom mean that it was *pasul* "for him"?

Rav Shalom did not leave him wondering. He fixed him with piercing eyes and said, "It's almost Yom Tov. Did you buy your wife something for Yom Tov? Did you buy her a nice dress, or some other appropriate gift to enhance her *simchas Yom Tov*?"

The young man sheepishly responded that he had not.

"Why not?" asked Rav Shalom.

"Because I cannot afford it. I am in *kollel*..."

"This," said Rav Shalom, "is the basis for my ruling. I said that this *esrog* is *pasul* for you, because you spent so much money for the *esrog*, but nothing for your wife. Return the *esrog* and get your money back. Then, buy a cheaper *esrog* and buy your wife a gift!"

The message of the story is one that is worthwhile for all of us to internalize. We, as *avdei Hashem*, feel a great sense of satisfaction when we do a mitzvah *bein adam l'Makom*. When we buy a beautiful and expensive *esrog* we feel really good about it. But do we experience the same satisfaction in our *mitzvos bein adam l'chaveiro*? Do we feel this same joy when we make our spouse, or any other person, happy?

In *Parshas Beshalach*, the Jews reached the climax of their *avodas Hashem* — they had just left Mitzrayim and experienced Krias Yam Suf where they saw tremendous revelations. They were in the middle of singing the *Shiras Hayam*, the Song at the Yam Suf, when they sang, "זֶה אֵלִי וְאַנְוֵהוּ — *this is my G-d and I will beautify Him*," expressing a joyous commitment to live their lives for the glory of Hashem.

What is the meaning of זֶה אֵלִי וְאַנְוֵהוּ? What does it entail? The Gemara (*Shabbos* 133b) explains it to mean הִתְנָאֵה לְפָנָיו בְּמִצְוֹת — *make your mitzvos beautiful*. This is the basis for the law of *hiddur mitzvah*. Buy a beautiful *esrog*. Make a beautiful sukkah. This is the simple meaning of the *pasuk*.

But then, the Gemara quotes Abba Shaul who has a different understanding of וְאַנְוֵהוּ. וְאַנְוֵהוּ can signify אֲנִי וָהוּא — *I and He*. This means הֱוֵי דוֹמֶה לוֹ — *be like Him*; pattern your *middos* after Hashem's *middos*. מַה הוּא חַנּוּן וְרַחוּם, אַף אַתָּה חַנּוּן וְרַחוּם — *Just as He is kind and merciful, so, too, you must be kind and merciful.*

How does one live זֶה אֵלִי וְאַנְוֵהוּ? One lives this way by being a thoughtful, considerate, and helpful individual. Working on these *middos* brings one to an elevated state, and a level that Hashem expects from us.

The very same *pasuk* that teaches us *hiddur mitzvah*, also teaches us compassion. A beautiful *esrog* is certainly a mitzvah, but being thoughtful to one's spouse is perhaps even greater.

## ❧ An Absolute Essential

I am afraid that many of us incorrectly view the pursuit of *bein adam l'chaveiro*.

Some people seem to be "natural" *ba'alei chessed*, such as Hatzolah members or *askanim*. Other people see them and may think, "It is wonderful to be involved, of course, but it's not really my thing… I am not a 'doer,' I am not the '*chessed* type.'" Such thoughts indicate that this person feels that *bein adam l'chaveiro* is some sort of specialty. It implies that focusing on others is an extra — a fine and worthy thing to do, but only if one has some leftover time, energy, and interest after one's "real" obligations are fulfilled.

This is an improper attitude. *Bein adam l'chaveiro* is not an extra; it is an integral part of our *avodas Hashem*.

The correct approach to *bein adam l'chaveiro* is found in a Mishnah that we say every single day.

Generally, the reward for our mitzvos is reserved for us in the Next World. But there are exceptions. The Mishnah in *Pe'ah* says: אֵלּוּ דְבָרִים שֶׁאָדָם אוֹכֵל פֵּרוֹתֵיהֶם בָּעוֹלָם הַזֶּה וְהַקֶּרֶן קַיֶּמֶת לוֹ לָעוֹלָם הַבָּא — *This is a list of mitzvos for which one enjoys some of his reward in this world…* What is on the list? Aside for the mitzvos of consistent Torah study and of *davening* properly, the entire list is made up of mitzvos that are *bein adam l'chaveiro*.

כִּבּוּד אָב וָאֵם וּגְמִילוּת חֲסָדִים — *honoring parents, doing chessed…*

וְהַכְנָסַת אוֹרְחִים וּבִקּוּר חוֹלִים — *hospitality, caring for the sick…*

וְהַכְנָסַת כַּלָּה וכו' וַהֲבָאַת שָׁלוֹם בֵּין אָדָם לַחֲבֵרוֹ — *bringing a bride to the chuppah…bringing peace among people.*

What is special about these mitzvos specifically that grants them the Mishnah's unique quality of אוֹכֵל פֵּרוֹתֵיהֶם בָּעוֹלָם הַזֶּה? The *Rosh* explains:

כִּי הַקָּדוֹשׁ בָּרוּךְ הוּא חָפֵץ יוֹתֵר — *Because Hakodesh Baruch Hu is more desirous*

בְּמִצְוֹת שֶׁיַּעֲשֶׂה בָהֶם גַּם רְצוֹן הַבְּרִיוֹת — *of mitzvos through which one helps others, and does their will;* in other words, *mitzvos bein adam l'chaveiro,*

מִמִּצְוֹת שֶׁבֵּין אָדָם לַקוֹנוֹ — *than those mitzvos which are bein adam l'Makom.*

We ourselves would not be able to make such a bold statement, but the Mishnah is teaching this to us: Hashem desires *bein adam l'chaveiro* more than *bein adam l'Makom*. Hashem has more *nachas* when we show devotion to another Yid than when we do a "real" mitzvah.

Rav Shach used to tell over the following exchange that he had with Rav Chaim Ozer Grodzinsky. In 1939 toward the end of his life, Rav Chaim Ozer printed the third volume of his *sefer Achiezer*, which is a compilation of his *she'eilos u'teshuvos*. Rav Shach assisted him in the effort, organizing the *teshuvos* and preparing them for printing. Rav Shach noticed that there were *teshuvos* that Rav Chaim Ozer had written sixty years earlier — *teshuvos* that he had waited sixty years to print.

Rav Shach asked Rav Chaim Ozer why he never printed these *teshuvos* from so many years before.

Rav Chaim Ozer gave him a most incredible reply: "As I aged, I realized the great importance of helping another Jew — helping an *almanah*, helping a *yasom*. I became very involved in *chessed*, and I didn't have the time to publish *sefarim*."

Rav Chaim Ozer, of course, valued and appreciated every word of Torah and understood that "וְתַלְמוּד תּוֹרָה כְּנֶגֶד כֻּלָּם." But he had to balance his responsibilities. He knew כִּי הַקָּדוֹשׁ בָּרוּךְ הוּא חָפֵץ יוֹתֵר בְּמִצְוֹת שֶׁיַּעֲשֶׂה בָהֶם גַּם רְצוֹן הַבְּרִיּוֹת מִמִּצְוֹת שֶׁבֵּין אָדָם לַקוֹנוֹ. And he lived with the understanding of כַּמָּה גְדוֹלָה בֵּין אָדָם לַחֲבֵירוֹ. He recognized the *zechus* of helping another Jew.

I enjoy telling the following story that I heard from Rav Zelik Epstein and Rav Tuvia Goldstein. I remember I was shocked when I first heard it.

Rav Akiva Eiger was once at home hosting Rav Yaakov MiLisa, the great Liser Rav, author of the *Nesivos Hamishpat*. They were in the midst of a deep discussion when there was a knock on the door. Moishe, one of the local collectors, was going collecting from house to house. Rav Akiva Eiger opened the door. It was a freezing cold night, and when Moishe stepped inside, Rav Akiva Eiger saw that he was freezing cold.

"Sit down, Moishe," ordered Rav Akiva Eiger, motioning to his own chair. Moishe sat in the offered chair, whereupon Rav Akiva Eiger kneeled down and began to rub his foot to warm it and bring back the circulation. While doing so, Rabbi Akiva Eiger turned his head back and said these incredible words to the Nesivos:

"*Liser Rav is mechubad mit de tzveiter fus* — the Rav of Lisa is honored with the *kibbud* of rubbing the other foot [of the beggar]."

Rav Akiva Eiger was not the type to make a joke. He truly believed that the greatest *kibbud* is helping another Jew.

## ᎒ᴥ᎒ Embracing the *Shechinah*

This understanding and attitude is not only a Mishnah, it is sourced in a *pasuk* in the Torah as well.

In the beginning of *Parshas Vayeira*, Avraham Avinu was *kaviyachol*, "hosting" Hashem. He was being מְקַבֵּל פְּנֵי הַשְּׁכִינָה when he saw the three traveling Arabs. What did Avraham Avinu do? He put Hashem "on hold," *kaviyachol* — he left his audience with Hashem, and ran to attend to the guests.

Says the Gemara (*Shabbos* 127a), from here we see that גְּדוֹלָה הַכְנָסַת אוֹרְחִים מֵהַקְבָּלַת פְּנֵי הַשְּׁכִינָה — *hosting guests is greater than greeting the Shechinah*. Hosting the *Shechinah* is spectacular, but *hachnasas orchim* is even greater.

The Maharal explains the above teaching. What he says is amazing, yet he writes it with such simplicity. קַבָּלַת פְּנֵי הַשְּׁכִינָה is a high level of *deveikus* — of connecting to Hashem. But there is a drawback. One cannot touch the *Shechinah*. One cannot embrace the *Shechinah*. As human beings we cannot really interact with Hashem; we cannot really be מְקַבֵּל פְּנֵי הַשְּׁכִינָה. All we can do is "go through the motions."

On the other hand, we can relate to a fellow human being in a direct and complete manner. One can embrace a fellowman, and one can pat him on the back, and give him some warmth…

And this goes one step further. Within every person is an element of the *Shechinah* — בְּצֶלֶם אֱלֹקִים בָּרָא אֹתוֹ. Every person is created in the image of Hashem; every person is a *shtik Elokus*. When one engages in קַבָּלַת פְּנֵי הַשְּׁכִינָה, nothing is happening on a human level. But when we perform *hachnasas orchim*, we are able to physically give to, and bond with, the *Shechinah* that is contained in a fellow human being.

Do we have that *emunah*? Do we really believe that when we take a guest into our house we are doing something greater than קַבָּלַת פְּנֵי הַשְּׁכִינָה? Do we see the *Shechinah* in another human being? Rav Akiva Eiger certainly did. He truly had the *emunah* that the greatest *kibbud* that he could give to the Nesivos is to offer to allow him to rub the foot of the beggar.

## ⟊ Serving Others

Imagine two young *bachurim* who travel to Eretz Yisrael and visit Rav Chaim Kanievsky. The elderly *gadol hador* personally ushers them into his home and begins to prepare tea and cookies for them.

While Rav Chaim is in the kitchen, one boy whispers to his friend, "How can we allow this to happen? The *gadol hador* should serve us? We have to tell him to please not trouble himself!"

The other boy whispers back, "Well, he's doing a mitzvah… I think it is a great *zechus* for him and we should allow him to continue."

Who is right?

This answer to this question is found in a Gemara in *Kiddushin* (32b).

The Gemara relates that Rabban Gamliel, the *gadol hador*, was celebrating the wedding of his son. All of his *talmidim* attended and Rabban Gamliel — of all people — was serving them! Rabbi Eliezer did not want Rabban Gamliel to continue serving them. But Rabbi Yehoshua disagreed.

Said Rabbi Eliezer, "Rabbi Yehoshua, why are you letting the Rebbi serve us?"

Answered Rabbi Yehoshua, "Why not? Avraham Avinu served his guests. Hashem Himself serves people! Why can't the Rebbi serve us as well?"

Note how the Gemara records this dispute — Rabbi Eliezer protests, but Rabbi Yehoshua is given the "final say." The Gemara holds that Rabbi Yehoshua was right.

Imagine — allowing a *rebbi* to serve *talmidim*! Allowing Avraham Avinu to serve Arab travelers! Honoring the Lisa Rav with the other foot! How can we understand this? כַּמָה גְדוֹלָה בֵּין אָדָם לַחֲבֵירוֹ. Helping another person, putting a smile on someone's face, alleviating the pain or suffering of a fellow human being — is the greatest *kavod* and the greatest *zechus*. It is something that Hashem Himself does day and night, and it is what Hashem wants us to emulate.

## ◖◗ Where Is the Sensitivity?

כַּמָה גְדוֹלָה בֵּין אָדָם לַחֲבֵירוֹ. Do we live with this reality?

Imagine sitting in shul on Shabbos morning when someone walks in carrying an item that is clearly *muktzeh*. What would we do? We would tell the person, hopefully in a tactful and discreet way, "You're not allowed to do that; that item is *muktzeh*."

But what about a situation where you are sitting at a table, and someone begins to talk *lashon hara*, or makes a snide or insensitive remark that is clearly *ona'as devarim*? Do we have the same reaction? Do we have the same sensitivity? Does it bother us as much?

Often, it does not. Why is that? When someone is carrying *muktzeh*, we feel compelled to object. So why would we tolerate it when someone says something derogatory about another person? It is because of the same incorrect attitude. We have a natural sensitivity toward everything *bein adam l'Makom*. This, of course, is a good thing. It should bother us when we see someone carrying *muktzeh* on Shabbos. But we do not have the same level of sensitivity toward things *bein adam l'chaveiro*. This is something that must be corrected.

If our child does not do well on his Gemara test, we are upset. But if he insults a sibling, does it bother us as much? If our child sat down at the *Shabbos seudah* without washing *netilas yadayim*, it would certainly shock us. But if our child used a tissue in shul and left it on the table, or was disrespectful to an English teacher, would we have the same reaction? Why not? Which is worse?

The Gemara (*Bava Basra* 88b) says: קָשֶׁה עוֹנְשָׁן שֶׁל מִדּוֹת יוֹתֵר מֵעוֹנְשָׁן שֶׁל עֲרָיוֹת — *The punishment for a breach in middos, which exhibits a lack in bein adam l'chaveiro, is harsher than the punishment for an infraction in forbidden relations,* one of the most serious areas of *bein adam l'Makom*.

In the context of this Gemara, "*middos*" means "measurements," and refers to the requirement to use accurate weights when selling merchandise. But the reasoning also applies to what we commonly refer to as "*middos*," and to all of our interactions *bein adam l'chaveiro*.

The Gemara is teaching us כַּמָּה גְדוֹלָה בֵּין אָדָם לַחֲבֵירוֹ.

## ✿ Not a Piece of Wood

The halachah is that one is not allowed to eat before *davening*. But the Gemara (*Shabbos* 9b) rules that if someone began eating a meal before *davening*, he may continue eating; he need not interrupt his meal to *daven*.

What constitutes the "beginning" of a meal? Halachically, a meal begins when the person sits down and loosens his belt. (In the Gemara's times, one would loosen his belt before a meal.) Once one loosened his belt he has "started" his meal, and he is allowed to complete it before *davening*.

Rav Yeruchem Levovitz derived an important lesson from this halachah. Note that the diner in question did not begin eating the main course, or even the soup. He did not even start eating at all. All he did was open his belt. Why did *Chazal* exempt him from *davening* at that point, just because he opened his belt? Let him close his belt and go *daven*! The answer is, as Rav Yeruchem put it, because *ah mentsch is nit kein shtik holtz* — a person is not just a piece of wood.

It is not a light matter to "just" tell someone, "Close your belt and go *daven*!" *Chazal* were very sensitive to avoid troubling a human being. If he already loosened his belt, leave him be. Let him finish eating and then he will go to *daven*.

Do we have that attitude? We value *davening*, we appreciate *Krias Shema*, but are we also cognizant to avoid inconveniencing another human being — whether it is a spouse, a parent, a neighbor, or other people at shul, work, or yeshivah?

Rav Yisrael Salanter was on his deathbed, a few moments before his *petirah*. It was the middle of the night, and he was alone in the room with a *talmid* who was attending to him. He began a conversation with his *talmid* and remarked that he does not know why people are scared to be alone with a dead person.

"There is no reason to be afraid of a *meis*," he said. "A *meis* has no power to harm anyone. It is just the body of a person whose *neshamah* has left him."

That conversation was his last act on this world; he was *niftar* several moments later. Unbelievable. What was he thinking during the last moments of his life? He was thinking about another person, trying to reassure his *talmid* who would soon be left alone with his body. Rav Yisrael Salanter taught us that perfection in *middos* means thinking of another human being.

There is another famous incident where Rav Yisrael Salanter was asked by a *talmid* which *chumros* he should implement when baking matzos. Rav Yisrael told him, "Think about the widows who are working on those matzos. Be thoughtful and don't yell at them; be considerate of them."

The twentieth chapter in *Mesillas Yesharim* is entitled "מִשְׁקַל הַחֲסִידוּת — *The Weighing of Piety.*"The entire chapter is devoted to discussing a great challenge in the life of an *eved Hashem* — finding the right balance in one's *ruchniyus* endeavors, or, in other words, finding the balance between *frumkeit* (outward piety) and *krumkeit* (crookedness). Much of the chapter is based on one idea: *frumkeit* cannot come at the expense of *bein adam l'chaveiro*.

\* Buying an *esrog* is a wonderful *frumkeit*, but at whose expense? If it is at the expense of a spouse, then it is not *frumkeit*, it is *krumkeit*. *Shalom bayis* experts report that much tension and friction between husband and wife is caused by misplaced *frumkeit*.

\* Doing a mitzvah, or being *makpid* on a *chumrah* that causes anguish to one's parents is not *frumkeit*; it is *krumkeit*.

\*Baking the best matzos shouldn't come at the expense of the widow who is making them.

Often the greatest *frumkeit* is to be completely concerned for someone else.

It is imperative that we as individuals, as parents, and as *mechanchim*, stress the importance of *bein adam l'chaveiro*. Today, we see such phenomenal growth and an extraordinary focus on *limud haTorah* — and that is as it should be. Our *yeshivos* and *kollelim* are brimming. We have many *shiurim* and learning programs for all types of people and schedules. We have an amazing amount of material and programming to get children to learn and do mitzvos — it is all wonderful. Now we need to apply that same focus to mitzvos that are *bein adam l'chaveiro*.

## 🕮 One Decision

The Chazon Ish (*sefer Emunah U'bitachon* 4:1) writes an important rule for life: success and failure often come about as a result of one decision. Allow me to explain:

A person may decide one day that he no longer has the strength to fight; he can no longer exhaust himself in the quest for self-improvement. This person decides that from now on, he is going to be relaxed, and "let things slide." This person has only made one decision — on one fateful day — but this one decision will be his downfall, because things will go from bad to worse.

Success, on the other hand is also hinged on "one decision." A person wakes up one day and thinks, "Enough is enough! This can't go on. I must work to improve the situation." This person, too, has really only made one decision, but once he decides to perfect a *middah* or to carry through with a mitzvah, then הַבָּא לְטַהֵר, מְסַיְעִין לוֹ — *one who comes to purify himself (i.e., to improve) is granted Heavenly assistance.* And his one decision will start a wonderful process that can lead him to great changes.

We need to make a conscious decision to focus more on *bein adam l'chaveiro,* and to develop a true understanding that *bein adam l'chaveiro* is an essential part of *avodas Hashem.*

Lest one say, "I know this, and I've tried to be better at *bein adam l'chaveiro,* but then I forget. If only I would have a constant reminder of how important *bein adam l'chaveiro* is!"

I would like to suggest a very simple reminder, based on the Gemara in *Yuma* (9b) that teaches that our *galus* was caused by *sinas chinam.* Look around and see the painful expressions of *galus* that engulf us. Every moment of *galus* is a reminder of כַּמָּה גְדוֹלָה בֵּין אָדָם לַחֲבֵירוֹ.

If we are still in *galus,* it is because we are still lacking in *bein adam l'chaveiro.* It is because we do not yet live with *emunah* that כַּמָּה גְדוֹלָה בֵּין אָדָם לַחֲבֵירוֹ.

We begin *Tachanun* with the *pasuk* (*II Shmuel* 24:14): נִפְּלָה נָא בְיַד ה' — *Let me, please, fall into the hands of Hashem,* וּבְיַד אָדָם אַל אֶפֹּלָה — *and into human hands I should not fall.*

Rav Chaim Shmulevitz (*Sichos Mussar* p. 446) explained this *pasuk* homiletically and viewed it as a plea: Man is inherently imperfect. When we say this *pasuk,* we should bear in mind the following plea, "If I am to have failings, נִפְּלָה נָא בְיַד ה' — let me fall short in my obligations *bein adam l'Makom.* וּבְיַד אָדָם אַל אֶפֹּלָה — but let me never fall short in my *bein adam l'chaveiro,* because that is a much more serious failing."

This is the message of the Ramban regarding Hagar, and the message of the *Gemara Yuma*. There's a *churban* that seems eternal, a two-thousand-year-long night. Every day that this *galus* continues, we have to hear the *galus* crying out, "*Yidden!* Realize what *bein adam l'chaveiro* is all about! See the impact of a lack of *bein adam l'chaveiro!*" And, perhaps more important, "Feel the *zechus* of being a thoughtful, thinking, considerate human being!"

## ᐒᔌ A Kosher Jew

Let me close with an incredible Midrash (*Koheles Rabbah* 12:14):

בְּשָׁעָה שֶׁאָדָם נִפְטָר מִן הָעוֹלָם — *When a man passes on from this world,*

הַקָּדוֹשׁ בָּרוּךְ הוּא אוֹמֵר לְמַלְאֲכֵי הַשָּׁרֵת — *Hashem tells the malachei hashareis,*

רְאוּ מָה הַבְּרִיּוֹת אוֹמְרוֹת עָלָיו — *"See what people say about this person?*

כָּשֵׁר הָיָה, יְרֵא שָׁמַיִם הָיָה — *Was he kosher? Did he fear G-d?"*

Two questions are asked. Was he a kosher person? Did he fear G-d? We know what fear of Hashem is, but what does it mean to be a "kosher" person? The *Eitz Yosef* (ibid.) explains: Kosher refers to his behavior *bein adam l'chaveiro.*

What an unbelievable lesson. We live our lives for that awesome moment, when we will stand under Hashem's scrutiny. But look at the sequence here. The first inquiry is about *middos tovos*, and only then does Hashem ask about *yiras Shamayim.* We would think that *yiras Shamayim* is the first step in *avodas Hashem.* After all, the *pasuk* (*Tehillim* 111:10) says, רֵאשִׁית חָכְמָה יִרְאַת ה'. The beginning of wisdom is fear of Hashem. That is certainly true — *yiras Shamayim* is the first step. But apparently one needs to make sure that he has *middos tovos* before he can take that first step and enjoy the unlimited *brachah* of הַבָּא לְטַהֵר, מְסַיְּעִין לוֹ.

# TORAH MACHT MENTCHEN
## The Torah's Training in Interpersonal Relationships

The Chafetz Chaim had a granddaughter who was enamored by the Haskalah movement. She once visited her illustrious grandfather as he was sitting and learning.

She asked him, "Why do you sit here studying Torah? It is from a bygone era! There is a whole new world out there; man has made such great strides in technology. How can this study bring light to the world?"

The Chafetz Chaim understood what was prompting her to talk this way.

He looked up and lovingly told her, "*Tochterel* (my dear daughter), I heard that they have just invented a plane that flies. Soon, they will manage to fly to the moon."

Bear in mind that this was when the flying "aeroplane" was a new phenomenon, and landing on the moon was still in the realm of science fiction.

The granddaughter nodded her assent. Technology was amazing. It would conquer the very heavens!

The Chafetz Chaim continued. "*Tochterel*, I heard that they have developed *bombehs* (bombs) that can be dropped from an airplane and kill many people. Soon, they will make a bomb that will be able to destroy a whole country."

The Chafetz Chaim, with his far-reaching vision, already envisioned the atom bomb and nuclear warfare. What he was telling his granddaughter was that man has made great strides, but where is it taking him?

"*Tochterel*," said the great sage, "*zei machen bombehs, un Torah macht mentchen* — technology makes bombs, and Torah makes people."

The Chafetz Chaim's vision, his *ruach hakodesh*, was amazing. But what is more instructive about the story is how the Chafetz Chaim, in the above statement, succinctly sets down a tremendous principle in our *avodas Hashem*: "*Torah macht mentchen* — Torah makes people."

The mission statement of the Torah has to be that Torah makes us better people.

## Kol HaTorah Kulah

The Gemara in *Shabbos* (31a) tells the amazing story about a non-Jew who wanted to learn the entire Torah on one foot. Hillel took up the challenge and said:

מַאי דַּעֲלָךְ סָנִי, לְחַבְרָךְ לֹא תַעֲבֵד — *What you don't want to be done to you, don't do to others.* Be considerate, be thoughtful.

זֶהוּ כָּל הַתּוֹרָה כּוּלָה — *That is kol haTorah kulah.*

וְאִידָךְ פֵּירוּשָׁה — *the rest [of the Torah] is the commentary of this principle,*

זִיל גְּמוֹר — *go and learn.* Go, now, and find out the explanation of this basic rule.

The question is obvious. וְאָהַבְתָּ לְרֵעֲךָ כָּמוֹךָ, being thoughtful and considerate is certainly important — but is that *the whole Torah?* What does it mean that the rest of the Torah is merely the explanation of this rule?

There are many explanations of this Gemara, but perhaps we can interpret the Gemara simply and literally. *Torah macht mentchen.* The purpose of the Torah is to transform us into thoughtful, considerate, and sensitive people.

There are countless examples of this in the Torah — in the Chumash itself, in the Gemara, and in the *Shulchan Aruch.* Let us take a look.

## Expensive Dog Food

We know that even a kosher species of animal, such as a cow, can be rendered *treif* if it is not *shechted* — slaughtered — properly. (The word "*treif*" actually means "torn," and refers to an animal that was killed by wild animals.) Now, what happens if your cow is attacked by wolves and you are left with a *treif* carcass? You can't eat it, so what should you do with it? I would think that the best thing to do would be to sell it to a non-Jewish butcher and recoup some of your loss. However, the *pasuk* (*Shemos* 22:30) says: לַכֶּלֶב תַּשְׁלִכוּן אֹתוֹ — throw [the dead cow] to the dog.

That is a very expensive dog food. Why can't you sell it to a non-Jew who is not prohibited from eating it? The *Da'as Zekeinim* and Ibn Ezra (ibid.) teach us a crucial lesson:

Why was the animal attacked? People usually have watchdogs to protect their animals — how did the wolf get to the cow? Evidently, the dog fell asleep on the job. The dog was "negligent" and a wild animal was able to attack. What is the farmer thinking now? He is upset and disappointed with the dog, which caused him to incur a large loss. The farmer's natural reaction would be to vent his frustration on the dog, and perhaps even hit the negligent dog.

Says the Torah — לַכֶּלֶב תַּשְׁלִכוּן אֹתוֹ. Give that dog the dead animal; let him feast on the meat. True, the dog was responsible for the damage, but the Torah is teaching us that you have to stop and think for a moment. What about yesterday, and what about last week, and what about last month and last year? The dog has been your faithful watchdog for all these years. Today, the dog let you down; it fell short of its responsibilities and caused you a loss. But don't be a *kafuy tov*, don't deny all the good it did for you; don't forget the dog's faithful service until now. Overcome your natural anger and reward the dog for all the good that you have received from it.

## ꧁ And Us…

What an incredible insight. What an amazing attitude.

Imagine what the world would look like if everyone lived with this lesson in his relationships with other people. We might not own watchdogs, but we all have friends, neighbors, and spouses. Sometimes they do things that may hurt us. What is our natural reaction? "I am angry. Look at what he or she did. How could one do that?" or "I told them to do this, and they forgot." In many situations, we might have every right to be upset. But the Torah teaches us to look at the good; don't focus on the negative. Don't focus on what was wrong today. Look at the positive from last week and last month and last year.

We live in a world that is torn apart by *machlokes*. If only we would live the Torah that we learn. *Hakaras hatov* means recognizing all of the good, filling our hearts with all of the good that this person has brought into our lives. Then there is no room in our hearts to be angry about a momentary shortfall.

*Torah macht mentchen.* The Torah trains us how to be better people, and how to get along with others.

## ✤ Between Man and Bread

Every Shabbos and Yom Tov we find another example of the Torah's goal to develop us into better people.

Before we make Kiddush on Shabbos or Yom Tov, we cover the *pas*, the challah that we will soon eat at the meal. Why? The *Yerushalmi* (quoted in *Tur, siman* 271) explains: in terms of the laws of *brachos*, bread has priority over wine. During the week, when one wishes to eat bread and drink wine, he first recites a *Birkas Hamotzi* over the bread and then recites a *Birkas Hagafen* over the wine. But on Shabbos, since we must recite Kiddush over a cup of wine before eating the bread, the wine takes precedence, and the *Birkas Hagafen* is recited first. The *Yerushalmi* teaches us that we cover the bread, שֶׁלֹּא יִרְאֶה הַפַּת בּוּשָׁתוֹ — *so that the bread should not be humiliated.*

We do not want the bread to see that it is being "demoted," and to feel marginalized or ignored. Isn't that odd? We have heard of *bein adam l'chaveiro*, but here we have a new category — *"bein adam l'pas."*

## ✤ Between Man and Stones

At the end of *Parshas Yisro* (*Shemos* 20:23), there is a similar law, one that is a *lav d'Oraisa*, a negative commandment of Torah law: It is forbidden to build the *Mizbei'ach* in the Beis Hamikdash with steps going up to the top. Rather, the *Mizbe'ach* must be built with a ramp.

Rashi explains: When one ascends steps, he lifts one leg at a time onto alternating steps, thereby slightly separating his legs as he ascends. If the *Mizbe'ach* is built with steps, as the *kohanim* ascend to the top there will be a slight display of immodesty — a small lack of *tznius* — to the stones that are underneath them. They would be guilty of treating the stones of the *Mizbe'ach* with a *minhag bizayon*, in a humiliating manner. Therefore, we must build a ramp so that the *kohanim* can ascend to the top of the *Mizbe'ach* in a more respectful manner.

Here we have a law that is *bein adam l'*stones. What is the point of this mitzvah?

Rashi goes on to comment that there is a message here for us. If we must be mindful of the humiliation of inanimate and unfeeling stones, then certainly we must be very careful with the honor and prestige of חֲבֵירְךָ שֶׁהוּא בִּדְמוּת יוֹצְרֶךָ, וּמַקְפִּיד עַל בִּזְיוֹנוֹ — *your friend who is patterned in the image of your Creator, and who is concerned with his humiliation.*

These laws are not about *bein adam l'pas*, or *bein adam l'*stones; these laws are meant to train us in *bein adam l'chaveiro*. We take care to treat the challah and the stones with honor and respect, in order to train ourselves in the proper way to treat a spouse, our friends, and our neighbors.

## Take It to Heart

Imagine a non-Jew who is told about the beauty and the *kedushah* of a Shabbos table and desires to see it for himself. He asks a Jewish friend if he can join him on Shabbos. Friday night, at the head of the table, he sees a mysterious lump covered by a velvet cloth.

"What are you hiding under that cover?" he asks.

"Oh, we're not hiding anything. We're just covering the bread. We are going to eat it soon."

"Why, may I ask, are you covering the bread?"

"Well, we don't want to embarrass the bread!"

The guest will probably run out of the house. He'll think that his Jewish friend has lost his mind. But these are not dry laws, or rules. *Torah macht mentchen.* This is the very essence of Torah training. לֹא נִתְּנוּ הַמִּצְווֹת אֶלָּא לְצָרֵף בָּהֶן אֶת הַבְּרִיּוֹת — *Torah was given to purify our character*, to refine our behavior (*Bereishis Rabbah* 44:1; see *Ramban* to *Devarim* 22:6).

We have to open ourselves to the training. Imagine a husband who is about to recite Kiddush on Friday night but then looks down to see that his wife forgot to cover the *pas*. He begins to yell at his wife, "I almost violated a halachah in the *Shulchan Aruch*! I was about to make Kiddush and the challah is uncovered. What did you do to me?"

You can almost hear the challah crying out to him, "You missed the point!"

We cover the *pas* to teach ourselves *not* to act that way. *Torah macht mentchen*; this is our training in how to become a better person. How wonderful it is to have this "thoughtfulness training" every Shabbos and Yom Tov.

## Prerequisite for Success

There is another halachah about bread that applies at the end of every bread meal: When we *bentch*, we should have bread on the table.

This halachah is based on a Gemara (*Sanhedrin* 92a): Whoever *bentches* without bread on his table, אֵינוֹ רוֹאֶה סִימָן בְּרָכָה לְעוֹלָם — *will never see success in life.*

Why is having bread on the table a prerequisite for success?

*Mishnah Berurah* (180:2), quoting Rashi, explains: You have just finished your meal; you are satisfied. Now, what will be if there's a knock on the door? A poor person is standing there and he is hungry. Will you have anything to give him? Don't think only of yourself. Make sure that after you eat, your table is capable of providing for someone else as well. If you do not do so, you are showing a terrible attitude that brings the curse of אֵינוֹ רוֹאֶה סִימָן בְּרָכָה לְעוֹלָם.

What an incredible halachah. When we put bread on the table before we *bentch* do we hear the message? Do we understand the implication? A person who is wrapped up in himself, and who is not thinking of others, will never be successful. A Yid's success in life comes when he is living for others — וְאָהַבְתָּ לְרֵעֲךָ כָּמוֹךָ. A person has to be thinking of others at all times.

We live in a selfish world, where the "I" is dominant — people are busy with iPods, iPads, and iPhones... But the Torah says that my life should revolve around the other person.

## Adameh L'Elyon

I know someone who is fond of saying: "Torah is not just information; it is *formation*."

I added to his pithy aphorism: "Torah is not information; nor is it mere formation; Torah is *total transformation.*"

Torah has to effect a total transformation within us.

Man is called "*adam*" because he was formed *min ha'adamah*, from the ground. The Torah's transformation is this: Take an *adam* who is essentially *adamah* and transform him to a being that can say, "אֲדַמֶּה לְעֶלְיוֹן — *I will be likened to the One on High*" (*Yeshayahu* 14:14). (See *Shelah, Toldos Adam.*)

Likening ourselves to Hashem is actually an obligation. The *pasuk* (*Shemos* 15:2) says, זֶה אֵלִי וְאַנְוֵהוּ, and the Gemara (*Shabbos* 133b) explains this to mean, הֱוֵי דוֹמֶה לוֹ — *make yourselves comparable to Him.*

How are we supposed to emulate Hashem? By emulating His *middos*. Be *rachum*, be *chanun*, be compassionate, be understanding.

The Torah expects us to effect a transformation within ourselves. We are meant to become people who emulate Hashem.

## ❧ Between Man and the Deceased

The *Shulchan Aruch* (*siman* 45), based on the Gemara in *Brachos* (18a), records the following halachah: When one is in a cemetery, he may not do a mitzvah in the presence of the dead who are buried there. In a cemetery, one must tuck in and conceal his *tzitzis*, and may not learn Torah or *daven* regular *tefillos* there.

This halachah is called *lo'eg larash*, which literally means "to make fun of a *rosh* — poor person." A dead person is "*rosh min hamitzvos*," he is poor from mitzvos, because he can no longer perform them. By performing a mitzvah in the presence of a *meis*, you make the *meis* feel bad; it is akin to saying, "I can still do mitzvos and you cannot."

Imagine a non-Jewish gravedigger working in the cemetery, who sees that every Jew who enters tucks himself in. He wonders at this strange behavior and he asks someone, "I see that every person who enters tucks his strings in; is this a Jewish custom?"

"We are simply concealing our *tzitzis*, because we do not want to make the dead people feel bad."

The gravedigger will have trouble believing what he is hearing. "You are concerned about the feelings of a dead person?"

*Torah macht mentchen.* By being considerate to the *meisim* in the cemetery, we are training ourselves to become sensitive and thoughtful to everyone.

## Between Man and Animals

There are sixteen places in the Torah where we are taught about the proper way to treat animals. Here are a few of them:

* The prohibition of *tza'ar ba'alei chaim*, causing unjustified pain to animals.

* *Shechitah* must be done deftly and with a razor-sharp *shechitah* knife, killing the animal swiftly and far more painlessly than other methods.

* It is forbidden to *shecht* a mother animal and her child on the same day (*oso v'es b'no*), or to take the eggs, or the young birds, out of a nest while the mother bird watches (*shiluach hakein*). The reason for these laws, according to the Ramban (cited by *Sefer Hachinuch*, mitzvah 545) is because harming the offspring in the presence of the parent is an act of cruelty.

Now, the Torah is not the ASPCA. What is the message here?

Such mitzvos are meant to imbue us with a sense of compassion (see *Sefer Hachinuch*, mitzvah 294). Through these mitzvos, the Torah trains us: When we are thoughtful and compassionate toward animals, we train ourselves how to be thoughtful and compassionate in our dealings with human beings as well. *Bein adam l'beheimah* is training for *bein adam l'chaveiro.*

## Between Man and the Egyptians

When we study *Yetzias Mitzrayim* we learn about all of the evil and wickedness of the Egyptians, and how they went to inhuman lengths to subjugate, humiliate, torture, and kill their Jewish slaves. Yet the Torah commands us (*Devarim* 23:8), לֹא תְתַעֵב מִצְרִי — *do not reject an Egyptian* who wants to convert and enter Klal Yisrael.

If *beis din* refuses to accept an Egyptian into Klal Yisrael they have transgressed this prohibition. Why? Says the *pasuk,* כִּי גֵר הָיִיתָ

בְּאַרְצוֹ — *because you dwelled in his land.* We must have *hakaras hatov* to the Egyptian, for we were hosted in his land.

The Egyptians enslaved us, they beat us, they killed us, they built our children into the walls. And yet we have to have *hakaras hatov* toward them.

One of the *chachmei umos ha'olam*, a non-Jewish writer who apparently knew his Bible, once commented that he sees the Divinity of the Torah from this commandment. A mere seven weeks after this abused people left the horror of the Egyptian bondage, they stood at Har Sinai and were admonished לֹא תְתַעֵב מִצְרִי. Only the Ribono Shel Olam Himself could give such a commandment.

If we are able to feel *hakaras hatov* to Egyptians, we are well on our way to becoming better and more grateful people who feel *hakaras hatov* to our parents, spouses, and everyone who helps us in any way.

There is another important "training lesson" in the Torah that pertains to our Egyptian "hosts":

On Pesach, like the other Yamim Tovim, there is a mitzvah of *simchah* (festive meal, wine, etc.). But in the Torah, there is no explicit mention of a mitzvah to have *simchah* on the Yom Tov of Pesach. Rather, the Midrash derives the mitzvah of *simchah* on Pesach from the mitzvah of *simchah* that is found by the Yom Tov of Sukkos, where it is mentioned twice. Since one mention of *simchah* is extra, we remove it from the laws of Sukkos, and apply it to the laws of Pesach.

Asks the *Yalkut* (*Vayikra* 23), why didn't the Torah give this mitzvah in a direct manner by simply stating the requirement of *simchah* in the passages that discuss Pesach?

Answers the *Yalkut*, because in the narrative of Pesach, we are told of the downfall of the Egyptians, and the *pasuk* (*Mishlei* 24:17) states, "בִּנְפֹל אוֹיִבְךָ אַל תִּשְׂמָח — *when your enemy falls, do not rejoice.*"

This is another brilliant application of וְאִידָךְ פֵּירוּשָׁה זִיל גְּמֹר — *The rest [of the Torah] is merely the commentary of this principle, go and learn.* This is a lesson in "*bein adam l'*Egyptian." This teaches us about the sensitivity that we must have toward a non-Jew. The nations of the world are also Hashem's creations, and we must train ourselves to feel sensitivity for their pain.

The Gemara (*Gittin* 61a) teaches that *chessed* is not reserved exclusively for our fellow Jews. If a non-Jew requests *tzedakah*, we must give him as well. We are also required to bury the non-Jewish dead, and to help non-Jewish people who are sick. Our non-Jewish fellowman is to be treated with respect and compassion.

As we know, the Torah allows for the institution of slavery. A Jew may own an *eved Ivri* — a Jewish servant, and an *eved Cana'ani* — a non-Jewish "slave." There are differences between these two types of *avadim*, including how the owner may use them. One may not command his *eved Ivri* to do any task that is humiliating or overly strenuous. On the other hand, one may give an *eved Cana'ani* any type of work. Yet look at how the Rambam records this halachah (*Hil. Avadim* 9:8): Even though this is the law (that one may assign his *eved Cana'ani* any type of hard labor), it is a *middos chassidus* (worthy and righteous behavior), and the way of the wise, for a man to be compassionate…and not bear down harshly, or cause pain, to [his *eved*].

The Rambam goes on to say that cruelty and brazenness are commonly found among the gentiles who serve idols, but the descendants of Avraham Avinu, the Jewish nation, to whom Hakadosh Baruch Hu imparted the *tovas haTorah* — the goodness of the Torah, and to whom He commanded righteous laws, they are compassionate to all.

Imagine — we are told that we must treat slaves, the least respected people in society, with compassion and dignity. What is the basis for such a law? The answer is those two words of the Rambam: "*tovas haTorah*." We were given the beauty of Torah, so we are expected to act with compassion.

I was once walking in yeshivah. The non-Jewish janitor had just mopped one part of the floor, and I saw a *bachur* walk across the wet, freshly mopped floor. He could easily have gone around the mopped area, but he did not bother to do so.

I approached the boy. "Didn't you see that the janitor just spent time and effort to mop the floor? How could you just walk on it, right in front of him?"

The *bachur* looked at me quizzically and said, "But he's a *goy!*"

"True," I replied, "but *you* are a Yid! And more than that, you are a *ben Torah*, whose every action must reflect *tovas haTorah*."

This is part of Torah, to treat everyone — the janitor, the English teacher, the non-Jew on the train, or at the office — with compassion. A Jew, and especially a *ben Torah*, must behave in a manner that is consistent with the idea that *Torah macht mentchen*. We are ambassadors of the Torah. When we mistreat the non-Jew, it is not just a *chillul Hashem*, it is a *chillul haTorah*, a misrepresentation of the essence of Torah.

## Between Man and the *Geulah*

There is yet another lesson to be gleaned from the Torah's narrative of *Yetzias Mitzrayim*.

In *Parshas Shemos* (4:13–14), the Torah recounts how Hashem appeared to Moshe Rabbeinu and told him that the time for the *geulas Mitzrayim* has arrived. But Moshe refuses to go. Why? Because he is afraid that Aharon will feel bad. Aharon is older than Moshe; how will he feel if his younger brother is chosen for this great act of destiny? Imagine that! Klal Yisrael is suffering in Mitzrayim, yet instead of springing into immediate action, Moshe holds back because of the feelings of one individual. *Bein adam l'geulah?*

Hashem's response validates Moshe's concern. Hashem tells Moshe that Aharon will *not* feel bad. In other words, Hashem agrees with Moshe — if Aharon would indeed be hurt then another plan is in order. But this is not the case. Aharon will not be slighted, and Moshe is therefore the one who should go.

This speaks volumes about the depth of *Torah macht mentchen*.

Rav Shlomo Zalman Auerbach used to point out the following: Before Sukkos people search for a beautiful *esrog*. They spend a small fortune for the perfect *esrog*, and treat it so gingerly, taking care not to damage it in any way. The *esrog*, as we know, represents the human heart. If we are so careful with our *esrog*, imagine the care that we must take when we are dealing with a real human heart.

On Pesach we begin our preparations for Shavuos as we begin *sefiras ha'omer*, counting the seven weeks leading up to the day of *Kabbalas HaTorah*.

It was on that awesome day that Klal Yisrael unanimously declared, "*Na'aseh v'nishma!*" What does *Na'aseh v'nishma* mean, on a practical level?

The Mishnah in *Avos* (3:17) states: אִם אֵין דֶּרֶךְ אֶרֶץ, אֵין תּוֹרָה. "דֶּרֶךְ אֶרֶץ" usually refers to *parnassah*, the earning of a livelihood. If a person does not have a steady and secure *parnassah* it is hard for him to learn Torah.

But Rabbeinu Yonah explains the term "דֶּרֶךְ אֶרֶץ" in its more familiar sense — it means having good *middos* and being a *mentsch*. Without *middos tovos*, there can be no Torah within a person: שֶׁאֵינָה שׁוֹכֶנֶת לְעוֹלָם — *for the Torah will never reside*, בְּגוּף שֶׁאֵינוֹ בַּעַל מִידוֹת טוֹבוֹת — *in a person who does not have good middos.*

Rabbeinu Yonah goes on to say that this is the explanation of the response of *Na'aseh v'nishma*. Before the *nishma* of hearing the Torah's words, comes the *na'aseh* of total transformation, namely, the refining of one's actions that will allow him to be a worthy receptacle for the Torah.

We need seven weeks to prepare ourselves to wear the crown of Torah by improving our *middos*, because without *middos*, there can be no Torah. Hillel's statement of "זֶהוּ כָּל הַתּוֹרָה" was quite literal.

## Priorities in Candle Lighting

A halachah in *hilchos Chanukah* is also based on the principle of *Torah macht mentchen*.

Erev Shabbos Chanukah, a person is required to light at least two *neiros* — one to fulfill the mitzvah of *ner Shabbos*, and one to fulfill the mitzvah of *ner Chanukah*. What happens if a person has very little money, and is only able to buy one *ner* — which mitzvah has priority?

The Gemara (*Shabbos* 23b) rules that *ner Shabbos* has priority — the person lights his Shabbos light, and must forgo the all-important mitzvah of *ner Chanukah*. Why? The Gemara explains: The basis for the mitzvah of *ner Shabbos* is to preserve the *shalom bayis* of the house. One lights a *ner Shabbos* so that he should not sit in a dark house on Friday night. When one sits in a dark room together with his family, invariably things will go wrong. People will bang into things and may become irritable and bicker and argue. That being the case, *ner Shabbos* — in other words, *shalom bayis* — has priority even over the exalted mitzvah of *ner Chanukah*.

The Rambam (*Hil. Chanukah* 4:14) records this halachah, and concludes with these unbelievable words:

גָּדוֹל הַשָּׁלוֹם — *Living in harmony with others is most important,*

שֶׁכָּל הַתּוֹרָה נִיתְּנָה — *for the entire Torah was given,*

לַעֲשׂוֹת שָׁלוֹם בָּעוֹלָם — *to maintain harmony between people,*

שֶׁנֶּאֱמַר — *as the pasuk [Mishlei 3:17] says,*

דְּרָכֶיהָ דַרְכֵי נֹעַם וְכָל נְתִיבֹתֶיהָ שָׁלוֹם — *Its ways are ways of pleasantness and all its pathways are peace.*

The essence of Torah, the mission statement of Torah, the objective of Torah, the purity of Torah, the *kedushah* of Torah is to create *shalom*, and to maintain *shalom*. זֶהוּ כָּל הַתּוֹרָה כּוּלָה!

## ⌒ Drivers' Ed.

The Gemara (*Brachos* 46b) rules: אֵין מְכַבְּדִין בִּדְרָכִים — When one is traveling on the road, he is not required to stop and allow someone else to pass him, even if that person is worthy of honor. For example, if one encounters an older person or a *talmid chacham* as he travels along the road, he is not required to extend him the honor of going first.

Why not? Don't we always show respect to other people, and especially to great rabbis and to older people? Why does this change on the road?

Rabbeinu Yonah (ibid.) explains: If you begin to accord honor to others as you travel on the road, what will happen? You are going to stop, and offer the other person to go first. Propriety dictates that he will decline the offer; he will say, "No, no…you go first…" But you will insist on showing him the proper respect and you will not go. Meanwhile, you are blocking traffic. You are slowing down everyone behind you; you are causing others to experience stress. Certainly we must honor those worthy of honor — but not at the expense of troubling people behind us.

I once saw a beautiful bumper sticker that read:

וְנָהַגְתָּ לְרֵעֲךָ כָּמוֹךָ — *When driving, treat your friend as yourself!*

We must drive with the attitude of וְאָהַבְתָּ לְרֵעֲךָ כָּמוֹךָ. That is really what this Gemara is teaching us: When driving on the road, be considerate of others and do not cause other drivers any unnecessary discomfort.

In New York City, there are signs posted warning drivers that they can incur a $350 penalty for honking their horns during times when the streets are meant to be quiet. I always felt that in an Orthodox neighborhood such signs are (or should be!) superfluous. Who doesn't understand that honking and making noise in the early morning or late at night can be terribly disturbing to other people? And it's really more than that — doing such a thing is not only a violation of New York City traffic codes, it is also a violation of *kol haTorah kulah*. So is parking in a way that blocks someone else's parked car or someone else's driveway.

The way we drive has to be dictated by our *heilige Torah* because *Torah macht mentchen*. Often, unfortunately, we hear non-Jews complaining that Jews are too aggressive on the road. Of course, as religious Jews, we are often in a rush. We have to make the *minyan*. We have to make *shkiah*. We have to make the *shiur*. We have to make the *chuppah*. But that can't be at the expense of misrepresenting our Torah, or, actually, humiliating our Torah. Our driving has to create a *kiddush Hashem*, not, *chalilah*, the opposite. We must bear in mind, "וְנָהַגְתָּ לְרֵעֲךָ כָּמוֹךָ."

## ᔐᔐ On the Road to Sensitivity

The Gemara (*Yevamos* 11b) teaches us an important attitude that we must strive toward:

לֹא יִשְׁפּוֹךְ אָדָם מֵי בּוֹרוֹ וַאֲחֵרִים צְרִיכִין לוֹ — *Do not pour out the water from your cistern if others may have a need for it.* Do not just live for yourself. If you have something that you do not need, give it to others.

When Rav Aharon Kotler was on a visit to Eretz Yisrael, he was told that a driver and car had been arranged for him during his stay. Rav Aharon was thankful for the arrangement, but was insistent on one condition: If his car were to pass someone waiting for a ride — at a bus stop or on the side of the road — they would stop and offer the person a ride.

"But it's inappropriate!" he was told. "Should the Rosh Yeshivah pick up hitchhikers?"

Rav Aharon responded, "Can I violate a Gemara? The Gemara (*Yevamos* 11b) says לֹא יִשְׁפּוֹךְ אָדָם מֵי בּוֹרוֹ וַאֲחֵרִים צְרִיכִין לוֹ — don't waste something that can help others. I cannot bear to 'waste' the extra spaces in my car."

Rav Aharon not only learned the Torah, but he lived the Torah; he breathed the Torah. He became the Torah that he learned.

If you are driving along and you see someone waiting for a bus, or someone carrying a heavy package, the principle of *Torah macht mentchen* would mandate that you offer him a ride. Isn't the Torah training our eyes to see the other person and his hardship?

In our neighborhoods, it is so difficult to find a parking spot. Yet sometimes people are not careful enough when they park, and they take up two spots. That is not driving *al pi Torah*, it is clearly a violation of the Gemara in *Yevamos*. That's not living the Torah that we learned. *Torah macht mentchen*; Torah is supposed to train us to be considerate of others, even when parking.

## 🌿 My Cup Runneth Over…

Let me give you one more example, which to me is astonishing.

The Rema (*O.C.* 296:1) records the *minhag* that when we make Havdalah we pour some wine on the ground. (Today most people let the wine spill over from the *kos* onto the tray, but the original *minhag* was to pour the wine onto the ground.)

וְעוֹשִׂין כֵּן לְסִימָן טוֹב בִּתְחִלַּת הַשָּׁבוּעַ — *We do this symbolic act at the beginning of the week as a good sign to start the week.*

Why is pouring wine on the ground a good *siman*?

The Rema cites the following *Chazal* as the basis for this *minhag*: כָּל בַּיִת שֶׁלֹּא נִשְׁפָּךְ בּוֹ יַיִן כַּמַּיִם אֵין בּוֹ סִימָן בְּרָכָה — *Any house wherein wine is not poured out like water will not see the signs of blessing.* This seems puzzling.

The Taz (ibid.) explains: We all want to have a good week, a week of happiness with our spouses and families. Do you know what threatens that? When we are not *mevater*.

When something breaks, or gets lost, or if money is misspent, we get angry. If someone in the house knocks over a cup of wine, and the wine spills out, what is our reaction? "Wine is expensive! What a waste!" If these things bother you, you will never be happy. The lesson we are learning during Havdalah is that if during the week the wine spills, view it as if it were water. The wine spilling should not bother you, just as water spilling would not. But if you cannot internalize the attitude that these losses are insignificant and that it is not worth being bothered by them, then your house will not be a house of blessed happiness.

It is a *siman tov*, at the beginning of the week, to pour some wine on the floor. Train yourself that this is really trivial, train yourself to be *mevater*. The ability to be *mevater* is the most magical tool in any interpersonal relationship; one who is able to be *mevater* can diffuse so much tension from a home.

Someone came to Rav Binyomin Zilber and asked for a *brachah* for *shalom bayis*. Rav Binyomin said, "You do not need a *brachah* to have *shalom bayis*. You just need to do one thing — be *mevater*."

This is the first halachah training of the new week, and it is the *brachah* of the week. It is also part of the total transformation that halachah is meant to effect within us. How great a human being can become if he lives and internalizes the Torah's messages.

These above are just a few examples among countless others. וְאִידָךְ פֵּירוּשָׁה זִיל גְּמֹר — the entire Torah is one long tribute to *Torah macht mentchen*. We must live with the *emunah* that Torah is supposed to impact every facet of our lives — our *bein adam l'chaveiro*, our *bein ish l'ishto*, our other interpersonal relationships, the way we treat non-Jews, and even the way we drive.

## ❧ Two Questions

I knew of a Yid who passed away not long ago, who endured unspeakable horrors during World War II. Often, those who were so brutally traumatized lost their faith, but this man remained *frum* and loyal to Hashem throughout all of his experiences. He once commented that he managed to keep his faith because of his *rebbi*, Rav Shimon Shkop; and in particular the memory of the *farher*, the entrance examination, that he took in order to gain entry into Rav Shimon's yeshivah.

"That *farher* was only two questions long, and I will never forget them. After that contact with the Rosh Yeshivah, nothing could shake me from my *Yiddishkeit*," he would say.

What were the two questions?

As a young *bachur*, he wanted to join Rav Shimon Shkop's yeshivah, but his parents were so poor that they could not afford to pay for transportation. The young *bachur* walked for many days until he arrived at Rav Shimon's house for the *farher*.

He came into the house and met Rav Shimon. "What can I do for you?" he asked.

"I want to learn in the yeshivah. I am ready for the *farher*."

"Well," said Rav Shimon, "the first question is, when was the last time you had a hot meal?"

The boy was shocked; he was not expecting that question. "Well, actually, my last real meal was before I left home, many days ago."

"Ah," said the Rosh Yeshivah, "that is what I thought. I want you to eat before we proceed. My wife is not home, but I can cook, too. You will have to settle for my cooking!" And Rav Shimon, *b'chvodo v'atzmo*, cooked him a hot meal.

While he ate, the *bachur* was reviewing his *shtickle Torah* to tell Rav Shimon. But when Rav Shimon came in he asked him the second question of the "*farher*":

"When was the last time you slept in a bed?"

What was Rav Shimon driving at? "Well, the last time I slept in a bed was at home. It has been a while."

"Yes, I thought so," said Rav Shimon. "Come with me, I want you to first sleep a bit. You must be so very tired."

The boy was tired, indeed, and did not protest at the offer of a bed.

He ended up sleeping through the night. But, as it turns out, he was not sleeping in an extra bed; he was sleeping in Rav Shimon's bed! Rav Shimon did not disturb the sleeping *bachur* and learned through the night.

"I knew then that if the Torah can make a person as great as Rav Shimon, I will never, ever, deviate an iota from the Torah."

This Yid saw a firsthand exhibition of *Torah macht mentchen*. He saw a *gadol* who not only learned Torah, but lived Torah, breathed Torah, thought Torah, and *became* Torah. Rav Shimon became the essence of Torah — דְּרָכֶיהָ דַרְכֵי נֹעַם וְכָל נְתִיבֹתֶיהָ שָׁלוֹם.

It is important to absorb the messages of Torah that we have all around us. Every day, every Shabbos, every Yom Tov — Pesach, Shavuos, Sukkos, Chanukah, and so forth — we encounter *halachos* that train us and transform us. May we be *zocheh* to that total transformation that will make us worthy of the exalted description "אֲדַמֶּה לְעֶלְיוֹן."

# GIVE AND TAKE

*Internalizing the Torah's Attitude toward Chessed*

I once delivered a *shiur* on the topic of *ma'aser kesafim*, the requirement to give one-tenth (or, ideally, one-fifth) of one's earnings to *tzedakah*. I mentioned that this is a very challenging mitzvah. For the poor man, who is barely making ends meet, this mitzvah entails giving away a tenth of his very survival. And a wealthy man may be required to part with hundreds of thousands of dollars.

After the *shiur*, I was approached by one of the attendees. My words had apparently struck a deep chord within him — a raw nerve, perhaps.

"Oy, you are so right," he said. "You have no idea how hard it is to give a *million dollars* to *tzedakah* every year!"

"Well," I said, "you certainly have that right. I imagine that I will *never* know what it means to give away a million dollars to *tzedakah* every year!"

Whether one's *ma'aser* is a tremendous amount of money, or if it's a tenth of his survival, it is always money that a person desperately wants for himself. So how can a person motivate himself to give away his money? How can one give it with joy and enthusiasm?

Actually, the question looms somewhat larger than the specific mitzvah of *ma'aser*. In reality, life is all about giving.

Aside from money, we must constantly share our time and resources with others. When we are in yeshivah or Bais Yaakov, we have to help others; when we get married, we have a spouse, and a family, to whom we are responsible. When we are in shul, there are so many collectors; when we come home, there are so many *tzedakah* letters. There are so, so many people that need our help.

In addition to our *chessed* load at home, and all of the *chessed* causes that we assist, it seems that everyone also has a "nudnik" or two in his life who claims another portion of his time, and, often, his money. A *gadol* once remarked that he is convinced that Hashem loves nudniks. "How do I know?" he asked. "Because Hashem made so many of them!"

And as we get older, our obligations seem to grow proportionately. Often, we have parents that are entering their elder years, and they also begin to need our time and care.

How is one supposed to juggle so many overwhelming responsibilities?

The answer to these questions is one word: *emunah*. Specifically, our *emunah* is the Torah's view of what giving is really all about.

Allow me to explain.

## 🌿 Live to Give

Rav Chaim Volozhiner used to say that a person was created to help others (see introduction to *sefer Nefesh Hachaim*) הָאָדָם לֹא לְעַצְמוֹ נִבְרָא, רַק לְהוֹעִיל לַאֲחֵרִינִי כְּכָל אֲשֶׁר יִמְצָא בְּכֹחוֹ לַעֲשׂוֹת — *Man was not created to see exclusively to his own needs; rather, he was created to help others in any way that he is capable of.*

I knew a *"pashute Yid"* who lived by these words. His motto in life was, *"Oib nisht fahr yenem, vos darf ich leben —* If not for someone else whom I can help, of what purpose is my life?" We live to help others. We live to give.

The *Mesillas Yesharim* (ch. 19) teaches us how Hashem views the *chessed* that we do. Imagine how you would feel toward someone who goes out of his way to help your *ben yachid*, your only son. You would feel so much appreciation to that person that you would do anything for him. That is how Hashem feels toward us when we take care of one of His "only children."

The *pasuk* in *Koheles* (7:2) says, וְהַחַי יִתֵּן אֶל לִבּוֹ — *and the living one will put it on his heart.*

The Midrash (*Koheles* 7:5) explains:

זֶה חֵי הָעוֹלָמִים — *This* [i.e., וְהַחַי, the living One] *refers to Hashem, the One Who lives forever,*

שֶׁהוּא מְשַׁלֵּם שָׂכָר לְבַר נָשׁ — *Who pays a reward to a person,*

עַל כָּל פְּסִיעָה וּפְסִיעָה בִּגְמִילוּת חֲסָדִים — *for each and every step that he takes for chessed.*

Look at the wording of the *pasuk*, וְהַחַי יִתֵּן אֶל לִבּוֹ — *Hashem will put our chessed into His heart.* Hashem will put the *chessed* that you did for His child *into His heart, kaviyachol,* and He will never forget it.

## ✑ Our Solution

Reuven was in deep trouble, both financially and emotionally. Moshe took Reuven under his wing, and spared no effort to assist him. As it often happens in these situations, Moshe's involvement in Reuven's problems began to take an emotional and financial toll on him.

After a particularly difficult day, Moshe unburdened himself to me.

"I can't go on like this. Reuven has terrible problems, and I would like to help, but the problems are his, not mine. Why must I suffer so much because of him?"

I told him that he is asking a very good question. Why, indeed, do we have to suffer because of other people's problems? This is not only a good question, but a very old question as well. And *Chazal* gave us the answer:

* The Gemara (*Bava Basra* 10a) recounts that Rabbi Meir would say that if a man asks you if Hashem loves the poor, why does He not sustain them? Answer him thus: So that *we* may be spared from the judgment of Gehinnom!

You got it all wrong. Of course Hashem could take care of His poor people. But Hashem made them needy so that we could help them, thereby earning Hashem's kindness.

* The Midrash (*Tanchuma, Mishpatim* 9) teaches that Dovid Hamelech asked this question as well. Dovid asked Hashem, "Why did You make such an imbalanced world? Some people have so much, and some have so little."

Hashem replied, "If everybody would have everything they need, how would there be *chessed* in the world?"

We have to believe that his problem is our solution. He has his problem so that we can do *chessed*. So if he is suffering **because of us,** how can we not help him? He is not our problem, he is our solution.

## ✑ Live to Give or Give to Live?

A wealthy Jew once visited the Chazon Ish, the unofficial "*melech Yisrael.*" He expected to see the Chazon Ish living in a mansion, or at least a comfortably appointed home. He was shocked to see the reality — the Chazon Ish lived in abject poverty, in a small and cramped apartment. He was so moved, that after his meeting he took out a wad of bills and put it on the Chazon Ish's table.

"Please, Rebbi, take this!"

But the Chazon Ish replied, "Thank you, but I don't take money for personal needs."

"*Uber fun vos lebt dem Rebbi* — but how does the Rebbi live?"

The Chazon Ish, with a twinkle and a smile, answered, "*Ich leb fun tuhn ah Yid ah tovah* — I live by helping others."

The Chazon Ish probably meant a play on words; helping others is what he "lives for." But there is a depth to his words, because *chessed* generates the greatest *zechusim*, which in turn benefit us directly.

In other words, it can be said that not only do we live to give, but, more accurately, we give to live. We all live from the *chessed* we do.

## Life Saver

The Gemara (*Shabbos* 156b) tells a fascinating story.

Rabbi Akiva was told by a stargazer that his daughter would die on the day of her wedding. The Gemara relates that Rabbi Akiva was very worried; he felt there was truth to that frightening prediction. The night before the wedding, everyone in Rabbi Akiva's household was busy preparing for the wedding. (There were no caterers then!) The *kallah* herself was off in a corner, and almost went unnoticed amid all of the activity. But someone realized that the *kallah* should be going to sleep soon, and must have something to eat before retiring — after all, she would be fasting tomorrow. A plate of food was set down in front of her.

Just then, a poor, hungry man came by to ask for something to eat. Everyone was so busy that no one paid attention to him. But the *kallah* herself noticed, and gave the man her plate of food. She literally gave him "the food from her mouth"; he ate her meal, and she went to sleep hungry.

The next morning, when she awoke, she went to take out her hairpin from the wall near her bed. (In those times, women would save their pins for the next day by sticking them into the wall.) To her great surprise, she saw that when she had stuck the pin into the wall she had unknowingly killed the poisonous snake that was destined to kill her, which was now dangling lifelessly from her pin.

It was a miracle! The story made headlines, so to speak; everybody was talking about it. Rabbi Akiva asked her, "Tell me, dear daughter, what happened? In what merit were you saved?" She told him about her gift to the poor man. Rabbi Akiva went out and proclaimed, צְדָקָה תַּצִּיל מִמָּוֶת — *charity saves a person from death* (*Mishlei* 10:2).

You tell a child a story to put him to sleep, but a story is told to an adult to wake him up.

What is this story supposed to awaken in us? What concept, or what attitude, should be given new light?

What the story teaches us is this: Not only do we live to give, but we must have the *emunah* that we give to live. Rabbi Akiva's daughter was granted a new lease on life because she helped someone else. עוֹלָם חֶסֶד יִבָּנֶה (*Tehillim* 89:3) does not just imply that when I am kind to someone else I build *his* world — through *chessed* I invariably build my *own* world.

## ᛒ᠊ᚱ Problems or Solutions

The *Zohar Hakadosh* (*Vayeira* p. 97a) writes that when Hashem feels love for a person, He sends him a gift — a poor person.

This "gift" can be anyone who needs help: a *meshulach* who needs money; a lonely person who needs *chizuk*; a parent who needs care. It could be what we call a "nudnik." When we encounter a "gift" like this, it is as if Hashem is saying to us, "I'm going to give you an opportunity to do *chessed*, so that I can repay you."

Imagine if you were the neighbor of Rabbi Akiva, living right across the street. You are watching the flurry of activity in the house, and you notice how the *kallah* is sitting off in the corner, and no one is paying any attention to her. The poor girl has to fast tomorrow and no one is feeding her. You feel bad; you feel like going over there yourself to bring her food. Suddenly, you say, "Oh, *baruch Hashem*! Someone gave her a meal! Now she'll eat." Just then, you see Reb Shmerel, the local collector, knocking on the door.

"I don't believe it! *Now* he comes? Where's his *mentschlichkeit*? Doesn't he know that they are making a *chasunah*?"

And then, to your great distress, you see the poor man take the *kallah's* own supper! You have to hold yourself back from running over and giving him a piece of your mind. How can you do that to her? Can't you come back tomorrow?

Rabbi Akiva's daughter, however, was able to see the poor man for what he was: a *doron*, a wedding gift, from Hashem Himself. This man is not a nudnik; he is my lifesaver. If not for him there wouldn't be a tomorrow just like the stargazer predicted! He was not a problem, he was a solution.

The *pasuk* (*Devarim* 13:18) says: וְנָתַן לְךָ רַחֲמִים וְרִחַמְךָ — *and He will give you mercy and be merciful to you.*

The *Zohar* (ibid.) explains: Sometimes Hashem sees that we need a *yeshuah*, a cure, or a solution to a problem, but we really do not deserve it. What does He do?

וְנָתַן לְךָ רַחֲמִים — *Rachamim* means an opportunity to display *rachamim*. Hashem will give you a chance to do an act of kindness. If you rise to the occasion, and take advantage of this opportunity, then, וְרִחַמְךָ — *He will grant* **you** *the rachamim* that *you* need; be it *gezunt*, or *parnassah*, a *shidduch*, or success with *chinuch habanim*.

We must have the eyes of *emunah* to see that. Sometimes we sit down, and think, "Ribono Shel Olam, I need help! My business is not going well; my daughter is getting older and needs a *shidduch*. I need *gezunt*; this child is sick; this grandchild is struggling. What should I do, Ribono Shel Olam? Send me a *yeshuah*!"

And right then, we notice someone who needs *our* help. The doorbell rings, and standing there is a person from Eretz Yisrael with a "hard luck story," or a neighbor who needs a little *chizuk*; the phone rings and it's a friend that needs help... A simple person may say, "This is so poorly timed! I am not in my element now; I am overwhelmed by my own problem. Right now I do not have the time, or the money, or the peace of mind to help anyone else."

A Yid living with *emunah* realizes that this *chessed* might be the key to the *yeshuah* that he just *davened* for. וְנָתַן לְךָ רַחֲמִים וְרִחַמְךָ. He won't throw it away!

## Hashem's Insurance

An individual from Far Rockaway, New York, who is personally acquainted with the people involved, told me the following story.

Reuven approached Shimon to ask him for a very important favor.

"I need a significant loan, but since I do not own my home, the bank will not lend me money. But if I can find a homeowner who will let his house be mortgaged, the bank will grant me a loan."

Shimon was not excited about the idea of mortgaging his home, but he thought it over and decided that this was an opportunity to do a big *chessed*. "I'll do it!" he told Reuven.

The two went to the bank, and began filling out the paper work, but the bank manager told Shimon that his house did not have enough insurance to satisfy the bank's requirements for a secure property.

"We can only use your house if you take out extra coverage, specifically flood insurance."

Now Shimon was faced with an overwhelming challenge. The whole idea was not really to his liking, and now he was being asked to buy extra insurance, which he did not even want. He never committed to spending his own money for this *chessed*. Shimon had the perfect excuse — he really wanted to help, but things did not work out...

But Shimon decided that although he could get out of his commitment, he was not going to. He took the opportunity to do this favor for Reuven, even at his own expense. Shimon bought the insurance.

A short time later, New York and New Jersey were hit by Hurricane Sandy, and Far Rockaway in particular sustained terrible flood damage. But Shimon was one of the few people who had the necessary insurance to make a claim and receive full coverage for all of his losses. Without that, he would have been left devastated.

A person who needs help is a source of *rachamim*; he is a gift who presents us with an opportunity to generate *rachamim* for ourselves.

## Taking by Giving

In the beginning of *Parshas Terumah* (*Shemos* 25:2), the Jews are commanded to give the materials for the construction of the Mishkan, דַּבֵּר אֶל בְּנֵי יִשְׂרָאֵל וְיִקְחוּ לִי תְּרוּמָה — *Speak to Bnei Yisrael and have them* **take** *for Me a donation*.

The Beis Halevi points out that the Torah uses a strange word here. In the context of this *pasuk*, a more accurate word would seem to be "וְיִתְּנוּ לִי תְּרוּמָה — *and they should* **give** *to Me a donation*," not וְיִקְחוּ, which means "take."

The Beis Halevi explains that the Torah uses the word וְיִקְחוּ because a Yid has to know that when he gives he is really taking.

This idea is encapsulated in the well-known observation of the Ba'al Haturim that the word (*Shemos* 30:12) וְנָתְנוּ — *they should give*, can be read forward and backward. What we give away, comes back to us.

Now of course we don't give *in order* to get back, because then we are just investors. But that is the way to begin. *Chazal* (*Pesachim* 50b) teach us, מִתּוֹךְ שֶׁלֹּא לִשְׁמָהּ בָּא לִשְׁמָהּ — *one who does a mitzvah for ulterior motives will eventually do it for the mitzvah's sake*. But we may begin "living to give" by internalizing the lesson that we "give to live"; that when we do *chessed* we ourselves are the biggest beneficiaries.

## Our Mission

The Midrash (*Vayikra Rabbah, Parshah* 34:4) cites the *pasuk* in *Mishlei* (22:2), עָשִׁיר וָרָשׁ נִפְגָּשׁוּ עֹשֵׂה כֻלָּם ה' — *The rich man and the pauper meet, Hashem is the Maker of them all*.

The Midrash then gives a penetrating analysis, a timely and timeless perspective, on the opportunity to help another Jew. If someone needs help, whether financially, or emotionally, or needs our time, we should say to ourselves, "Why did Hashem give me what I have, and make him so needy? So that I should help him. Hashem has given me extra so that I may share my good fortune with him."

If we help the needy person, both of us will be happy, and Hashem will reward the one who gives.

But, says the Midrash, if the person who has it all, starts to think, and reason: "Why should I be busy with him? Why do I have to help him? Let him take care of himself."

Then, says the Midrash, remember — עֹשֶׂה כֻלָּם ה'. Hashem makes all. The One Who gave the rich man his wealth can make him poor, *chas v'shalom*! And the One Who made the pauper poor, can make him wealthy.

Remember that we have extra in order to give others. Hashem could have taken care of the other person, but He wants us to understand that by helping someone else we are not the benefactor, but the beneficiary. Don't think, "Why do we have to suffer for him?" because in reality, he might be suffering for us.

Life is dependent on giving. Parents give to children, children give to parents, spouses and friends and neighbors give to one another — so much of the happiness in life depends on giving. The greatest threat is when a person does not see the privilege he has, and the benefit he gets, from giving.

## What Can You Do for Me?

I had a neighbor, who has a wonderful sense of humor. When I would knock on his door, he would open the door, give me a big smile and say, "Yes? What can *you* do for *me*?"

It was a funny greeting — a twist on the formal, "Yes, what can *I* do for *you*?"

My neighbor, of course, was joking. But there are people who live like that. When they meet another person, they begin to think, "What can you do for me?" They live in the pitiful world of כְּשֶׁאֲנִי לְעַצְמִי, מָה אֲנִי — *if I live for myself, what am I* — a selfish and self-centered existence, where people live only for themselves.

Then, there are those people who live with the proper attitude toward *chessed*. These individuals see another person and they think, "What can I do for him? How can I make his day more pleasant? How can I put a smile on his face?"

That attitude — seeing the gift and the opportunity in helping another human being — is the secret of living a life of *chessed*.

* How do you give away a million dollars of your hard-earned money?

By remembering the *Chazal* (*Ta'anis* 9a), עַשֵּׂר בִּשְׁבִיל שֶׁתִּתְעַשֵּׁר — *give ma'aser in order to become wealthy...* By strengthening your *emunah* that you are not giving away one million, you are being given nine million. By feeling privileged — not threatened — by needy petitioners.

* How do you find time to spend time with parents, especially when you have no time for yourself?

By realizing that you are not just living to give, you are giving to live. By bearing in mind that although כַּבֵּד אֶת אָבִיךָ וְאֶת אִמֶּךָ is indeed a time-consuming mitzvah, it is for this very reason that the Torah promises לְמַעַן יַאֲרִכוּן יָמֶיךָ — you are going to get back the time you spent.

* How do you help the "nudnik" in your life?

By taking that word out of your vocabulary. This person is not a nudnik, he (or she) is a gift from Hashem, the *yeshuah* you need. He may just be your lifesaver. By remembering that the world operates on the concept of וְנָתַן לְךָ רַחֲמִים וְרִחַמְךָ. By internalizing the fact that when you give, you may be the biggest taker.

## Our Frightening Times

A Yid recently asked me, "Our generation is suffering from so many problems. Many struggle with *parnassah*, and with issues of *chinuch habanim*. We are experiencing a *shidduch* crisis. Illness claims too many of our young people. We are seeing technology and decadence ruining so many others. There is so much pain in our world. Tell me, why is this so?"

I told him that I cannot venture to answer that question, but I can relate what I heard from two of our generation's great *mashgichim* — Rav Moshe Wolfson and Rav Mattisyahu Salomon, who expressed a very similar thought.

In *Parshas Vayeira*, the Torah tells us the story of the three *malachim* who went to Sedom in order to save Lot and to destroy the city. But first the Torah relates how the *malachim* were invited into Lot's home and threatened by the city's citizens. Then Lot bravely placed himself between the angry mob and his guests, whom he sought to protect with great *mesirus nefesh*.

Rav Wolfson pointed out that the above part of the narrative is not an unrelated incident; rather, it is the preface and the basis for the rest of the story.

Lot had to be saved because he was Avraham's nephew, but Lot was undeserving of salvation. What did Hashem do? He engineered a situation where Lot would be able to do *chessed* with *mesirus nefesh*. וְנָתַן לְךָ רַחֲמִים — Hashem gave Lot an opportunity of *rachamim*. Lot utilized the opportunity, and that saved his life.

A similar lesson is taught in *Parshas Shemos*. The *pasuk* tells us (*Shemos* 5:14) that the *shotrim*, the policemen who directly supervised and enforced the Jews' labor in Mitzrayim, were beaten by the Egyptian taskmasters for the slaves' failure to fulfill their daily quotas. Rashi explains that these *shotrim* were Jews themselves, who felt compassion for their brethren, and would not beat them to force them to fulfill the essentially impossible quotas that were set for them. Their compassion entailed *mesirus nefesh* on their part, for the *shotrim* took the beatings on themselves.

Rav Mattisyahu pointed out that the compassion of the *shotrim* was not only a great *zechus* for them personally (these *shotrim* later merited positions on Moshe Rabbeinu's Sanhedrin), but this was the *zechus* that helped bring about the *geulah*.

It was time for the *geulah*, but the Jews were hardly deserving of it. They were sunk in the forty-nine gates of *tumah*; they were unworthy. So Hashem engineered a situation wherein *Yidden* would be given the opportunity to be *moser nefesh* for one another. The *shotrim* rose to the occasion and Klal Yisrael as a whole merited the *geulah*.

Perhaps, this is why we see so much suffering and pain in our times. הִגִּיעַ זְמַן גְּאוּלַתְכֶם — *it is time for our geulah*. Any person with open eyes and open ears can see and hear Mashiach's imminent arrival! The painful question is, are we deserving of it? Fortunately there's a solution to this crisis.

The Gemara (*Sanhedrin* 98b) asks:

מַה יַּעֲשֶׂה אָדָם וְיִנָּצֵל מֵחֶבְלוֹ שֶׁל מָשִׁיחַ — *What should a person do to save himself from the birth pangs of Mashiach?*

יַעֲסֹק בַּתּוֹרָה וּבִגְמִילוּת חֲסָדִים — *Involve himself in Torah study and acts of chessed.*

Torah study, as we know, is the greatest *zechus*. But what role does *gemilus chassadim* play?

*Chessed* is a necessary tactic in the *Ikvesa d'Meshicha* because *chessed* generates *rachamei Shamayim* that we so desperately need.

In our current world situation, Hashem is giving us untold opportunities for *chessed*. Wherever you go, unfortunately, there are so many needy people. And He is trusting us to do our part, and to turn וְרַחַמְךָ into רַחֲמִים.

We must have the *emunah* to realize that when we give a helping hand, we are really taking Hashem's hand — the hand that we describe in *bentching*: יָדְךָ הַמְּלֵאָה הַפְּתוּחָה הַקְּדוֹשָׁה וְהָרְחָבָה — *Your Hand which is full, open, holy, and expansive.*

Hashem's hand is מְשַׁלֵּם שָׂכָר עַל כָּל פְּסִיעָה וּפְסִיעָה בִּגְמִילוּת חֲסָדִים. *Der Eibishter bleibt nisht shuldig.* Hashem is cherishing all of our *chassadim*, so that we will merit וְרַחַמְךָ, thereby turning *galus* into *geulah*.

# BUILDING WORLDS...WITH WORDS
## *The Power of Chessed B'dibbur*

Did you ever find an amazing bargain? Did you ever chance upon an unbelievable sale? When that happens, people usually get very excited, and share the "great news" with all of their friends.

I want to share with you a phenomenal bargain that we can all benefit from.

Rav Chatzkel Levenstein (*Ohr Yechezkel* 1:5) once noted in a letter that when a person says a few nice words to someone else, all he has "given" is a few words, but, in return:

הַקָּדוֹשׁ בָּרוּךְ הוּא נוֹתֵן לוֹ בְּעַד זֹאת — *Hashem gives him for this act,*

בְּיָדוֹ הַמְּלֵאָה הַקְּדוֹשָׁה — *with His full and holy Hand,*

שֶׁפַע בְּרָכָה מַמָּשׁ — *an abundant flow of brachah.*

For a few words, you can receive an abundance of *brachah*. What a tremendous bargain. The practice of speaking positive words, words of encouragement and praise, is an exceedingly worthwhile investment.

Rav Chatzkel concludes:

מַה גּוֹדֶל הַצְלָחַת הָאָדָם — *How great is that man's success.* How wonderful it is. You can give away nothing and receive everything.

אֲשֶׁר קָנָה לְעַצְמוֹ הַמַּעֲלָה שֶׁל אַהֲבַת הַבְּרִיּוֹת — *that he acquired for himself the virtue of loving people,*

הִנֵּה תָּמִיד הוּא מוּשְׁפָּע בְּבִרְכַת השי"ת — *he will always be showered will Hashem's blessing of,*

טוֹב עַיִן הוּא יְבֹרָךְ — *one with a good eye* — who sees others in a positive way, and trains himself to use the power of words in a kind and constructive way — *will be blessed.*

## ◌ An Irresistible Offer

Imagine: A few days before Purim, Moshe receives a phone call from a very wealthy friend.

"Reb Moshe, I need a favor," says the wealthy man. "Usually, over Purim I give out $100,000 cash. Not just to people who need *tzedakah*, but to everybody I see, just to make people happy! I've been doing this for years."

"That's wonderful!" says Moshe. "But how can I help you?"

"Well, this year, I will not be home for Purim and won't be able to bring my 'happiness' to anybody. Do me a favor. I'm going to give you a box with $100,000 cash. Give it out to anybody you want — all of your neighbors, family, and friends, anyone and everyone! Just make people happy."

Who could say no to such a request? But there's more to this irresistible offer. Imagine if this wealthy man added the following:

"I would really appreciate it if you can do this for me. In fact, as an expression of my thanks to you, I am going to give you an additional $10,000 cash to keep for yourself."

What a windfall! What an amazing opportunity.

Now imagine if Moshe declines the offer!

"I'm sorry, but I do not have the time for this. I am too preoccupied..."

Is that not ridiculous? Moshe is being given the opportunity to help so many people, including the people closest to him, and to be rewarded handsomely for doing so, and he is refusing to do so. Is it not tragic to see him throw that all away?

But do you know what is more tragic? All too often, we are the *nimshal*.

With positive words, we can help everyone around us, and all of the people who are closest to us. And it is a cost-free endeavor — Hashem gives us the words; He doesn't charge us for them! And to top it off, He rewards us so handsomely for doing this. But all too often, we throw away the opportunity.

## ⟨⟩ Double Your Blessings

The Gemara (*Baba Basra* 9b) teaches that if someone gives a poor person *tzedakah*, he receives six *brachos*. This, of course, shows us the greatness of *tzedakah*. But then the Gemara goes on to say something quite amazing:

וְהַמְפַיְּיסוֹ בִּדְבָרִים מִתְבָּרֵךְ בְּאַחַת עֶשְׂרֵה בְּרָכוֹת — *And one who appeases the poor person with kind words is blessed with eleven brachos.*

*Tosafos* (d.h. *v'hamefayso*) explains that in this second case, the solicited person has no money to give to the poor person. But he doesn't just dismiss him, he gives him a good word; he speaks to him kindly and encouragingly. One who does so will receive almost double the *brachos* than the one who actually gave *tzedakah*.

Now this is surprising. If you give away your hard-earned money, you receive six *brachos*. We can understand that. But why is it that if you give words, you receive almost double that amount? In America there is an expression, "Talk is cheap." That is true in one sense, because words do not cost anything. So, why should a person who merely gave away words deserve more *brachos* than someone who gave away something with monetary value?

I want to explain this by asking you to decide the following question: Two friends, Reuven and Shimon, go together to a *drashah* given by a well-known *rav*, who makes a powerful presentation about the importance of *chessed*. The two friends are greatly inspired; after the **drashah,** both decide to implement what they have heard, and to add more *chessed* into their lives.

Reuven is creative and ambitious, and has some extra money. He goes out that night and buys a pushcart, and a lot of fresh, delicious milk. The next morning, he goes to a street corner near his home and gives out milk, free of charge, to anyone who passes by. Everyone needs milk. Here you can get milk for free. Reuven has found a practical method to do *chessed* for others.

Shimon does not have as much money as Reuven, and cannot afford to be as generous, but he also wants to bring *chessed* to others. What does he do? He goes to another street corner and stands there smiling and warmly greeting every single passerby. Everyone he sees is given a friendly "Good morning!" and a wish for a great day.

Who is a greater *ba'al chessed*?

One would be tempted to say that the question is ridiculous. Reuven is obviously doing so much more. But, as we will see, the opposite is true.

## ✑ Better Than Milk

The Gemara (*Kesubos* 111b) actually rules on this very question, based on a *pasuk* in *Parshas Vayechi*.

When Yaakov Avinu blesses his son Yehudah, he says (*Bereishis* 49:12): וּלְבֶן שִׁנַּיִם מֵחָלָב. Literally, this means that the people of *shevet Yehudah* will have healthy white teeth from the abundance of milk in their territory.

The Gemara expounds the *pasuk:* טוֹב הַמַּלְבִּין שִׁנַּיִם לַחֲבֵרוֹ יוֹתֵר מִמַּשְׁקֵהוּ חָלָב — *One who "flashes his white teeth"* (i.e., one who smiles) *to his friend, has done something better than one who gives his friend a drink of milk.*

Imagine that. Giving someone milk is wonderful. But smiling at him and telling him a kind word is a greater act. Why is that?

A person might have all the milk in the world, but if no one cares about him, everything that he has is worthless. The Gemara says (*Ta'anis* 23a): אוֹ חַבְרוּתָא אוֹ מִיתוּתָא — *Give me a chavrusa, a friend, or give me misusa, death.*

Rashi (*Bava Basra* 16b, *d.h. oh chevrah*) expresses this thought as follows: אִם אֵין לָאָדָם אוֹהֲבִים, נוֹחַ לוֹ שֶׁיָּמוּת — *If a person has no friends he is better off experiencing death.*

There is a powerful message here. If someone does not have milk, it is not so difficult to get some. But when a person feels unimportant, when he feels alone, he undergoes the most painful human experience in this world. When you smile at him, or when you greet him with that warm "Good morning!" you are recognizing and acknowledging him. You are the *chavrusa* that replaces the *misusa*. When you do so, you have given him something far more valuable than milk.

## ✑ Talk Is Life

Shlomo Hamelech, the wisest of men put it succinctly (*Mishlei* 18:21): מָוֶת וְחַיִּים בְּיַד לָשׁוֹן — *Death and life are in the hand of the tongue.*

Words are powerful. Words can wreak havoc in a person's life. מָוֶת בְּיַד לָשׁוֹן.

But there is another half to the equation as well: חַיִּים בְּיַד לָשׁוֹן. Words are therapeutic. Words are healing. Words are uplifting. Words give life.

We don't really need proof for this; we have all experienced the truth of this elementary concept. We have all had "one of those days" when we wake up in the morning on the wrong side, and the day goes from bad to worse. You think to yourself, *I can't go on like this...* Just then, someone comes over and compliments you. He tells you that he thinks so highly of you, that he is impressed with how you managed this or that, or with how nicely your child or grandchild behaves. A few well-placed words and the world is suddenly bright again.

A kind word or a nice compliment is so important and meaningful. Don't we all see how true חַיִּים בְּיַד לָשׁוֹן is?

The Rambam (*Hil. Dei'os* 6:3) discusses the mitzvah of וְאָהַבְתָּ לְרֵעֲךָ כָּמוֹךָ. After stating the requirement to love your fellow Jew, the Rambam offers practical applications of this mitzvah.

Says the Rambam, "Therefore, based on what I have just told you [that you are obligated in this great mitzvah], here are some examples of what you must do in daily life."

Let's pause for a moment to ask — what do you suppose is the Rambam's very first example, his primary illustration, of *ahavas Yisrael?*

You would probably say, "Give a large amount of money to *tzedakah*," or, "Help people with anything they might need." Let us see what the Rambam actually says: לְפִיכָךְ צָרִיךְ לְסַפֵּר בְּשִׁבְחוֹ — *Therefore, you must relate your fellow Jew's praises.* You should compliment others.

The Rambam understood the human psyche. There is simply nothing as important, or as meaningful, as a compliment. The world around us says, "Talk is cheap." But Shlomo Hamelech says, talk is life, חַיִּים בְּיַד לָשׁוֹן.

Compliments breathe new life into someone's *neshamah.*

## ❧ Constant Compliments

Rav Elya Lopian would often reminisce about the time in his life when he studied in the great Kelmer Yeshivah, under his illustrious *rebbi*, the Alter from Kelm.

The Alter's *rebbetzin* was an outstanding woman in her own right, who single-handedly ran the yeshivah. She cooked for the *bachurim*, took care of the finances of the yeshivah and the maintenance of the building…she did everything. Originally Rav Elya attributed her unusual accomplishments to the fact that she was a very idealistic and motivated person, and that she must have unique strengths. But, said Rav Elya, he once discovered the true secret of her greatness.

It happened when Rav Elya ate at the Alter's home one Shabbos. There he saw one simple thing — the Alter profusely complimented his wife. Rav Elya even remembered some specific compliments: When the Alter tasted the challah, he said, "This challah is so delicious we really ought to make a *Borei Minei Mezonos* on it. It is like a good cake!" And so it went throughout the *seudah*.

Rav Elya said that he then understood how the *rebbetzin* was able to accomplish so much. When someone feels appreciated, when someone feels recognized and acknowledged, that person becomes energized and empowered to do so much more than they might otherwise have been capable of.

## The Gift of Everything

Toward the end of his life, the Vilna Gaon left Europe to settle in Eretz Yisrael. At this time, he wrote a now-famous letter to his family — to his wife, to his daughters, and to his aged mother who lived with them. While instructing his wife about creating the proper atmosphere in the home, the Gaon writes something unbelievable:

אִשָּׁה אֶת רְעוּתָהּ תְּשַׂמַּח בִּדְבָרִים טוֹבִים — *Everyone should use kind words to make each other happy,*

כִּי זֶה מִצְוָה גְדוֹלָה לְכָל אָדָם — *for this is a great mitzvah for every person,*

וּבָזֶה רֹב הַתּוֹרָה לְשַׂמֵּחַ לָאָדָם — *and the majority of the Torah is to make someone else happy.*

Note the Gaon's instructions: It is a great mitzvah to make someone else happy. And how does one do so? בִּדְבָרִים טוֹבִים — with kind words. The greatest tool to bring happiness to others is positive words.

The *Avos D'Rabbi Nosson* (I 13:4) teaches:

הַמְקַבֵּל אֶת חֲבֵירוֹ בְּסֵבֶר פָּנִים יָפוֹת — *If someone greets his friend with a shining countenance, with warmth,*

אֲפִילוּ לֹא נָתַן לוֹ כְּלוּם — *even if he does not give him anything tangible,*

מַעֲלֶה עָלָיו הַכָּתוּב כְּאִלּו נָתַן לוֹ כָּל מַתָּנוֹת טוֹבוֹת שֶׁבָּעוֹלָם — *it is as if he has given his friend **all of the best gifts in the world.***

Words are not cheap. Words are כָּל מַתָּנוֹת טוֹבוֹת שֶׁבָּעוֹלָם — *all of the best gifts in the world.*

## ଚ See the Person

There is another practical lesson that I believe we must learn to incorporate into our lives.

We are conditioned to see mitzvos. When we see a poor man, we see the opportunity for us to fulfill the mitzvah of *tzedakah*. But what happens if we have no money to give him? Most people just walk away; after all, what else can I do to help him?

However, a greater, more sensitive person also sees the **person** behind the mitzvah. He understands that this collector left his home, and perhaps even his country, due to his financial hardships. His dignity is shattered; his self-esteem is at an all-time low. Why not say a few nice words to him? He's not a *pushke* that happens to be able to walk and talk. He is a suffering human being. Why not say, "I'm sorry I don't have money, but I hope your child will have a *refuah sheleimah*," or, "I hope that you'll be able to celebrate your wedding with much *simchah*."

This applies even when we are giving money to a poor person. Where there's a *meshulach* circulating in shul, instead of silently handing him a dollar as if you are paying a toll, give him a good word. "*Refuah sheleimah*." "Mazel tov." "You should have much *hatzlachah*." Remember that he is a person with feelings — not just a *pushke* that happens to have feet.

My friend once told me a very disturbing story. A *meshulach* was going around from house to house in one of our prominent communities, and knocked on my friend's door. It was already a bit late in the evening. My friend invited the *meshulach* in. "Please come in, sit down, rest a bit. Can I offer you something to eat or drink? Perhaps you would like to use the phone, or the bathroom?"

The *meshulach* was very thankful, and became a bit emotional.

"I have been walking around the whole day, and you are the first person who invited me into his home."

*Yidden* are wonderful people; we give incredible amounts of *tzedakah* and that is to our eternal credit. But how could it be that a fellow Jew circulating in our neighborhoods is not invited in to anyone's home? We see the mitzvah of *tzedakah*, but we don't see the person. We can accomplish so much with just a few kind words.

It is noteworthy that the Rambam's description of *tzedakah* (*Matanos Ani'im* 10:4) is primarily *how* to give, not how *much* to give.

בְּסֵבֶר פָּנִים יָפוֹת וּבְשִׂמְחָה — *With a shining countenance and with joy,*

וּמִתְאוֹנֵן עִמּוֹ עַל צָרָתוֹ — *bemoan with him about his problem,* inquire about his problem, feel his pain,

וִידַבֵּר לוֹ דִּבְרֵי תַנְחוּמִים — *speak to him words of condolence and comfort.*

Evidently, more important than the *tzedakah* itself are the words that accompany it, as well as the manner in which the money is given.

The Rambam adds that even if he has no money to give, he should appease the pauper with words.

## ‭〰 Practical Training

Unfortunately, many of us do not have the proper training to see the individual. I would like to give a few scenarios to consider, besides the *ani* collecting *tzedakah*, so that we can train ourselves in this most important attitude.

### * Torah

Why is it that after hearing a *drashah* or a *shiur*, very few people approach the speaker to thank and compliment him on a wonderful speech? Apparently we are trained to see mitzvos — *limud haTorah*, *chizuk* in our *ruchniyus*, which is wonderful. But we also have to see the person — in this case the speaker — behind these mitzvos.

### * Tefillah

I used to sit next to Rav Pam during *davening*. (Not that I sat in the front of the *beis midrash*, rather he would sit toward the back.) I noticed that he complimented every *ba'al tefillah* that led the *davening* on Shabbos or Yom Tov. And when he did so, he crafted a custom-made compliment for each one. Rav Pam was focused on seeing people and used words effectively.

### *Chinuch

When we meet our son's *rebbi* or *menahel*, or our daughter's teacher or principal, do we compliment them on the job that they're doing? Do we give them the well-deserved *yasher ko'ach* for their incredible dedication to being *mechanech* our children? Don't they deserve our thanks and recognition?

When we see our child's *rebbi*, or our daughter's teacher, we see the importance of our child's *chinuch*. But let's also see the people behind that *chinuch*. Take a moment to compliment them. And if you do not meet them, give them a call to express your gratitude.

I was once in the bank, shortly before Pesach, and I met a former neighbor, who was also the wife of my son's *rebbi*. She told me, "You should just know how much *chizuk* my husband received from your letter." I had no idea what she was talking about. "Which letter?" I wondered to myself. She continued, "My husband works so hard, and more than the kind gift, your letter really meant so much to him." Then I realized what she meant. She was referring to the note that I had sent the *rebbi* when I sent him a Chanukah gift, which is a customary expression of thanks. I feel that it is inappropriate to send such a gift to school/yeshivah with a child. It is as if the child is saying, "Here *rebbi*, this is a tip." Instead I mailed it to him, and with it a short letter expressing my gratitude. It didn't take me very long, but look how long the effect lasted. From Chanukah until Pesach, that letter was having an impact. It was an unbelievable lesson. Words are not cheap.

### * Shabbos

When we enjoy a *Shabbos seudah*, do we make sure to compliment those who made the *seudah*? They put in hours to prepare a beautiful Shabbos or Yom Tov meal and deserve to feel our appreciation, even if it's our own spouse or parent.

All of these things are obvious when we are thinking. Unfortunately, sometimes we don't think. We need to be thoughtful. We need to train ourselves to think along the lines of חַיִּים בְּיַד לָשׁוֹן. Then we will find countless opportunities throughout the day to put that *pasuk* into practice.

## 🙡 Life and Death

The *Zohar Hakadosh* (*Parshas Tazria* p. 46b) writes that just as there is a punishment for saying negative words, such as *lashon hara*, there is also a punishment reserved for someone who is in a situation where he could have said positive words but did not.

We are all aware that we have an obligation to refrain from forbidden speech. But here we see that we have the same obligation to speak kind words.

This *Zohar* brought me to a deeper awareness of the awesome double responsibility inherent in the *pasuk*, מָוֶת וְחַיִּים בְּיַד לָשׁוֹן.

The first part of the *pasuk*, מָוֶת בְּיַד לָשׁוֹן, has become synonymous with the battle cry for *shemiras halashon*. The Chafetz Chaim Heritage Foundation, among other great people and organizations, has done tremendous work educating people on the *churban* wrought by *lashon hara*. When people speak *lashon hara*, one can almost hear Shlomo Hamelech crying, "מָוֶת בְּיַד לָשׁוֹן! *Yidden!* Words can do so much damage. We have to stop this!"

But after seeing the *Zohar*, I hear Shlomo Hamelech crying in pain, "חַיִּים בְּיַד לָשׁוֹן! *Yidden*, there is so much that we can accomplish with words — we can compliment someone, we can greet someone, we can thank someone, we can acknowledge someone, we can inspire someone!" Are we utilizing the powerful gift of *dibbur*? We must realize that doing these things is not only an incredible kindness, it is also an obligation that we have. When we fail to use words in a positive way, we are as guilty as someone who uses words in a negative way.

## 🙡 Building Worlds

This brings us to a new set of common scenarios that we should contemplate. There are so many people who need encouragement, and when we withhold our good words from them we are depriving them. And that too is part of Shlomo's painful cry, "חַיִּים בְּיַד לָשׁוֹן!"

## * Our Children

Children who feel appreciated and recognized are able to reach higher levels of success. Children need "watering," like plants. The more they are showered with kind words and compliments, the more they grow.

Someone once asked the mother of Rav Nosson Tzvi Finkel, the Mirrer Rosh Yeshivah, about her parenting methods. How did she raise a *gadol* like Rav Nosson Tzvi? Her answer was, "I always complimented him." Indeed, חַיִּים בְּיַד לָשׁוֹן!

## * Our Family

Within our homes, we must utilize the enormous *ko'ach hadibbur*. We can bring joy to our spouses, our parents, our friends, and our relatives with what we say, and with what we don't say. Often, our words control other people's moods, and can make a person have a good day or a bad day. Each and every one of us is much more powerful than we realize.

## * The Despondent

We all know people who need *chizuk*. Perhaps they lost a loved one, or were just laid off, or recently divorced, etc. Give these people an occasional call before Shabbos or Yom Tov.

I know great people who do not have a spare moment, but routinely make phone calls to people going through difficult situations. They make sure that people who need *chizuk* get that needed phone call. Can't we do the same?

The *pasuk* (*Tehillim* 89:3) says: עוֹלָם חֶסֶד יִבָּנֶה. This *pasuk* invokes the vision of building a world through **buildings** of *chessed* — *mosdos* of *chessed*, organizations of *chessed*. That is true, of course. But you can also build worlds with **words** of *chessed*. Words help build other people's days, other people's lives. Words build worlds of life and happiness.

## ⟲ Power of a Compliment

I once gave a speech about this topic. After the speech, a woman approached me and told me her story.

"What you said is so true," she began.

She was a young mother, but she hadn't been feeling well, so she went to the doctor. After his initial examination, the doctor ordered some tests. Then a few days later he ordered more tests. After a week or so, she went to his office to discuss his diagnosis and was told that the tests had confirmed his worst fears: the young woman had the dreaded illness.

She walked out of the doctor's office, and her world seemed to collapse before her eyes. She did not know what to do. She had to go home; she had young children. Her husband didn't know anything, her children didn't know either. She decided that she was in no frame of mind to cook supper; she was going to take the family to the pizza shop, which was not something she typically did. Perhaps the children suspected that something was wrong, and were acting more subdued than usual.

At one point, the mother got up from the table to go to the sink. A woman who was standing there said to her, "You know, I have been observing your family. You have such a beautiful *mishpachah*. Such nice, well-behaved children. You should be *gezunt* and have much *nachas* from them."

This woman became very emotional as she told me, "I went through two and a half years of excruciatingly painful treatment. And do you know what kept me going? Those words, 'You have such a beautiful family; you should have *nachas* from them.'"

Two and a half years of unbearable treatment were made tolerable because of a well-placed compliment.

What did it cost, and what did it take, to utter those few words? I am envious of that other woman. She harnessed the power of words and literally rebuilt another person's shattered world.

## ❦ Traveling Alone

I was once speaking with someone who had just flown in from Eretz Yisrael. "Did you come with anyone else?" I asked him.

"No, I traveled all alone," he replied.

The way he said it seemed funny. "You traveled alone? Did you charter a personal jet to fly from Eretz Yisrael?"

He started laughing. "Actually it was a packed flight — four hundred people! What I mean is that I didn't know anybody on the plane. In that sense, I really was alone."

A person could be sitting on a plane with four hundred people, but he is traveling all alone. This struck me as an incredible lesson. There are people in our heavily populated neighborhoods who are living all alone. With a few words, we can improve their lives. Can't you hear Shlomo's cry "!הַחַיִּים בְּיַד לָשׁוֹן" Use words to build lives.

Some people are passed over by life. There are some people who no one really thinks of; no one includes them in his daily living. There are people in our neighborhoods who do not receive too many *mishloach manos* on Purim. There are people in our neighborhoods — I wish I was wrong, but I know I am not — who are rarely invited to *simchos*.

Do you know what it means to go through life with the feeling that you are totally unimportant? With the thought, *If I disappeared, no one would care. If I wouldn't come to shul for two months no one would even notice.* Such a person is experiencing what the Gemara describes, אִם אֵין לָאָדָם אוֹהֲבִים, נוֹחַ לוֹ שֶׁיָּמוּת. He is "traveling alone."

But then one person cares enough to go over and utilize the power of words.

"I did not see you in shul last week — where were you? I missed you."

"I'm making a *simchah*; it would mean a lot to me if you could make it. Please come."

"*Ah freilichin Purim!* Enjoy the *mishloach manos*!"

A greeting may be much more than a kind formality. Those words can be restoring a person dignity. They are giving him a dose of desperately needed self-esteem. They are saying, "You are important, you count, we *do* appreciate you." They are the *chavrusa* that replaces the unbearable *misusa*.

## ☙ One-Man *Gemach*

The *pasuk* (*Mishlei* 19:22) says: תַּאֲוַת אָדָם חַסְדּוֹ — *The longing of a person is for kindness.* *Taivah* means desires and pleasure. Generally, *taivah* is something negative; Jews eschew the pursuit of pleasure. But Shlomo Hamelech is saying that there is a permissible *taivah*. What is it? *Chasdo* — kindness.

The Ibn Ezra (ibid.) explains: a person should have a desire, a pleasure, in helping others.

A Yid's DNA is programmed for *chessed* (see *Yevamos* 79a). Just look around; our involvement in *chessed* is awe-inspiring. We have literally thousands of organizations and *gemachim* that are devoted to helping others.

I recently saw a directory of all the various *gemachim* that exist in our community — a free or next-to-free service for every need imaginable. I became emotional; I remember thinking, *Ribono Shel Olam, look how wonderful Your children are.*

If I may suggest, each person in his own life could make a personal *gemach* — a kind words *gemach*. Use the *ko'ach hadibbur* for what it was intended for. Give compliments, give warm words, and give greetings. You won't need funding for your *gemach*; you just need a *Yiddishe hartz*. You just need to care enough to stop and see the other person, and to think, "How can I use *chessed b'dibbur* to brighten this person's day?"

Every Yid can become a one-person *chessed* organization by generously dispensing *chessed b'dibbur*.

If I may humbly suggest, let us all try to implement our newfound appreciation of *chessed b'dibbur* in a practical way. Try this for one week. Every day, once by day, and once at night, go out of your way to give a compliment, or say a nice word. We have so many opportunities to use words to make others happy. But I warn you — this behavior is addictive. It is habit-forming because when you focus on others and decide that you are going to use words to breathe life and *simchah* into other people's *neshamos*, you enter the blissful world of *chessed b'dibbur* and of עוֹלָם חֶסֶד יִבָּנֶה. You will experience the sublime feeling of תַּאֲוַת אָדָם חַסְדּוֹ, the simple pleasure of making someone else happy. And you won't be able to stop building worlds with words.

# NOTHING BETTER, NOTHING WORSE
## The Perils of Ona'as Devarim

Many years ago, Rav Pam approached a small group of people, including myself, and asked us to do him a favor. (This was out of character for Rav Pam, who never asked for anything.) Every year, the Chafetz Chaim Heritage Foundation produces a video presentation, which is shown in communities around the globe on Tishah B'Av. This video features speeches from *roshei yeshivah* and *darshanim* who speak on themes of the day. Typically, the speeches are videoed well before Tishah B'Av, and the speakers deliver their remarks to an empty *beis midrash*. But Rav Pam felt awkward speaking to an empty room. He asked us to help him by coming to the *beis midrash* to form an audience. The speech that I heard that day had a profound impact on my life.

Rav Pam discussed a topic that receives far less attention than it deserves. He spoke about *ona'as devarim*, causing others pain and anguish through insensitive, thoughtless, or angry words.

Rav Pam remarked that we have merited to see a veritable revolution in *shemiras halashon* in our days; there is a heightened awareness about the danger and damage that *lashon hara* causes. But, he lamented, "If only we would channel the same efforts to focus on the equally terrible effects of *ona'as devarim*!"

## ❧ Intolerable

If we look at how the Torah speaks about *ona'as devarim* we will see — perhaps surprisingly — that there is no other *issur* of which Hashem speaks so harshly.

In *Parshas Behar*, the *pasuk* says (*Vayikra* 25:17): וְלֹא תוֹנוּ אִישׁ אֶת עֲמִיתוֹ — *And a man shall not pain his fellow*. Rashi, quoting the Gemara, explains that this is the Torah's prohibition against *ona'as devarim*, hurtful words.

The Torah continues: וְיָרֵאתָ מֵאֱלֹקֶיךָ כִּי אֲנִי ה' אֱלֹקֵיכֶם — *and you shall be fearful of your G-d, for I am Hashem, your G-d.*

The end of the *pasuk* comes as a warning, as if to say, "You had better be careful about this…"

The Torah also writes in *Parshas Mishpatim* (*Shemos* 22:21–23): אַלְמָנָה וְיָתוֹם לֹא תְעַנּוּן — *Do not oppress a widow or an orphan.*

Rashi comments that this does not refer exclusively to a widow or an orphan; it means anyone who is vulnerable to being hurt by words. Do not cause pain to anybody.

The *pasuk* continues:

אִם עַנֵּה תְעַנֶּה אֹתוֹ — *If you will oppress him,*

כִּי אִם צָעֹק יִצְעַק אֵלַי — *if he will but cry out to Me in pain,*

שָׁמֹעַ אֶשְׁמַע צַעֲקָתוֹ — *I will heed his cry.*

Then the Torah says shocking words — words that are almost hard to repeat:

וְחָרָה אַפִּי — *and I will be angry;*

וְהָרַגְתִּי אֶתְכֶם בֶּחָרֶב — *I will kill you by the sword,*

וְהָיוּ נְשֵׁיכֶם אַלְמָנוֹת וּבְנֵיכֶם יְתֹמִים — *and your wives will be widows, and your children orphans.*

Remember, this is Hashem Himself — *Avinu Av Harachamim* — Who is talking so harshly to us. "I will be angry. I will kill you. Your wives will become *almanos*. Your children will be *yesomim*." As if this isn't enough, the Gemara explains that the wife won't be a regular *almanah*, because the husband will disappear and his body won't be discovered. She will be an *agunah* — which is even worse than an *almanah*, for she can never remarry. And the children will be unable to inherit from their father, because they will not have the necessary proof that he is dead.

Do you know of any other prohibition where the Torah speaks in such a severe manner?

Hashem will not tolerate *ona'as devarim*. Hashem never overlooks or ignores words that are used to hurt someone else. Why not? What is so terrible about *ona'as devarim*?

## ᠍᠍᠍ A Slap in the Face

When someone speaks hurtful words to a fellow Jew, he is causing pain to Hashem's own child. The *pasuk* (*Devarim* 14:1) says: בָּנִים אַתֶּם לַה' אֱלֹקֵיכֶם — Every Jew is a child of Hashem.

But there is more to this. The Alshich (*Parshas Behar*) and the Maharal (*Nesiv Ahavas Rei'a*, 2) both explain that every Jew has within him a *chelek Elokai mima'al* — a little part of him that comes from the *Shechinah*. If you hurt a fellow Jew, you are actually hurting Hashem Himself, *kaviyachol*. In fact, the Kli Yakar writes that this is alluded to in the double *lashon* of the *pasuk* in *Parshas Mishpatim* (cited above):

אִם עַנֵּה — *If you hurt a Yid,*

תְעַנֶּה — *you are hurting Me as well.*

I remember once talking to a *bachur* who looked like he was about to explode. I asked him, "What is the matter?"

He answered me, "I can't take it anymore. People treat me like a piece of dirt!"

How terrible! Is he a piece of dirt or a piece of *Shechinah?* The *pasuk* cries out, "Be careful with the way you treat another person, because he is not a piece of dirt; he has in him a piece of the Ribono Shel Olam.

Lest you think that this is an exaggeration, look at the Gemara in *Sanhedrin* (58b):

הַסּוֹטֵר לוֹעוֹ שֶׁל יִשְׂרָאֵל — *If someone slaps another Jew in the face,*

כְּאִילוּ סוֹטֵר לוֹעוֹ שֶׁל שְׁכִינָה — *it is as if he slapped [kaviyachol] the Shechinah.*

The Maharsha explains this in the same manner that we have explained above. Every Jew has within him a piece of *Elokus*, a *chelek Elokai mima'al.* By hurting a fellow Yid, we hurt, *kaviyachol*, Hashem Himself.

## ᠍᠍᠍ *Chodesh Av*

There is a well-known Gemara in *Gittin* (57a):

בּוֹא וּרְאֵה — *Come and see; let us internalize the message,*

כַּמָּה גָּדוֹל כֹּחָהּ שֶׁל בּוּשָׁה — *how terrible is the effect of humiliation,*

שֶׁהֲרֵי סִיַּע הַקָּדוֹשׁ בָּרוּךְ הוּא אֶת בַּר קַמְצָא וְהֶחֱרִיב אֶת בֵּיתוֹ וְשָׂרַף אֶת הֵיכָלוֹ — *for* Hashem helped Bar Kamtza, and destroyed His House and burned His Heichal.

The Gemara (*Gittin* 55b) recounts the well-known story which was the prelude to the *Churban Bayis* — the story of Kamtza and Bar Kamtza. The host of a party humiliated Bar Kamtza, who then began the chain of events that ultimately brought about the destruction of the Beis Hamikdash. The Gemara directly attributes the *Churban* to the humiliation that Bar Kamtza suffered. Hashem would not tolerate such behavior. Only one individual was humiliated, but that was enough to cause the Beis Hamikdash's destruction. כַּמָּה גָדוֹל כֹּחָהּ שֶׁל בּוּשָׁה!

Let us learn the lesson; let us finally tackle this horrible problem of hurtful words. We have been suffering for almost two thousand years because we do not realize the danger of words.

I am haunted by Rav Pam's words: Are we doing enough? Are we focusing enough on *ona'as devarim*?

## ❧ Lethal Weapon

There is another reason *ona'as devarim* is such a terrible *aveirah*. One who is guilty of *ona'as devarim* is taking the most meaningful gift of speech and turning it into a lethal and brutal weapon that inflicts so much pain.

The Midrash (*Parshas Behar*) tells a very interesting story. Rabban Gamliel sent his trusted servant Tevi on a mission: he told him to go out and buy "a good item." Tevi went to the butcher and bought tongue.

The next day, Rabban Gamliel again sent Tevi out to the market — this time with instructions to buy "a bad item." Once again, Tevi returned with a tongue.

Rabban Gamliel asked Tevi, "When I told you to buy a good item, you brought me a tongue, and when I told you to buy a bad item, you bought a tongue again!"

Tevi's response was very profound.

כַּד יְהֵוִי טַב — *When the tongue is good,*

לֵית טָבָה מִינֵיהּ — *there is nothing better than it.*

וְכַד בִּישׁ — *But, when the tongue is abused,* when it is bad and is used for hurtful words,

לֵית בִּישׁ מִינֵיהּ — *there is nothing worse than it.*

The Midrash concludes with the *pasuk* in *Mishlei* (18:21), מָוֶת וְחַיִּים בְּיַד לָשׁוֹן.

When the tongue is used to utter kind words, there is nothing better. Words can be the greatest source of *simchah* and *chessed*. But the tongue can also be used as a brutal force inflicting so much damage in someone else's life. When that happens, לֵית בִּישׁ מִינֵיהּ, then words are מָוֶת.

Haven't we all experienced this firsthand? Your day is going wonderfully, and then someone makes a negative comment, and everything turns sour. Those wrong words, that insensitive statement, cuts so deeply into you that you can appreciate what the *pasuk* (*Mishlei* 12:18) says, יֵשׁ בּוֹטֶה כְּמַדְקְרוֹת חָרֶב — *There are words that cut like the sharpness of a sword.* When used improperly, the tongue is a lethal weapon, as we find in *Tehillim* (57:5) וּלְשׁוֹנָם חֶרֶב חַדָּה — *and their tongue is a sharp sword.*

Words can be uplifting; words can be healing; words can be therapeutic. But instead, *ona'as devarim* uses words to cause anguish and to wreak havoc. Instead of accessing the חַיִּים בְּיַד לָשׁוֹן, one misuses the power and brings about מָוֶת בְּיַד לָשׁוֹן.

Hashem will not tolerate it when people abuse the gift of speech and turn life into death.

## ✎ Sticks and Stones

The *Sefer Chassidim* (54) writes: אֵיזוֹ הִיא רְצִיחָה שֶׁאֵינָהּ נִכֶּרֶת לָעֵינַיִם — *What is murder that it is not visible to the eye?* There is something that is a "silent killer." What is this silent killer? הַמַּבְיִישׁ פְּנֵי חֲבֵירוֹ בָּרַבִּים אוֹ מְצַעֲרוֹ — *one who embarrasses his friend in public or causes him pain.*

The Vilna Gaon (*Mishlei* 18:8) writes something similar: hurling *dibbur hara'ah*, harmful words, at someone is much worse than hitting him. When you hit someone, you injure his hand, foot, or face. But words hurt the *neshamah*. They cut into the person himself; they attack the entire person. In addition, the Gaon says:

שֶׁהַכָּאָה יִתְרַפֵּא — *When someone gets hit, the wound heals,*

אֲבָל דִּיבּוּר לֹא — *but words never heal.*

Words remain within the wounded person's soul and continue to inflict perpetual pain. He goes to sleep thinking, "He said I am lazy," and he wakes up thinking the same.

We grew up with that silly rhyme, "Sticks and stones will break my bones, but names will never harm me." That is so wrong:

* The *pasuk* cries מָוֶת בְּיַד לָשׁוֹן.

* The Midrash teaches לֵית בִּישׁ מִינֵיהּ.

* *Sefer Chassidim* refers to harmful words as a silent killer.

* The Vilna Gaon says that for two reasons words are worse than being physically beaten.

I would say, "Sticks and stones will break my bones, but words will never leave me." A hurtful word remains, and often does tremendous damage.

## ❧ Identity Crisis

Words are especially dangerous when they are used to characterize the person. If you say, "You are selfish," you are defining the person. It is almost as if you are invalidating the person.

I recall an incident that almost turned into a great loss for Klal Yisrael. A very successful *rebbi* once told me that if not for a certain friend he would never have entered the field of *chinuch*. I was shocked. "You are a born *rebbi*! How could it be that you almost missed your life's calling, your mission that you are so obviously suited for?"

This *rebbi* explained to me what happened, and I was stupefied.

One of his *rebbeim* once told him, "You are a *k'shei havanah*; you don't grasp things quickly." I imagine that this comment was made in some sort of context, and perhaps it was even meant constructively, but the young student took these words very much to heart. His *rebbi paskened* that he was a *k'shei havanah*.

All through his *kollel* years, this young man never entertained the thought of entering *chinuch*. He thought, *I can't be a mechanech, I am a k'shei havanah!* But when he started looking for a job, someone approached him and told him about an available job in a yeshivah.

"Why don't you apply?" he asked.

"Oh no, not me! I can't be a *rebbi*…"

"What do you mean you can't? You are a born *mechanech*!"

The young man then confided to this person what his *rebbi* had said to him years before.

*Baruch Hashem*, that concerned person spoke to the young man and uprooted the negative self-image that he had for so many years. The young man went into *chinuch* and has seen great success. But Klal Yisrael almost lost that great talent, all because of one negative comment. One statement can cause so much damage.

Isn't it true לֵית בִּישׁ מִינֵיהּ? Isn't it true מָוֶת בְּיַד לָשׁוֹן? That is the danger of words. Words penetrate to the very essence of the human being, and they do not heal.

## Children

Rav Pam mentioned that he has seen parents who make the grave mistake of labeling their children. He once saw a mother tell her child, "You are a bad boy!" The boy burst out crying and was inconsolable. With his perceptive eye, Rav Pam drew an important lesson from what he saw.

When a parent says something to a child, the child is labeled. The child gets the message, "This is what my father or mother thinks of me." We must be ever so careful with what we say to our child, especially when we are upset or disappointed. Even if we have a right to be disappointed, be careful what you say, because words penetrate very deeply. Words label and characterize and, unfortunately, can destroy a child.

Rav Pam related that he heard of children who went off the *derech* because of harmful words. Words spoken by a parent or by a *mechanech* or by other children turned them away from *Yiddishkeit*. At one of the annual Agudas Yisrael conventions, Rav Pam devoted his address to this problem and he included it in his *sefer Atara Lamelech* (p. 89) discussing how careful we have to be when we speak to children.

Are we doing enough to solve this problem?

# A Widow with a Husband

The damage that can be wrought through words spoken to a spouse is frightening. A *gadol* once told someone who was having a *shalom bayis* issue, "Why are you causing anguish to an *almanah* (widow)?" The person was frightened by this stark pronouncement. "*Rebbi*, she is my wife. And I am still alive!" But the *gadol* told him, "Your wife is an *almanah b'chayei ba'alah* — an *almanah* with a live husband."

The *gadol* went on to explain. "Why is the Torah so careful about protecting the feelings of an *almanah*? The *Chinuch* (mitzvah 65) writes that when a married woman is hurt, she can always turn to her husband for comfort and solace. An *almanah*, on the other hand, has no one to turn to. She has no husband; thus, she is terribly vulnerable, and the Torah demands that we must be extra careful not to hurt her.

"If someone hurts his *own* wife — if the husband who is supposed to be the source of her comfort and protection is the source of her misery and anguish — isn't she as vulnerable as an *almanah*? So why are you hurting an *almanah*?"

A husband is supposed to be the source of good words and good feelings. If he uses words in the opposite way, his words cut so deeply and leave a pain that does not go away.

The Gemara (*Bava Metzia* 59a) says: לְעוֹלָם יְהֵא אָדָם זָהִיר בְּאוֹנָאַת אִשְׁתּוֹ — *A man should be ever wary of his wife's pain.* Rashi explains that the pain the Gemara is referring to is *ona'as devarim*. Be careful with what you say to your wife; be ever wary that you do not pain her with your words.

I was once helping a couple who was having difficulties in their *shalom bayis*. The husband had said something very insensitive to his wife, and I was trying to explain to her that he didn't mean it. She looked at me and asked, "But how could he *say* such a thing?"

I then felt the truth of an expression I once heard, "Before you say something, you control the words, but after you say it, the words control you."

Under the *chuppah*, a new husband hands his wife a *kesubah* in which he commits himself, אֲנָא אוֹקִיר — *I will cherish you*; I will treat you with great respect. He is obligated to honor her with his words, and certainly not to cause her pain and anguish. Rav Pam once told me, "When the fire of marital strife is burning in a home, it is all too often because of a wrong word."

## ᏝᎣ Widening the Front Lines

Am I not justified in saying that on a day-to-day basis the most common source of aggravation and anguish for many people are insensitive words? Whether at home, in shul, at work, with a relative or neighbor, between parent and child, isn't it true that לֵית בִּישׁ מִינֵיהּ. Are we doing enough about *ona'as devarim*? We can and we must put more effort into awareness and prevention of this verbal scourge.

We have seen tremendous success in the battle against *lashon hara*. We have seen thousands, or probably tens of thousands, of men, women, and children who have been victorious over the archenemy that is called *lashon hara*. (To a great extent, this revolution can be credited to the tireless work of the Chafetz Chaim Heritage Foundation.) We must not lessen our efforts in the battle against *lashon hara*, but we must widen the front lines to battle *ona'as devarim* as well. We can use those same strategies and techniques that have proven successful.

Here's the good news. In a certain sense, the battle against *ona'as devarim* is easier than the battle against *lashon hara*. *Lashon hara* has many complicated *halachos* — what to say, what not to say. *Sefer Chafetz Chaim* is a detailed halachic guide of what one is permitted to say.

But the *halachos* of *ona'as devarim* are very simple, and straightforward: דְּעֲלָךְ סָנֵי לַחֲבָרָךְ לָא תַעֲבֵיד — *[Words] that you would not like, don't [say] to others.* Sometimes you make a snide remark with the excuse, "I am only kidding, can't he take a joke?" Would *you* like to be the victim of that joke? When it comes to *ona'as devarim* the rules of what to say and what not to say are very simple: וְאָהַבְתָּ לְרֵעֲךָ כָּמוֹךָ, what you don't like, don't do to others.

## ᏝᎣ Think Before You Speak

The first step in the battle against *ona'as devarim* is very simple. We have to train ourselves to think before we talk. We have to follow the wise advice of Shlomo Hamelech (*Mishlei* 15:28):

לֵב צַדִּיק יֶהְגֶּה לַעֲנוֹת — *The heart of a righteous person contemplates what to say.* Rashi explains that he thinks before he talks. He doesn't just talk impulsively.

Before you talk, think, "Did I come down to this world to make someone else suffer from my words? Did I marry this woman to make her life miserable? Was I *zocheh* to have a child to inflict wounds with words?"

This tactic has proven very effective in the battle against *lashon hara*; many of us have successfully trained ourselves to think before we say something that might be *lashon hara*. Now let us also train ourselves to think before saying words that may be hurtful.

I was once advising a man whom I felt was verbally abusing his wife. "You have to start thinking before you talk," I told him.

He blurted out, "But it's not my nature to think!"

"Let me ask you a question," I said. "Did you ever go to a kiddush in shul?"

"Yes, of course."

"I have never seen you at a kiddush, but I assume that you are like most people. At a kiddush, there are always trays of assorted cut cakes. As a person reaches to take a piece of cake, he hesitates for a brief moment. He is thinking. 'Which piece of cake should I eat? The seven-layer cake? The sponge cake? A brownie?'

"Now the decision which cake to eat is not a particularly important one. Yet a person stops for a moment and thinks! He makes a decision and chooses between the cakes.

"So why don't you stop for a moment and *think* before choosing between *chaim* and *maves*? You think before choosing cakes but don't think before saying something that is either לֵית טָבָה מִינֵיהּ or לֵית בִּישׁ מִינֵיהּ!"

There is another point worth considering. Hashem blessed us with many senses: our eyes see, our ears hear, our nose smells. These senses work automatically. If there is something in front of us that we may not look at, we must avert our eyes, and if there is something that we are not supposed to hear, we have to close our ears, because we see and hear involuntarily. The same is true regarding the sense of smell. But the *chush hadibbur* is not automatic. No one speaks involuntarily; a person has to *decide to talk*. If we can train our eyes to avert seeing forbidden sights, and "close" our ears from hearing forbidden speech, then we can surely train our tongues to refrain from speaking painful words.

## ⊛ We Can Do It

Rav Itzele Peterburger once said that he always thought before he spoke. He added that he would usually hear his *yetzer hatov* telling him, "Don't say that; Hashem is listening."

I believe in people. People want to be good, but they fail to realize the obvious. That is why I often speak about *tikun hamiddos*. When guided, people are very responsive. If we realize the impact of words, we would think before we talk.

We can do it. We have been victorious with the enemy of *lashon hara*. Now we have to focus and channel our strength against *ona'as devarim*.

At the funeral of his *rebbetzin* of fifty-four years, Rav Shlomo Zalman Auerbach made an astonishing statement. He said that typically at the *levayah* a husband asks his wife for *mechilah*. But, he said, "I do not have to ask for my *rebbetzin's* forgiveness, because I never hurt her. We always lived happily and *b'shalom*."

What an amazing declaration. Imagine living together for fifty-four years and never hurting your spouse's feelings! How can you do it? I can tell you how to start. Start by training yourself to hesitate for a moment, and think before you speak.

This will also help: Before speaking in a challenging situation, remember this Midrash, which is cited by the Vilna Gaon in his *Iggeres HaGR"a*:

כָּל רֶגַע וְרֶגַע שֶׁאָדָם חוֹסֵם פִּיו — *Every moment that a person is quiet and doesn't say what he is tempted to say,*

זוֹכֶה לָאוֹר הַגָּנוּז — *he merits the hidden light,*

שֶׁאֵין כָּל מַלְאָךְ וּבְרִיָּה יְכוֹלִים לְשַׁעֵר — *that even a malach can't fathom.*

It is obvious that the Midrash is not only referring to someone who refrains from talking *lashon hara*. It is also referring to someone who does not say words that might be *ona'as devarim*. When a person thinks before he speaks and refrains from saying the nasty comment that has occurred to him, he is rewarded by Hashem with the *ohr haganuz*. He has earned an ethereal and unfathomable delight. Why is there such a great reward for this person? He did not really do anything; he just held back negative words. What he did was merely a passive inaction.

Evidently that "inaction" is infinitely precious to Hashem. You are being careful with Hashem's child. You are being careful with a piece of Hashem. You treat him with respect, not like a piece of dirt. And the reward that you deserve is equally infinite.

Let us take up Rav Pam's call to action, to give proper focus to *ona'as devarim*. Let us replace the most painful feelings of לֵית בִּישׁ מִינֵיהּ with the uplifting feelings of לֵית טָבָא מִינֵיהּ. Let us train ourselves to think before we speak, and to reserve our most precious gift of words for use in a positive way — to do *chessed b'dibbur*, to mend broken hearts, and to lift broken spirits.

# THE *VAYAR* PERSON
## *Empathizing with Others*

Look out the window; look down the street. What do you see?

We see hundreds of people every day, but we do we really see them? Do we acknowledge them? Do we appreciate them, or make them feel appreciated?

Rare is that special person who is thoughtful and considerate and does indeed see everybody. But shouldn't we all strive to become that outstanding person? And how can we become that person?

The way that one becomes that wonderful person is by first becoming a *"vayar* person," with a *vayar* outlook — the root of all personal greatness. A *vayar* person really sees the people that he encounters.

Let me tell you about a *vayar* person.

## ᎧᏫ᠍ The First *Vayar* Person

In *Parshas Vayeira*, the Torah introduces us to the *amud hachessed*, the pillar of *chessed* of Klal Yisrael — Avraham Avinu. What was his greatness? I think it is encapsulated in one word: *"vayar."*

Avraham was sitting outside his tent on the third day after his *bris milah*. It was terribly hot and he was in a lot of pain, making it is very difficult for him to sit there. Nevertheless, the *pasuk* (*Bereishis* 18:2) tells us:

וַיִּשָּׂא עֵינָיו **וַיַּרְא** וְהִנֵּה שְׁלֹשָׁה אֲנָשִׁים נִצָּבִים עָלָיו... — *And he raised his eyes **and he saw**, and behold, there were three men standing before him…*

And then the Torah seems to repeat itself:

**וַיַּרְא** וַיָּרָץ לִקְרָאתָם — **and he saw**, and he ran toward them.

Rashi points out the obvious redundancy — the *pasuk* says *vayar* twice; why does the Torah repeat itself? Rashi answers:

הָרִאשׁוֹן, כְּמַשְׁמָעוֹ; וְהַשֵּׁנִי, לְשׁוֹן הֲבָנָה — *The first* [mention of וַיַּרְא] *is meant in the simple sense; the second is a "lashon havanah" — it connotes understanding.*

This *lashon havanah*, this sense of understanding, is the secret of the *vayar* person, and it is the key to greatness. What is it?

We are blessed with the gift of eyesight. When we encounter someone, our eyes take in the image of that person; we see his physical being. This is the first "*vayar*," seeing in the simple sense. Then there is a person who has a "*vayar*" attitude, who takes a deeper look with the second *vayar* — *lashon havanah*. The *vayar* person looks at the individual before him and contemplates; he seeks to understand: What can I do for this person? What does he need? How can I help him?

## Mission Statement

The mission statement of a *vayar* person is described in a beautiful quote from Rav Chaim Volozhiner, quoted by his son in the forward to *Nefesh Hachaim*: "My father would often rebuke me when he saw that I was not affected by other people's suffering, and he would constantly tell me: הָאָדָם לֹא לְעַצְמוֹ נִבְרָא רַק לְהוֹעִיל לַאֲחֵרִינִי בְּכָל אֲשֶׁר יִמְצָא בְּכֹחוֹ לַעֲשׂוֹת — *Man was not created to care for his own needs; rather, he was created to help others in any way that he is capable of.*"

We are on this world for others.

## Rather Be a Worm?

I once met a wonderful *talmid chacham*, an older man, who travels every day within the city from one neighborhood to another. He goes to the bus stop to wait for a bus, but hopes for a ride. The bus stop is located in a well-traveled area; many people drive by and could easily stop to offer him a ride, but very often they do not stop. People drive right past him, leaving him standing in the bitter cold or in the sweltering heat.

"Why do people drive by and let an old man stand there?" he asked me. "Why don't they offer me a ride?"

I told him what he had already realized: "The people don't see you. They see you, but they don't see your *needs*. They don't put two and two together; they don't think to themselves, 'I am traveling in his direction, and I have an empty seat. Why not stop and offer him a ride? He doesn't look threatening.' They see you, but aren't thinking about you."

And then he rephrased his question, and it made such an impact on me. "Today we live in a generation where there is a great awareness about the problem of insects in vegetables. How is it that people can see and notice these miniscule worms, yet they don't see *me*?"

And then he said in jest, "When I stand at the bus stop hoping that someone will stop for me, I think of the *pasuk* in *Tehillim* (22:7) וְאָנֹכִי תוֹלַעַת וְלֹא אִישׁ — *I am a worm, and not a man.* I wish I would be a worm because then I would be seen."

A witty comment, but a very sad observation. Why do we see tiny insects but not people? A *vayar* person *does* see people. He is focused on seeing people and their needs. He feels the privilege, the thrill, of helping another Jew, because that's his mission in life.

Giving someone a ride is a wonderful opportunity to perform *hachnasas orchim*. When a *vayar* person goes to a *simchah*, and he knows of someone who needs a ride there, he does not wait to be asked — he offers. That is a *vayar* person; he sees people, and he sees their needs. He not only helps with the ride, but he also seeks to save that person the trouble and the discomfort of having to find the ride and ask for the ride himself.

When a *vayar* person sees a guest in shul, he does not just think, *Oh, an out of towner…* Rather, he sees someone who is out of his familiar surroundings, in a new place, who may feel awkward, a bit uncomfortable. The *vayar* person thinks about this visitor; he thinks into the situation, *If I acknowledge him with a warm shalom aleichem, if I befriend him, I am going to alleviate that uneasy feeling that he's experiencing.* A *vayar* person not only sees human beings, but he sees their needs, and he thinks, *What can I do now to make this person more comfortable?*

## ⬥ "You Don't Look Good Today"

Let us meet about another *vayar* person, who lived a few generations after Avraham Avinu.

Toward the end of *Parshas Vayeishev*, we find Yosef Hatzaddik languishing in prison, with no hope in sight. He is, as the *Sar Hamashkim* describes him (*Bereishis* 41:12): נַעַר עִבְרִי עֶבֶד — *a young boy, an Ivri* (all alone on foreign soil), *a slave.* In short, his situation is very bleak.

And then one day, a day of tremendous destiny, he enters the room where his fellow prisoners are, and the *pasuk* (*Bereishis* 40:6) says: וַיָּבֹא אֲלֵיהֶם יוֹסֵף בַּבֹּקֶר וַיַּרְא אֹתָם וְהִנָּם זֹעֲפִים — *And Yosef came to them in the morning, and he saw that they were depressed.*

What would the average person do? The average person might not even notice the look on their faces. He is dealing with his own bitter situation.

But Yosef was not the average person. He was a *vayar* person. He took an interest and asked them that magical question (v. 7), מַדּוּעַ פְּנֵיכֶם רָעִים הַיּוֹם — *Why does your face look sad today?* "Hey, fellows, you don't look good..."

And that began a chain of events that changed history. The prisoners tell him about their dreams, and Yosef interprets them. Then, Pharaoh has the dreams, and Yosef — now known as one who can interpret dreams — is summoned to interpret Pharaoh's dreams. Amazing. Yosef's life changed so dramatically — from the נַעַר עִבְרִי עֶבֶד languishing in prison, he is catapulted to greatness to become the viceroy of Mitzrayim.

Do you know what changed all this? One word: *vayar* — he cared enough to notice and he acted upon what he saw. He did not just shrug his shoulders and brush it aside. He did not think to himself, *What can I do? I have my own problems!* Instead he said those therapeutic words: "You don't look good. What's the matter? Maybe I can help you." He conveyed the feeling that "your problem is my problem."

Yosef was a *vayar* person; he did not just see two prison inmates — he saw their pain and worries, and he took it to heart.

The *pasuk* in *Tehillim* (89:3) says: עוֹלָם חֶסֶד יִבָּנֶה. This means that with *chessed* you can build someone else's world. Through *chessed* we can help alleviate other people's pain and we can build them. Yes. We can build worlds with words. But there is also a different meaning to the *pasuk*. By doing *chessed*, you build your *own* world. Whatever you invest into *chessed* is repaid and you reap the benefits. After all, "*der Ribono Shel Olam bleibt nisht shuldikt* — Hashem repays His debts." When you help others, you are helping yourself.

Yosef was a perfect example of this. He cared enough to think of others; he sought to alleviate the suffering of his fellow prisoners, and that was the very source of his own salvation. Because he was a *vayar* person, who acted upon what he saw, he was saved, and he attained unimaginable greatness.

Imagine hearing the tragic story of a fellow Jew who is sitting in jail through no fault of his own, the sad victim of a libel. Which Yid would not get involved in the mitzvah of *pidyon shevuyim* to free him from his suffering?

So I ask you, what about a person who is imprisoned by a problem which overtakes and overwhelms him? Isn't he also a helpless captive? Is that not what Dovid Hamelech asks of Hashem (*Tehillim* 142:8): הוֹצִיאָה מִמַּסְגֵּר נַפְשִׁי — *Release my soul from imprisonment.*

Sometimes a person is a prisoner of his problem, and to help him is a form of *pidyon shevuyim*. When the *vayar* person sees another person who appears to be worried, who seems to be having a difficult time, he sees an opportunity for *pidyon shevuyim* through a few pleasant words or a nice gesture. When he sees a person who looks unhappy, he will say something to bring a smile to his face. When he sees a person who does not have a job, he cares about it, and he gets involved. When he knows a person isn't well, he will remember to call him every so often. Even if he cannot do anything in a practical sense, he will at least convey the message, "I care about you. I am thinking of you. You are not alone." If a person is undergoing difficulties, words can help lift his spirits.

The *vayar* person lives in the world of לֹא לְעַצְמוֹ נִבְרָא, not in this world for his own needs. He is not living in the pathetic world of "Me, Me, and Me…"

Yosef Hatzaddik saw people who did not look good, and it bothered him enough to inquire about it. Yosef gave us a shining example to follow; this is something that we can implement on a daily basis. Often, we see people who do not look good — who look discouraged or dejected. If we are the *vayar* person, we will go over to them and say something, which will hopefully cheer them up.

If you come home, and your spouse does not look good, it is important to say something. "You don't look good. What's wrong?" Sometimes, it is not advisable to say, "You don't look good…," but you can't just ignore the problem. Use wisdom to lift up the other person's spirit.

## ❧ Chessed B'dibbur

It is important to stress that helping someone in need does not necessarily require significant time or effort. Often, much can be accomplished by just talking to someone. Go over and compliment him. Say something nice. Relate how you were impressed with something that he did, how nicely his children — or even grandchildren — are doing. A nice greeting can do wonders. You can build worlds with words. *Chessed b'dibbur* is an incredible way to do so much with so little. It is a cost-free, time-free investment, which yields tremendous benefits.

If you enjoyed someone's *simchah*, tell him how beautiful it was. If a person made a *shidduch*, tell him what a wonderful *shidduch* it is.

Think of your child. If you compliment him, he will probably learn better that day and be a finer person. You can paint a better image of what you want him to be, and invariably he will be that. Think of your son's *rebbi* or your daughter's teacher. Praise them for all that they do for your child.

Men have opportunities to compliment the person who gave a *shiur* or the *ba'al tefillah* who *davened* for the *amud*. Women have opportunities to compliment other women at a *simchah* on how well behaved their children are. These are simple gestures that yield tremendous results. The *vayar* person is living in a magnificent world of *chessed b'dibbur*. Used properly, words can be so uplifting, so therapeutic, so healing.

There is a frightening passage in the *Zohar Hakadosh* (*Parshas Tazria* p. 46b): Just as there is a punishment for one who says evil words, there is also a punishment for one who does not say kind words. Why is there a punishment for that? If we *could* say something nice, we *should* and *must* say it.

If I compliment or thank the bank teller, I am exhibiting the trait of a *vayar* person. That teller is not just a machine trained to perform a service — he is a human being. When I thank the mailman, or the store cashier, I create a *kiddush Hashem* by acting in a manner that allows others — even non-Jews — to realize that Jews are considerate people. A Jew is not just religious; a Jew is *observant*. He observes, recognizes, and acknowledges other people.

That is the *vayar* person; he sees a person — that's step one. And then there is the second *vayar* — he thinks, *What can I do to make his day? What can I say to bring him relief or comfort, nachas or simchah?*

## Where's the Smile?

Imagine the following scenario: During *Shacharis* one morning, you notice a stranger *davening* without *tallis* and *tefillin*. He may not be married, but he surely is bar mitzvah. So where are his *tefillin*?

Would you ignore this? I don't think anyone would. You would probably ask him, "Do you need to borrow *tefillin*?"

It certainly would bother you to see a Jew *davening* without *tefillin*.

Now imagine that we notice someone without a smile. Would that bother us as well? Would we be uncomfortable leaving this fellow Jew to his own devices? Why would it bother us to see someone without *tefillin*, but it wouldn't particularly bother us to see someone without a smile?

What is a more painful sight to Hashem — a Yid *davening* without *tefillin*, or a Yid without a smile? I would venture to say that it is more painful for Hashem to see a Yid without a smile.

The Mishnah (*Sanhedrin* 46a) describes the execution of a sinner. The Mishnah then adds: בְּשָׁעָה שֶׁאָדָם מִצְטַעֵר שְׁכִינָה מָה אוֹמֶרֶת — *when a Jew is suffering, what does Hashem say?* "קַלַּנִי מֵרֹאשִׁי, קַלַּנִי מִזְרוֹעִי" — *My head is heavy upon Me! My arm is heavy upon Me."* Hashem is pained, so to speak, because of this person's suffering. He cannot tolerate seeing this happen!

And the Mishnah comments: אִם כֵּן הַמָּקוֹם מִצְטַעֵר עַל דָּמָם שֶׁל רְשָׁעִים שֶׁנִּשְׁפַּךְ, קַל וָחֹמֶר עַל דָּמָם שֶׁל צַדִּיקִים — *If Hashem is so distressed over the blood of the wicked, how much more so is He pained by the suffering of the righteous.* The suffering of the righteous Jew causes Hashem that much more pain.

Look how it bothers Hashem when a Jew is in distress, when a Jew is suffering. We do not find this type of strongly worded statement to describe Hashem's reaction when a Jew cannot, or does not, perform a mitzvah. But look how it bothers Him when a Yid is suffering.

A *vayar* person is patterned in the image of Hashem Himself; if a fellow Jew is not happy, it bothers him terribly. When someone seems worried, it becomes *his* worry and he tries to do something. Invariably, there is always something to be done if you care enough to want to do it. The *vayar* person notices the lack of a smile just as much as he notices the lack of *tefillin*.

## A Wrong Picture

What is wrong with the following picture?

Reuven and Shimon planned to go to a *chasunah* together. However, on the morning of the *chasunah*, Reuven calls Shimon.

"I am sorry, Shimon. My child is really not feeling well, and I can't go tonight. Please make other arrangements."

"Well, thank you, Reuven, for letting me know. I guess I'll have to travel alone. Thanks anyway for your offer."

And Shimon hangs up.

What was wrong with this dialogue?

Shimon is not acting like a *vayar* person. He was polite and grateful, but his only concern was his ride. Reuven just told him that he has a big problem. His child is obviously quite unwell if he cannot get out of the house later that evening. Shimon should show his concern and offer an appropriate response:
"Reuven, I am so sorry to hear that your child isn't well. I hope he has a *refuah sheleimah* quickly. Can I help in any way?"

Even if Shimon cannot offer any help, he should still show concern. People feel comforted when others show they care. That would be the reaction of a *vayar* person. He recognizes other people's needs and tries to help them.

## Elder Care

There is another example that must be highlighted. Today *baruch Hashem* many people are living long lives, which wasn't as common in earlier generations. For many people, this presents a new challenge. Middle-aged people have come to be known as the "sandwich generation" — they are raising their own large families, with children and grandchildren, and their parents are aging and require extra care and attention.

People must earn a living and they have community responsibilities, as well. They must *daven* and learn. They must take care of themselves and their children, and be there for their grandchildren. They don't have a moment to breathe. And now, on top of all that, they must devote time to care for their aging parents as well. How are they supposed to do the impossible? How can they juggle their many responsibilities?

For a *vayar* person the answer is obvious. In fact, for a *vayar* person there is no question.

When he sees his parents, he sees all the time and effort they devoted to him and his needs. He cannot even think, *I don't have time for my parents.* How can anyone dare think these thoughts? Did parents ever "not have time" for their children? In a *vayar* person's life, there is no such thing as not having time for a parent's needs.

Rav Yaakov Galinsky once saw Rav Shach, who was then in his late nineties, running.

"Why is the *rosh yeshivah* running?" he asked.

Rav Shach answered with his typical wisdom: "I don't have *ko'ach* to walk, so I must run!"

If we don't have time to go help our parents, then we must run to help them. Having older parents is not a new challenge that we face; it is a new privilege, it is a new opportunity to fulfill the sacred, beloved mitzvah of *kibbud av v'eim.*

A *vayar* person capitalizes on this and takes advantage of every opportunity — every visit, every errand, every phone call. He notifies them of every milestone — the grandchild's good report card, the birthday, the Chumash *mesibah*, the *siyum*, the graduation, etc. This sends a very important message. We are constantly thinking of you. We are never too busy for you.

If we don't have the time, then we have to run to make the time! To a *vayar* person, it is obvious. "This is my father; this is my mother. How can I *not* have time?"

## ᐧᑫᓬᐤ The Mark of Greatness

There is a third great *vayar* person in Klal Yisrael's history, from whom we never cease to be inspired — Moshe Rabbeinu. לֹא קָם בְּיִשְׂרָאֵל כְּמֹשֶׁה. What was at the root of his greatness? What made Moshe the great Moshe Rabbeinu?

In *Parshas Shemos*, we are introduced to Moshe Rabbeinu. Says the *pasuk* (*Shemos* 2:11): וַיִּגְדַּל מֹשֶׁה וַיֵּצֵא אֶל אֶחָיו **וַיַּרְא** בְּסִבְלֹתָם — *Moshe grew up, and he went out to his brothers **and he saw** their suffering.*

The Midrash in the beginning of *Shemos* (*Shemos Rabbah* 1:27) elaborates:

*And he saw their suffering.* What is the nature of this "*vayar*"? Moshe saw his brothers' suffering and cried. He said, "Woe to me over you! I would give my life to help you…" And Moshe would give his shoulder, and help each one of them… This is as it states (*Shemos* 3:4): "*And Hashem saw that he turned **to see**…*" Hashem saw in Moshe that he turned from his own affairs to **see their suffering**; therefore (ibid.), "*and Hashem called out to him from within the bush…*"

Moshe was brought up by Basya bas Pharaoh; he was living a life of royalty in Pharaoh's palace. But he knew of the plight of his fellow Jews, so he left the comfort of his palace to see the suffering of his brethren. He went to see and internalize their suffering.

Rashi puts it succinctly: נָתַן עֵינָיו וְלִבּוֹ לִהְיוֹת מֵיצֵר עֲלֵיהֶם — *He focused his eyes and his heart to be pained over them.* Moshe's sensitive heart, and his caring eyes, were focused on his brethren. Moshe was the quintessential *vayar* person. His eyes were trained to see the other person's problems. And his caring heart viewed his brothers' problems as his own problems. He went to see their suffering, so that he could feel their pain.

## ᐧᑫᓬᐤ Our *Gedolim*

There is a well-known story:

A few days before Pesach, a man asked the Beis Halevi the following question:

"Rebbi, can I be *yotzei* the mitzvah of the four *kosos* with milk?"

The Beis Halevi listened to the question, thought for a moment and said, "You should use wine. Here, take this…," handing the man a sizable sum of money, "and have a *kahsher uhn freilichin Pesach*."

When the grateful man left, a student who was present asked, "This man needed wine. But the *rav* gave him significantly more money than a bottle of wine would cost. Why?"

Answered the Beis Halevi, "If he was planning on drinking milk for the four *kosos*, including the third and fourth *kosos* which we drink after *shulchan orech*, he obviously has no meat for the *seudah*. He not only lacks wine, he also has nothing for his Yom Tov meal."

If someone asked us that question, we would research the subject in rabbinic literature, because we see *she'eilos*. But the Beis Halevi saw people. He saw the person before him; he could hear the grumbling of his stomach. He realized that he had nothing to eat. That is a *vayar* person — someone who sees people's needs.

Anybody who learned in Ponevezh or lived in Bnei Brak knew about Rav Shach and his *Dinstig*. *Dinstig* is Yiddish for Tuesday. On Tuesdays Rav Shach would deliver his famous *shiur klali*, on which he worked very hard to prepare. He would become so involved in preparing the *shiur* that there was an unspoken rule in Bnei Brak that Rav Shach was not to be disturbed on Tuesday. Not that Rav Shach was inaccessible; he was never inaccessible. But people understood not to approach Rav Shach on Tuesday because he was busy preparing.

One Tuesday a *bachur* from Yerushalayim who was unaware of the unwritten *Dinstig Rule* traveled to Bnei Brak and rang Rav Shach's bell. Rav Shach came to the door.

"I am sorry to bother the Rosh Yeshivah," the boy began, "but I have a problem and haven't been able to eat or sleep properly for three days. May I please speak with the Rosh Yeshivah?"

Now don't forget, this is *Dinstig*, when no one bothered Rav Shach.

Rav Shach ushered the boy into the house. "Come in, come in. Excuse me for a moment." And Rav Shach left the room.

Let's pause to wonder for a moment. Why did Rav Shach run out on this *bachur*? Was Rav Shach too busy to talk to him? *Chas v'shalom!* Listen to the rest of the story:

Rav Shach came back a few minutes later with a plate of food.

"You said that you haven't eaten properly for days, so I had to make you breakfast. First sit down and eat, and then we'll talk about your problem."

And Rav Shach served the *bachur* a meal.

That's a *vayar* person. Rav Shach's world did not end with his *shiur klali*. He not only helped people solve problems, but he also **saw** that there was someone who did not eat and rushed to feed him.

## ☙ We Can Do It!

One would think that the level of a *vayar* person might be beyond the reach of the average person. But *Chazal* believed in our potential and expected each and every one of us to think and act like a *vayar* person.

The Gemara (*Shabbos* 67a) examines the prohibition of engaging in superstitious activities. The Gemara discusses a custom that was prevalent in those times. If someone had a tree which was not producing fruit, he would wrap a red ribbon around the tree. The Gemara questions why such an act is permissible.

The Gemara explains that this is not a senseless act; rather, it has a practical benefit: it alerts anyone who passes by that the tree is not producing fruit and the passerby will *daven* that the tree should recover.

I find this to be amazing. In the times of the Gemara, people who saw a ribbon wrapped around someone else's tree would *daven* for it. People were expected to notice a problem, feel empathetic toward the tree's owner, and pray for his success. This is the *madreigah* of a *vayar* person. Today we don't expect anyone to *daven* that his neighbor's tulips should bloom nicely. But there are many other situations where we should try to help others:

* When we hear the name of a *choleh*, and we are asked to say Tehillim, does the *choleh's* distress become a real problem for us? Do we just say Tehillim because we have to? Or are we a *vayar* person who sees a person struggling for his life, who sees a stricken family, anxious — or terrified — of what might happen? Do we visualize a woman who fears becoming a widow? Do we picture a child who desperately wants his father to live to lead him to his *chuppah*?

* What if we hear about a person who needs a job? Do we hear the information in an abstract way; do we think vaguely about an overall "*parnassah* crisis?" Or do we feel the pain of a fellow Yid who lost his livelihood, who lost his dignity. How can I help him in a practical way? Does his problem become my problem?

* How do we view the "*shidduch* crisis?" A *vayar* person does not think in terms of numbers and statistics. When he sees a young lady who has not yet found her *bashert*, he thinks about people suffering — the girl herself, anxious parents and grandparents, perhaps a younger sibling who cannot even begin listening to *shidduchim* suggestions.

A *vayar* person does not just see problems, he sees people behind problems, real people and very real suffering. When we put ourselves in the other person's shoes, if we care enough that his problem is our problem, we are so much closer to finding the solution. But without a proper *vayar* outlook, we will view the problem as something unfortunate, but we will not be motivated to help. If we are told of an old person who lives alone, and who needs help, we can just file the information away or we can see the person in pain and feel his loneliness and frustration. If we do so, we will almost certainly find the time to give him a call and show him that he is important in our eyes.

## ◐✎ Put Yourself in His Shoes

I am always inspired (maybe I should say guided) by the mitzvah to lend another Jew money. The *pasuk* (*Shemos* 22:24) says:

אִם כֶּסֶף תַּלְוֶה אֶת עַמִּי אֶת הֶעָנִי עִמָּךְ — *When you lend money to My people, to the poor man with you...*

What does אֶת הֶעָנִי עִמָּךְ — *the poor man with you* mean? Rashi explains: הֱוֵי מִסְתַּכֵּל בְּעַצְמְךָ כְּאִלוּ אַתָּה עָנִי — *look at yourself as if you are the poor one.*

What does this mean? I am not the poor one. I have money.

This I believe is the secret of being a *vayar* person. When someone needs a loan, we can find many good excuses why we cannot lend him the money. But if we look at him and say, "If I would be an *ani* and I would need this loan, wouldn't I want him to help me?" If I put myself in his shoes, I will find the ability to extend the loan. That is the *vayar* person's attitude in life. He sees the other person, realizes his need, and asks himself, "How would I want people to help me if I were the one in need?" The *vayar* person then acts accordingly.

וְאָהַבְתָּ לְרֵעֲךָ כָּמוֹךָ does not mean that if I only have one pair of shoes, I have to give it to the other person. The rule in such cases is *chayecha kodmim*, you go first (as the Ramban [ibid.] points out). So what does it mean? Not to give the other person your shoes, but to put yourself *in his shoes*. If we live this way, we will be overwhelmed with the *simchah* of helping Jews, because we will realize that we can do so much with so little. We can help so many people if we care enough to be focused. The *vayar* person is living in the incredible world of עוֹלָם חֶסֶד יִבָּנֶה, but more important, he lives in the world described by another *pasuk* (*Mishlei* 19:22), תַּאֲוַת אָדָם חַסְדּוֹ — *his pleasure in life is to help others.*

The Chazon Ish writes in one of his letters: עָשִׁיר אֲנִי בְּאַהֲבַת הַזּוּלַת — *I am wealthy with the opportunity to love* [and to help] *other people.* This is the bliss of the *vayar* person.

## Turn the Ringer On

Let me conclude with an incident that occurred many years ago, yet remains vividly in my memory. I learned from this the lesson of the *vayar* person in a very practical way.

Someone once had to reach me to discuss an important matter. He met me one day in shul.

"I have to speak to you," he said. "I called your house, but every time I call the line is busy."

"Well," I said, "I admit, it is often hard to get through on my house phone."

We both had busy schedules and were running off to other commitments.

"How should I reach you?" asked my friend.

"I'll tell you. Call me tonight at exactly nine o'clock. I will stay by the phone and I will make sure that the line will be free. But I ask of you one favor. An unused phone line can't stay 'off limits' in my house for too long. So please call at nine o'clock sharp and we'll be able to talk."

My friend agreed.

That night, at one minute to nine, I took up my position at the desk in the study, with the telephone right in front of me. The line was free, but no call came in — not at 9:00, not at 9:15, and not at 9:30. I was disappointed. My family and I were inconvenienced for nothing. But I assumed that something came up for my friend, and he simply was unable to call.

The next morning I met him in shul. Before I had a chance to say anything, he asked me, "What happened to you last night?"

"What happened to *me*? What happened to *you*? I was waiting at the phone until 9:30!"

"What do you mean? I kept calling and calling. I was not getting a busy signal, but no one picked up the phone."

"It can't be!" I replied. "I was waiting right by the phone."

"I'm telling you, I must have called ten times in a row. And I even checked and rechecked to make sure that I was dialing the right number."

I went home determined to solve the mystery. I went straight to the study and examined the phone. Sure enough, the ringer was turned off. Obviously, earlier in the evening, someone wanted quiet and turned the ringer off, and forgot to turn it back on.

A person can be desperate; he can call and call again, countless times. But if the ringer is off, the call will never be heard. A *vayar* person has his ringer on. He hears the other person's call. And sometimes he hears a silent call, a silent cry, an uncalled call, because he is sensitive to the other person's needs.

Avraham Avinu, Yosef Hatzaddik, Moshe Rabbeinu — they were *vayar* people, and that was the source of their greatness. They cared enough to see the needs of others. And they cared enough to think of solutions to their problems. Someone needs a job, someone needs a *shidduch*, an older parent, a lonely person, a person who doesn't have a smile on his face — these are just a few examples of the countless people whom we meet on a daily basis. We may meet our child's *rebbi* or a *ba'al simchah*. Will we truly see them, or simply nod and pass them by?

Turn your ringer on…and enter the world of עָשִׂיר אֲנִי בְּאַהֲבַת הַזּוּלַת and enjoy!

# FRUMKEIT AND CHUMROS...
# GALUS TO GEULAH
## Finding the Delicate Balance

Pesach — a time of frenzied preparations, of an intense search for any vestige of *chametz*...a time of *chumros*.

The *Meshech Chachmah* (*Parshas Bo*) explains why our passion for *chumros* comes to the fore specifically at this time of the year: It is because the event that we are commemorating — the *geulah* from Mitzrayim — was a direct result of our willingness to go beyond the letter of the law.

At that time, Klal Yisrael was wallowing in the forty-ninth level of impurity, sinking quickly into a quagmire from which there could be no escape. What saved them "שֶׁלֹּא שִׁינוּ אֶת שְׁמָם, שֶׁלֹּא שִׁינוּ אֶת לְשׁוֹנָם וְשֶׁלֹּא שִׁינוּ מַלְבּוּשָׁם — *they didn't change their names, their language, and their clothing.*" Hashem saw their adherence to the barriers they erected to safeguard the *mesorah*, and this steadfastness — *chumros*, not halachah — was the catalyst for the redemption.

Perhaps, says the *Meshech Chachmah*, this is what we are celebrating with our frantic pre-Pesach labors: the value of *chumros*, the prelude to the *geulah*.

History proves that this devotion to nuances, these "*frumkeiten*," was not only the secret of the redemption of old, but is also the secret of our flowering as a nation, the reason we have been able to thrive against horrific odds.

Personal *chumros*, then, are an important — even laudable — component of our *avodas Hashem*. But they come with an equally important caveat. *Chumros* are worthy only when they are applied properly. But in so many situations in life, one who seeks to act in a stringent manner can bring about heartache and even *churban*.

## Disproportionate Devotion

Ironically, *chumros* were the cause not only of the *geulah*, but of *galus* as well — both in the days of the First Beis Hamikdash, and the Second Beis Hamikdash.

After the destruction of the First Beis Hamikdash, there was still a remnant of Jews in Eretz Yisrael, under the leadership of Gedalyah ben Achikam. But Gedalyah was brutally murdered, and that was the final blow to the Jews of the time. After his death, many thousands were killed, and the remnant was banished to exile.

Describing the tragedy of the murder of Gedalyah ben Achikam, Yirmiyahu Hanavi says of the Jews, "אֲשֶׁר הִכָּה בְיַד גְּדַלְיָהוּ — *who were killed by Gedalyah*" (*Yirmiyahu* 41:9). Of course Gedalyah, a tzaddik, didn't actually kill *Yidden*, but it is considered as if he did. Why? Because when he was warned that someone was coming to assassinate him, he refused to accept what he considered to be *lashon hara*. He innocently closed his ears to the "slanderous" reports without checking into them as he was halachically permitted to do, and so when they proved correct he was held accountable (*Niddah* 61).

Look at the *churban* wrought by a *chumrah*.

In the times of the Second Beis Hamikdash, a *chumrah* was the catalyst for the actual *Churban haBayis*.

The Gemara (*Gittin* 56a) tells us that the misplaced humility of Rabbi Zechariah ben Avkulas caused the destruction of the Second Beis Hamikdash. When a blemished sheep was sent by the Roman king, the *chachamim* wanted to permit it to be brought as a *korban* in the Beis Hamikdash, for safety's sake. But Rabbi Zechariah protested, feeling that doing so might lead to an error in halachah. So the animal was not sacrificed. This enabled Bar Kamtza to slander the Jews to the king, claiming that they insulted him by rejecting his offering. Thus the humility of Rabbi Zechariah — based on heightened sensitivity to halachah — led to the destruction of the Second Beis Hamikdash.

## ❧ The Balance

Rabbi Moshe Chaim Luzzatto devotes an entire chapter in *Mesillas Yesharim* (ch. 20) to "מִשְׁקַל הַחֲסִידוּת — *The Weighing of Piety*." He tells us that achieving the proper balance in *chassidus* is an "עִנְיַן עִקְרִי מְאֹד מְאֹד — *a very basic fundamental* to *avodas Hashem*." He cites the two examples above, pointing out that both tzaddikim, Gedalyah ben Achikam and Rabbi Zechariah ben Avkulas, were fooled by a *yetzer hara* that clouded one's judgment, and that ultimately turns mitzvos into *aveiros*.

Do we sometimes see this in our times as well?

* The phone rings. Someone wants information about a friend. You are aware of a serious problem, but because of *shemiras halashon* you decide not to mention it; after all, it is negative information... What a *churban*! Don't be what the Gemara calls a *chassid shoteh*, a pious fool. The truly pious thing to do would be to excuse yourself from the call, and tell the person that you will be sure to call him back. Then ask a *rav* about how to proceed in order to responsibly relay the necessary information, while avoiding unjustified *lashon hara*. In this way, you will spare other people so much potential anguish.

* You're running late to Minchah, and you do not want to miss Kaddish, or miss starting the *Shemoneh Esrei* exactly with the *tzibbur*. As you approach the shul you notice that there are no available parking spots. But what's this? You can "*chap*" a spot — but only if you block someone's driveway... Your concern over arriving at the *minyan* in good time is laudable, but surely not at the expense of inconveniencing another person — an inconvenience that can be quite extreme.

The *Yalkut Shimoni* in *Koheles* (§976) says it this way:

אֵין בֵּין גֵּיהִנֹּם לְגַן עֵדֶן אֶלָּא כְּחוּט הַשַּׂעֲרָה — *There is only a hairsbreadth separating Gan Eden from Gehinnom.* Indeed, *frumkeit* and *krumkeit* seem quite similar!

## ❧ Don't Be Too *Frum*!

The *Mesillas Yesharim* gives another example, a third proof to the critical necessity of *mishkal hachassidus*:

The Mishnah (*Brachos* 1:3) records a dispute between Beis Shammai and Beis Hillel regarding the evening recitation of *Krias Shema*. Beis Shammai requires one to actually lie down to recite it, while Beis Hillel maintains that *Krias Shema* can be said in any position — whether sitting or standing.

"*Said Rav Tarfon, 'I was traveling on the road, and I [alighted from my horse in order to] lie down, according to Bais Shammai's ruling and I put myself in danger from bandits.' They said to him, 'You deserve to have been killed, for transgressing the ruling of Beis Hillel!'*"

What is the reason for that harsh condemnation of Rav Tarfon Usually the rule in halachah is *"hamachmir tavo alav brachah"* — on who is stringent deserves a blessing, not a death sentence!

But at that time in history, the disputes between Beis Shammai and Beis Hillel — forming two distinct schools of halachah — threatened to divide Klal Yisrael, until it was established that the halachah follows Bei Hillel. By transgressing the ruling of Beis Hillel which had been given halachic primacy, Rav Tarfon was in effect renewing the controversy His *chumrah* had the potential to lead to *machlokes*, to a schism in Kla Yisrael, and it was therefore detrimental.

It's amazing. *Chumros* can lead to *churban*. Mitzvos can become *aveiros*, and *"frumkeit becomes krumkeit."* It's frightening.

So how can we achieve the balance? Obviously, one's good intention are not sufficient. The challenge is so very great. How do we get on the path to Gan Eden and pay heed to the almost invisible line that separates it from Gehinnom.

## ᧤ The Solution

The solution, I believe, is to follow the advice of Rav Pam, who often said, *"Nemt arois dem mishkal hachassidus* — Take out the scale of *chassidus."* Learning this most important balance is the solution.

Rav Pam gave the *mashal* of baking a cake. When baking, you have the option of estimating the measurements of the ingredients; with experience you may recognize how much an ounce of yeast or a half cup of sugar is — but you can't be absolutely sure. For that you have to use a measuring cup or a scale. That is the function of *mishkal hachassidus* carefully measuring the relative importance of things before doing something that affects others.

\* A *bachur* comes home for *bein hazmanim* and his mother asks for his help. "I have a *chavrusa*," he calls to her, as he runs out...

This *bachur* sincerely wants to do *ratzon Hashem.* But he lacks *mishkal* If only he would follow Rav Pam's advice, and take out the "measuring cup" of *mishkal hachassidus.* He would then weigh and measure the options carefully, and arrive at the correct course of action.

Rav Chaim Kanievsky (*Orchos Rabbeinu* 3:108) relates how the greatest of *masmidim*, the Chazon Ish, who personified complete and total submersion in Torah, would go visit his aged mother every single day, and it wasn't an easy route. Rav Chaim attests that he spent a half hour on each visit! The Chazon Ish was in possession of that *mishkal.* He had a balance.

## Getting Practical

The *Midrash* (*Shemos* 3:16) says that when Hashem instructed Moshe Rabbeinu to redeem Klal Yisrael, Moshe held back. "How can I go?" he asked. "Perhaps my older brother, Aharon, will be hurt because I was chosen rather than him."

Moshe Rabbeinu preferred to delay the *geulah* of Klal Yisrael rather than risk hurting Aharon's feelings. What did Hashem say?

Hashem assured Moshe that Aharon didn't mind, but actually rejoiced over his brother's glory.

What *didn't* Hashem say? Hashem did *not* say that this wasn't Moshe's concern, or that Aharon was just one person and his sensitivities couldn't count in the face of the nation's salvation.

No! The sensitivities of individuals must be taken into account even at historically important moments. Consideration for the feelings of others is a non-negotiable factor in aiming to do *ratzon Hashem*. The problem is that we tend to minimize the importance of *bein adam l'chaveiro* — Moshe Rabbeinu taught us that we must glorify *bein adam l'chaveiro*!

This, too, is an essential component of *mishkal hachassidus.*

* Avraham Avinu perceived that the *ratzon Hashem* was for him to postpone the exalted conversation with the *Shechinah* and busy himself with the needs of his "guests" (*Shabbos* 127a).

* Arriving home on a *leil Shabbos*, the Chafetz Chaim made Kiddush before singing *Shalom Aleichem*. He explained that "*di malachim kennen varten* — the angels can wait," but the guest he brought home hadn't eaten all day.

* If it rains on the first night of Sukkos, the Chafetz Chaim rules (*Sha'ar Hatziyun* 639:67) that since the mitzvah to eat in the sukkah is

*d'Oraisa*, we should postpone the meal until *chatzos* if necessary. But if there is a guest who is a poor person, one should only wait a short while. Evidently, the *dveikus* attained by the performance of this precious mitzvah is suspended due to a greater mandate: to concern oneself with the poor person's rumbling stomach.

* Many of us know the story of Rav Yisrael Salanter's *talmidim* who approached their Rebbe to ask him to instruct them in the *chumros* that they should employ when baking matzos for the mitzvah of the Seder. Rav Yisrael's reply? "Be very stringent not to speak sharply or critically of the poor women (who were often *almanos*) who work in the bakery, rolling out the matzos..."

* I once asked Rav Pam if an individual *davening* should quicken his pace to finish the *Shemoneh Esrei* if he feels the person in front of him wants to take his three steps back already and is growing annoyed by having to wait for him. "I think he should," said Rav Pam. "*Mitt der Ribono Shel Olam kehn mehn zich adurchmachen, mit nuch a Yid veiss ich nisht* — with Hashem you can work it out. With another Jew, I'm not so sure."

I believe that this is the gauge that we should use in our own *mishkal hachassidus*.

### ᎶᏅᎧ True *Frumkeit*

Of course, a crucial part of *mishkal hachassidus* is mastery of halachah, for an *am ha'aretz* cannot be a *chassid*. One has to be clear as to what the halachah is before he can forgo a *chumrah*.

Our *gedolim* know where the hairsbreadth lies.

* Someone proudly told Rav Yaakov Kamenetsky that although his workplace was open on Purim, he would be calling in sick in order to observe *mitzvos hayom*. "The mitzvah of *seudas Purim* is *d'Rabbanan*," responded Rav Yaakov in his inimitable pleasant way, "whereas not to speak *sheker* is a *d'Oraisa*."

* When the Belzer Rebbe was sitting with his mother on Pesach she put some matzah into her soup. She passed the plate to her son, the Rebbe, who took a spoonful of the soup though it meant eating

gebrokts." *Kibbud eim* is a *mitzvah d'Oraisa*, while *gebrokts*, though a *heilige minhag*, is still just that — a *minhag*," said the Rebbe.

* Rav Yaakov Kamenetsky finished saying a *shiur*, and the shul immediately started Maariv. Many people rushed outside to wash their hands for *tefillah*, and a long line formed at the sink. Rav Yaakov walked to head of the line and took away the washing cup. Washing the hands before *davening* is a halachah. Using a cup for that is a *chumrah*. Nowhere does it say that others have to miss Maariv because of your stringency.

* The *minhag* in Skver is not to sing the *piyut Kah Keli* on a Yizkor day. One Yom Tov, the *chazzan* was unaware of this *minhag* and started a rousing rendition of the *piyut*. The chassidim knew the Rebbe's zealous protection for every *minhag Skver*, but the Rebbe raised no protest at all. Asked about it later, the Rebbe explained, "*Minhag Skver* is not to embarrass another Jew."

* The Manchester Rosh Yeshivah, Rav Yehudah Segal, said that although he felt the optimal place to perform the ritual of *negel vasser* is at the bedside, all the years that his wife was alive he did it outside the room. "To do it the way that I wanted to would have meant disturbing her sleep, and that would have been wrong."

* One year, as Rav Shlomo Zalman Auerbach prepared to recite *Birkas Ha'ilanos*, someone pointed out that there was only one tree in the garden, and it is a *hiddur mitzvah* to make the *brachah* in front of two trees. Rav Shlomo Zalman explained that there was a *hiddur mitzvah* to make the *brachah* there as well. "Look at that window and notice the smile on the face of the *almanah* who owns this house. It brings her joy that we chose her tree for our *brachah*! That is a bigger *hiddur*."

* A Jew entered the great Gerrer Beis Medrash and asked if someone could lend him a *gartel* for Minchah. Someone did — the Rebbe himself, the legendary Imrei Emes. The Rebbe *davened* without a *gartel*, later explaining, "A *gartel* has two functions: to enhance the sanctity of the *mispallel*, and to do *chessed* with another Yid."

*Mishkal hachassidus* dictates that we look beyond the black and white, beyond the clear delineations of halachah, to see if perhaps we have obligations that are implied, even though they are not spelled out.

## ✥ Fighting for Our *Minhag*

Often we grow agitated over a breach in halachah or *minhag*, and we feel that it's our duty to protest. The *Magen Avraham* (53:26) says: אֵין לְהִתְקוֹטֵט עֲבוּר שׁוּם מִצְוָה — *one should not fight for any mitzvah*. The *Mishnah Berurah* gives a similar ruling. The *Shulchan Aruch* rules that a *tzibbur* should take care to appoint a pious and learned person to lead the *tefillos* on the Yamim Nora'im (*siman 581*). The *Mishnah Berurah* writes (§11) that even though it is a great merit to be the *ba'al tefillah*, if a candidate sees that a fight will ensue if he takes the position, he should withdraw — even if it means that the *ba'al tefillah* will be less suitable than he is.

* At a *nichum aveilim*, Rav Michel Yehudah Lefkovitz was asked by the mourners for a *kabbalah* as a *zechus* for their father's *neshamah*. The *gadol* replied that perhaps they should commit never to argue over the *amud* during the year that they were "*chiyuvim*."

* Rav Yaakov Kamenetsky was once asked by a *talmid*, "How should I walk down with my child to the *chuppah*? Should the *chassan* and *kallah* be escorted by their parents? Or should both fathers escort the *chassan*, and both mothers escort the *kallah*? Rav Yaakov replied that his *talmid* should do what the *mechutanim* wanted to do. The *talmid* persisted. "But what did the Rosh Yeshivah [referring to Rav Yaakov] do? Rav Yaakov smiled. "For three of my children I did it one way, and for three I did it the other way..."

* A *talmid* once approached Rav Pam with a dilemma. He was making a *bris*, and each of his two grandmothers insisted the child be named after her deceased husband. What should he do? Rav Pam felt that one of the grandmothers had a stronger "claim," and then called the other grandmother and explained that the greatest *zechus* that she could do for her husband would be to be *mevater*, to withdraw, in the interest of *shalom*. A short while later, Rav Pam was visited by that *talmid* who reported the "problem" they encountered when the other grandmother learned of what Rav Pam had said. She too wanted to "give in" to earn such merit!

How many friendships have been broken, *kehillos* destroyed, *chassanim* and *kallos* escorted to the *chuppah* with their *simchah* marred by *machlokes* over *minhag*? How many births have ushered in long and bitter arguments revolving around names and *kibbudim* at the *bris*? The controversy and antagonism is always *l'shem Shamayim*, expressed with righteous indignation. But no argument is worth the price of compromising *shalom*, especially within a family. It is a beautiful thing that *Yidden* are ready to defend their *minhagim*, but not at the expense of *shalom*, as the *Magen Avraham* clearly states. There is no bigger *zechus* than to be *mevater* and to keep the peace.

## Integrity…Even in Performance of Mitzvos

Rav Pam often quoted the *Yerushalmi* (*Sukkah* 3:1), "אוֹי לוֹ לָזֶה שֶׁנַּעֲשָׂה סַנֵּיגוֹרוֹ קַטֵּיגוֹרוֹ — *Woe to him whose source of merit testifies against him.*" As an example, he mentioned a worker who comes late to work or a *rebbi* arriving late to class, because he was *davening* for a long time.

* Rav Segal once came to America for Pesach with several boxes of matzos. The *talmid* accompanying him suggested he pack the boxes in such a way that they would not be obvious to the customs agents, thus avoiding paying tax on them. Rav Segal looked at him in horror, the look of a man whose only gauge is the *mishkal hachassidus*. When Rav Segal did, in fact, end up paying a hefty tax for the boxes, he turned to this *talmid* and exulted, "*Ah, noch a hiddur in di matzos!*"

* Some sixty years ago, shortly before Rosh Hashanah, Rav Pam told his class: "My landlord wants to raise our rent by five dollars a month, but I can't afford it. I have two options. The first is to offer him half of that, two dollars and fifty cents extra a month, and he'll probably accept it, though reluctantly. But I have an idea. Every year, I buy the *arba'ah minim* for Sukkos. This year I can use the shul's *arba'ah minim*, and save thirty dollars toward paying the full raise in the rent. What do you think, *bachurim*? Which is more important — having *arba'ah minim* of my own, or *shalom* and integrity?"

## With Parents

One Shabbos, Rav Shlomo Zalman Auerbach noticed a father and son approaching him. The father was carrying a chair, while the son walked empty-handed. They explained that the son was *machmir* not to use the *eruv*, so he couldn't assist his father.

Rav Shlomo Zalman was terribly upset. He devoted *an entire shmuess* in yeshivah to this, wondering how, for the sake of a *chumrah*, a son could trample on the *mitzvah d'Oraisa* of *kibbud av*.

While *mishkal hachassidus* is essential in our dealings with everyone around us, it is all the more so when dealing with our parents.

The Chida (in *Shiyurei Brachah* [notes to *Shulchan Aruch, Yoreh De'ah*], *siman* 241) records a shocking statement of the *Zohar*: Rachel Imeinu died prematurely, and did not merit to raise her son Binyamin because she caused her father Lavan pain when she stole his idolatrous *terafim*!

I once asked Rav Pam to explain this most unusual statement. How could Rachel be punished for doing what was certainly the right thing?

Rav Pam answered that, of course, Hashem is more meticulous when judging tzaddikim. But there is also a practical message for us: "Rachel's actions did not achieve any real improvement. Lavan just went out and bought more *terafim*, and was only pained and enraged that the original ones were taken. Were her actions really justifiable? Rachel was married to a resident *"posek,"* Yaakov Avinu. But she did not consult with him! Were the repercussions of her actions fully thought out, to the final degree? Since Rachel failed in this regard (on her level), she was punished for the outcome that she caused her father pain."

The lesson we must take out of this is the extraordinary care that we must exercise when we run the risk of causing aggravation to our parents. In such situations, *frumkeit* is so very often *krumkeit*.

## ⌘ Regarding *Shalom Bayis*

*Shalom bayis* professionals attest that much needless friction in Jewish homes is caused by zealous adherence to unnecessary *chumros*. Still more *churban "habayis"*!

* When the Chafetz Chaim was a *bachur*, he went to his Rebbe, Reb Nochum'ke, to be with him as he lit his Chanukah *neiros*. He noticed that Reb Nochum'ke let the optimum *zman* of *hadlakas ner Chanukah* pass as he waited for his wife to return home. "The halachah is that *ner Shabbos* has precedence over *ner Chanukah* for the sake of *shalom bayis*. I reasoned that I had no right to deprive my wife of her pleasure in being

present for the *hadlakah* — and to disturb our *shalom bayis* — for the sake of the *hiddur* of lighting with the ideal *zman*."

* Rav Chaim Vital said: A person may do many good deeds and learn much Torah, but ultimately when he is called before *Beis Din shel Ma'alah*, he will be asked: Were you as careful about the feelings of your wife as you were with others?

* The halachah recommends *davening* Minchah on Erev Shabbos Chanukah before lighting the menorah. "But if your wife needs your help," Rav Pam would tell his *talmidim*, "*daven* Minchah after the lighting of the Chanukah candles!"

* Rav Pam once gave a similar *psak* to his *talmidim* in a pre-Pesach *shiur*. On the night of the Seder, the halachah requires one to eat the *afikoman* before *chatzos*, and of course, after eating the *afikoman*, one may not eat anything else. It is often a difficult deadline to keep, and sometimes one must rush *shulchan orech* (the Yom Tov meal) or skip parts of it entirely. There is a famous device known as the *t'nai* (the stipulation) of the Avnei Neizer which allows one to "conditionally" eat a *kezayis* of matzah in the middle of the meal before *chatzos*, and then to continue the *seudah* and later eat a second *afikoman*. Some *poskim* are against doing so for various reasons. But Rav Pam would instruct his *talmidim* that if the situation arose, they should employ the *t'nai* of the Avnei Neizer. His reasoning? "Your mothers/wives worked hard to prepare a beautiful *seudah* in honor of Yom Tov, and it would pain them if their families could not enjoy it properly."

The *Maharitz Chiyus* quoting the *Ya'aros Devash* gives an amazing explanation of the Gemara in *Brachos*, 27a.

A delegation approached Rabbi Elazar ben Azaryah and asked him to accept the post of Nasi — to lead Klal Yisrael. Rabbi Elazar's immediate response was that he must go and ask his wife!

What does this mean? Rabbi Elazar ben Azaryah was being offered the most coveted and important position in Klal Yisrael. Did he need his wife's advice to make his decision?

The *Maharitz Chiyus* explains: A married man must set aside special times to be with his wife, but the halachah lessens a husband's obligation in this area if he has other obligations. Since the job of Nasi entails a tremendous obligation to the *tzibbur*, the Nasi is less obligated to his wife. Certainly, the offer of the position of Nasi was a phenomenal opportunity and a great merit for Rabbi Elazar ben Azaryah. But before he allowed himself to consider it, he had to make sure that his wife agreed to give up some of the times that she was currently entitled to.

## ✢ Think!

The Gemara in *Mo'ed Katan* (5a) records what I believe is the ideal lesson of *mishkal hachassidus*.

The Gemara expounds the *pasuk* in *Tehillim* (50:23): *One who sets a way, I will show him the salvation of Hashem."* The word "set" is spelled שָׂם (i.e., "set in place"). But the Gemara states, אַל תִּקְרִי וְשָׂם אֶלָּא וְשָׁם דֶּרֶךְ — *Do not read this word as "set," but rather as "one who **evaluates** (from the word שׁוּם or שׁוּמָא) his path."*

The Gemara continues:

*Rabbi Yannai had a certain talmid who would ask him questions [on his shiur] every day. But on the Shabbos preceding the holiday, he would ask no questions.*

The Shabbos preceding a holiday is when the general population would join together to hear public lectures about the upcoming holidays. Rashi explains that on these occasions, when the people would come to hear Rabbi Yannai's lesson, this *talmid* understood that if he would ask a difficult question, and Rabbi Yannai would not be able to answer it, Rabbi Yannai would be embarrassed.

What could be more of a mitzvah than to have a give and take with one's rebbe in Torah? Yesterday the *talmid* was fulfilling the greatest mitzvah with his questions, and tomorrow he will find himself engaged once again in this great mitzvah. But today the general populace is in attendance. Today this "mitzvah" could very well lead to a problem — even to an *aveirah*.

This is the essence of *mishkal hachassidus* — evaluate and assess. **Think**. Is what was good yesterday, and what will be good tomorrow, necessarily good today? Is this really a mitzvah in the current situation?

I once heard a father chastising his son, "*Al tehi tzaddik harbei!* Don't be so *frum!*" I believe that that is a wrong message. The discussion of *mishkal hachassidus* should never be viewed in that light. We have to cherish our *frumkeiten*; *dikduk b'halachah* is something to strive for. We are not permitted to deviate or compromise on even one word of halachah. *Mishkal hachassidus* does not mean taking care not to be "too *frum.*" What it means is to define "*frumkeit*" properly, to be aware of what true *chassidus* entails, and then to act accordingly. It means to look around and anticipate the effects of what we do and how we do it. It means to evaluate, assess, and think our actions through. As *l'shem Shamayim* as they surely are, they still must be carefully weighed with the "measuring cup" of the *mishkal hachassidus*.

Treasure this important tool, carry it with you always, for it can make all the difference. Allow *mishkal hachassidus* to guide you to correctly applied stringencies and properly evaluated adherence to halachah, and once again bring us the *geulah!*

# REACHING IN

## *Developing Our Sense of*
## *Bein Adam L'atzmo*

# שער
# בין אדם לעצמו

לזכר נשמת

**הגאון הצדיק רבי חיים יעקב סאפרין זצוק"ל זי"ע**

**האדמו"ר מקאמארנא יצ"ו**

נתבקש לישיבה של מעלה

ה' סיון ערב חג השבועות תשכ"ט לפ"ק

הונצח ע"י נכדו

# LISTEN TO YOUR MESSAGES
## *Being Receptive to Inspiration and Guidance*

Imagine a businessman invested a huge sum of money into building a factory with the most advanced automated equipment. This factory can produce thousands of products per hour — hour after hour, day after day. The factory has the potential to generate tremendous income automatically and effortlessly — all with the press of a button.

Now imagine if the new owner forgets one minor detail — he forgets to press the button. The machinery lies dormant, and nothing is produced. What a waste.

The world around us can be an automatic, effortless, and constant source of inspiration to help us grow and become better people.

But there is one thing that we must do before the beautiful and intricate machinery of the world can begin to produce — we have to press a button that opens our hearts and minds to inspiration. When we attune ourselves to becoming inspired, and we see the world properly, we turn on this grand machinery of inspiration.

## ✄ Constant Inspiration

First and foremost, the natural world — this magnificent planet that we live on — can be so inspiring.

Our world bears eloquent testimony to the fact that "בְּרֵאשִׁית בָּרָא אֱלֹקִים." Every blade of grass, every insect, every sunrise, cries out "שְׂאוּ מִי בָרָא אֵלֶּה — *See Who created these!*" "מַה גָּדְלוּ מַעֲשֶׂיךָ ה' — *How great are Your deeds, Hashem!*" The world is bursting with *emunah*.

Rav Pam once recounted that he met a Jewish scientist who was so inspired by the symmetry and beauty of a molecule of water that it sparked her journey back to *Yiddishkeit*. This is the message of a drop of water — there must be a Creator!

The people around us are another source of inspiration.

My greatest heroes are *ba'alei teshuvah*. They changed their lifestyles, they changed everything about themselves, at twenty, thirty, forty, even fifty years old. They call out to us, "Look, I changed everything. I changed the way I lived, the things I ate…you can change a little bit, too. You can stop talking *lashon hara*, or stop talking during *Chazaras Hashatz*." Women who adopted a Torah lifestyle call out to their sisters, "I changed my entire wardrobe. You, too, can change a few items that are of questionable *tznius*." Meeting people with such strength of character should inspire and uplift us, and motivate us to grow.

A *bachur* once came to the Gerrer Rebbe. The Rebbe asked him, "Where are you learning?" The *bachur* replied, "I learn in Ohr Somayach, but I'm not a *ba'al teshuvah*." (Yeshivas Ohr Somayach generally caters to students who are new to *Yiddishkeit*.) The Gerrer Rebbe looked at him and asked, "*Fahr voss nisht?* Why *aren't* you a *ba'al teshuvah*? Everybody else is doing *teshuvah* and you are not?" Shouldn't we all hear this message when we see a *ba'al teshuvah* who epitomizes change?

What about your neighbors or your friends? They can also be a source of tremendous inspiration. Have you ever been invited to a friend's *siyum*? He is also very busy — just like you. Nevertheless, he made a *siyum* because he was determined. He worked hard, day after day, in order to accomplish his goal. Is that not inspiring? Just think back to the last *Siyum HaShas* — literally thousands of people made a *siyum*. Many were inspired by the *Siyum HaShas* that preceded this one. They were motivated to do the impossible — and they did the impossible.

And, of course, the events and occurrences that happen in the world should inspire us to improve ourselves.

Sometimes we hear, *Rachmana litzlan*, of a tragedy — a young person afflicted with a terrible illness, or passing away in the prime of his life. Isn't that also a most effective wake-up call, stirring us to appreciate life? It should encourage us to think, "*Baruch Hashem*, I have life. Am I fulfilling my potential?"

These are just a few examples from among the countless opportunities that we have daily to hear the world's messages of inspiration. But we need to press the button. If we are not tuned in, we are not going to hear anything.

# ✿ The Listening Ear

The *pasuk* (*Yeshayahu* 55:3) says: שִׁמְעוּ וּתְחִי נַפְשְׁכֶם — *Listen and you will give life to your soul*, you will invigorate your *nefesh*.

The Midrash (*Rabbah*, *Yisro* 27:9) expounds on the *pasuk* as follows: If a person fell off the roof and was injured "from head to toe," he must treat each wound individually. When considering our spiritual selves, we also have 248 spiritual *eivarim*, limbs. Being that a person's ear, and its spiritual counterpart, is only one of these *eivarim*, one would think that by treating the ear, one heals only the ear. But, says the Midrash, this is incorrect. If the person treats his ear, and makes it into an *ozen shoma'as*, a receptive ear, he grants a *chiyus*, a healing life force, to his entire *nefesh*. שִׁמְעוּ וּתְחִי נַפְשְׁכֶם — If a person is listening, he changes his entire being. He does not need to focus different treatments on different parts of his being; the treatment of the ear is an effective cure-all.

This Midrash conveys an important lesson. A person who is tuned into receiving his messages, effects a total transformation within his soul.

This was Yisro's greatness. *Chazal* tell us that Yisro served every *avodah zarah* in the world. But what changed him, and brought him "under the wings of the *Shechinah*"? וַיִּשְׁמַע יִתְרוֹ — *And Yisro heard* what Hashem did to Klal Yisrael. In truth, everybody heard; the *pasuk* says that all of the nations heard of the great events that took place — *Yetzias Mitzrayim*, *Krias Yam Suf*, *Milchemes Amalek*, *Mattan Torah*. But Yisro not only heard, "*Yisro hut derhert*" as they say in Yiddish, Yisro heard and understood. He was a *receptive* listener. He heard the message; he heard the world crying out, "Become a better person. Come serve Hashem!"

Contrast this with Bilam who was a colleague of Yisro; they both served as advisers to Pharaoh. Yisro made a most incredible change, but Bilam who had the same opportunity to improve, ignored the messages. If anything, Bilam should have been more likely to change; he was, after all, a *navi*. But Bilam was not a good listener, as evident in the incident with his donkey (*Bamidbar* 22:29). When Bilam's donkey spoke to him, he should have been astounded. Instead, he merely talked back to the donkey. How silly; how foolish. That was Bilam's downfall. He heard the message, but he ignored it. He lost the opportunity to fulfill שִׁמְעוּ וּתְחִי נַפְשְׁכֶם.

The Kli Yakar asks: We know that דְּבָרִים הַיּוֹצְאִים מִן הַלֵּב נִכְנָסִים אֶל הַלֵּב — *Words that emanate from a heart enter the heart.* Yet we see throughout Tanach that Klal Yisrael sometimes ignored even our greatest *nevi'im*. The *nevi'im* certainly spoke דְּבָרִים הַיּוֹצְאִים מִן הַלֵּב. So why didn't their words penetrate the hearts of the Jewish People?

The Kli Yakar answers with a very powerful message. Certainly the words of the *nevi'im* emanated from the heart. But there has to be a heart on the receiving end, as well. Klal Yisrael did not heed the words of the *navi* because they lacked the heart; their hearts weren't listening to the messages.

## ◌୧ A Moment of Truth

Rabbeinu Yonah (*Sha'arei Teshuvah* 2:10) writes that sometimes, when a person hears something inspiring: בְּרֶגַע קָטָן יוֹצֵא מֵאֲפֵלָה לְאוֹר גָּדוֹל — *In a split second, he can leave the darkness and enter the great light.*

How true are these wonderful words. A person sometimes experiences a "moment of truth." If he hears the message and takes it seriously he can transform his life.

וְאַשְׁרָיו — *How fortunate* and lucky he is, continues Rabbeinu Yonah, כִּי צָדַק נַפְשׁוֹ בְּשָׁעָה קַלָּה — *for in one brief moment*, in a moment of destiny, *he changed his life.* That was Yisro, and that can be us as well.

\*\*\*

Rav Chatzkel Levenstein was one of the greatest influences in his generation. But in his youth, he was not very learned. He was an orphan and worked as a delivery boy. One Friday, after a hard week of work, he was paid his wages and he went to the *mikvah*. He hung up his jacket, and when he returned, the money was gone. Someone had stolen it.

This was a life-altering moment for him. *I worked an entire week for this money*, he thought to himself, *and in a moment it's gone! This is what money is? I can't spend my life running after money.*

And he immediately made a decision. "I am leaving my job. I am going to learn Torah."

We all know of Rav Chatzkel's great mind. But think of his listening ear. He took the inspiration of the moment and transformed himself, and the world.

\*\*\*

It was Shabbos Chanukah during World War I and in a shul in Vienna a *rav* was delivering a *drashah*.

"The *Chashmona'im* were a small group of courageous individuals who changed the world. We also need courageous individuals who will change the terrible downward trend that we are witnessing in Jewish education."

Then the *rav* added something novel for his day:

"And who is worrying about *chinuch habanos*, about our girls' education? No attention at all is given to them! We need a few *Chashmona'im* to change this terrible reality."

Unbeknown to the *rav*, there was a young woman from Cracow sitting in the *ezras nashim* listening intently to the *drashah*. The young woman's name was Sarah Schenirer, and she heard the message. She decided then and there to take on that role, to be that *Chashmona'i*. And she changed the world, having an indescribable impact on Klal Yisrael, both during her life as well as after her death, through the Bais Yaakov school system that she founded.

I'm sure there were many people that heard that same speech, both men and women. But, like Yisro, Sarah Schenirer not only heard, she was also tuned in to what she was hearing.

***

A businessman related to me this incident, and he earned my greatest respect from it. This man was offered to be a partner in a business venture that had the potential to yield astronomical profits. He was already successful in his current businesses, but this venture was of a different magnitude; this could propel him into the world of the super wealthy.

However, he refused the offer, for the most amazing reason. He thought about what is happening in our world, all of the frightening headlines and events. He remembered that our *gedolim* have told us that we are living in the era of *Ikvesa d'Meshicha*. One *gadol* recently said that we are not only hearing the footsteps of Mashiach, we can actually hear him turning the doorknob to open the door of the *Geulah*.

"We are living in very special times. I prefer spending any extra time that I have preparing myself for Mashiach's arrival. I have enough *parnassah*, and there is no reason for me to get involved in another business venture."

This man listened well, and truly heard the message of the world around us.

## ◐〜 Take It Personally

I always marvel at the Gemara in *Maseches Yuma* (86a): הֵיכִי דָּמֵי חִילּוּל הַשֵּׁם — *What is chillul Hashem on a practical level?*

If I were to ask you this question, you would probably say, "Well, maybe it's Reform or Conservative Jewry that makes a mockery of *Yiddishkeit*, or maybe it is the government in Eretz Yisrael that wants to uproot Torah… These are practical examples of *chillul Hashem*."

But this is what the Gemara says:

*What is chillul Hashem?* אָמַר רַב, כְּגוֹן אֲנָא — *Rav said, "I am an example of chillul Hashem.* If I buy meat and do not pay for it immediately this is a *chillul Hashem*, because people will say, 'The rabbi is not paying for what he takes.'"

Rav Yochanan also responded, "כְּגוֹן אֲנָא — *Like me.* I am a *chillul Hashem* if I walk *daled amos* — approximately six feet — without Torah or *tefillin*, because people will think lightly of *talmidei chachamim*."

When these *Amora'im* heard something, they looked into themselves. "What does it mean to me; how can I improve?" And almost with excitement they called out "כְּגוֹן אֲנָא — *It is me*, it is me! How can I use the inspiration to improve myself?"

Imagine when a lottery number is drawn, and everyone looks to see if he has the winning number. The lucky winner cries out, "I have it! It's me! It's me!"

When those great *Amora'im* heard about something that calls for change, they automatically applied it to themselves. "It's me! I have to be careful not to buy without paying." "I have to be careful to be constantly immersed in Torah."

When a speaker says: "People must…" or "*Yidden* should always…" the listening person changes those words into: "I must…" "I should always…" He thinks, *The speaker is talking to me; his message is meant for me.*

## ❦ This Means You

Rav Pam once recounted an incident with his father, who was the *rav* of Beis Midrash Hagadol in Brownsville. A member of the *kehillah* did something that warranted strong reproof. In this particular case, Rav Pam's father felt that it would be counterproductive to talk to him directly. Instead, he made his point in his next *drashah*. Without directly attacking the guilty party, the *rav* made it very clear, and in very strong terms, that what that person did was unacceptable. After the *drashah*, that very man came over to Rav Pam's father, and said, "*Rebbi, oiy hust du zey guht areingezugt* — you really told him off!" The man heard the entire *drashah*, but he was not listening.

I once heard a beautiful *shmuess* in Chodesh Elul from Rav Shlomo Wolbe. At the end of the *shmuess*, he said that he wanted to close with the most important point: "With regard to everything I said tonight, *ich mein du, mit du, mit du, mit du…* — I meant you, and you, and you, and you…" He symbolically pointed to everyone in the audience.

Beautiful and inspiring words are meaningless if the listener does not apply them to himself.

\*\*\*

The story is told of a traveling *maggid* who came to a town to deliver a *drashah*. In front of the crowded shul, he thundered, "The time to do *teshuvah* is now. We won't live forever! Every single member of this town is destined to eventually pass on from this world." The *maggid* could see that his words were having an effect on the people — except for one man sitting in the back who seemed completely unmoved. In fact, he was actually smiling.

The *maggid* repeated himself. "Each and every person in this town will die one day." Phrasing the thought in such a blunt manner brought many to tears, but the man in the back was now smiling broadly!

The *maggid* focused a severe look at the man, and cried out with great emotion, "Is there anyone here who does not realize with absolute certainty that everyone in this town will eventually die?" The people were now weeping, but that man was chuckling softly to himself.

When the *maggid* finished his *drashah*, he could not contain himself. He approached the man who was laughing and asked him, "How could you smile and laugh in the face of such a stark eventuality?"

"Oh, you don't understand — I'm not from this town. I'm just a guest for Shabbos."

It is as Rabbeinu Yonah (*Sha'arei Teshuvah* 2:26) expresses: אִם הָאָדָם לֹא יְעוֹרֵר אֶת עַצְמוֹ, מַה יוֹעִילוּ הַמּוּסָרִים — *If a person does not rouse himself, of what value will those who give mussar be to him?*

A person must have a *lev shomei'a*. When he hears a *shmuess* he should internalize it and apply it to himself. "כְּגוֹן אֲנָא — *Like me.*"

## Tichbad Ha'avodah

There are messages of inspiration abound for those wise people who have developed a listening ear. But the *yetzer hara* knows this too. And, of course, he is not going to sit idly while we pick up these life-altering messages.

The *Mesillas Yesharim* (at the end of chapter 2) describes in detail the various strategies that the *yetzer hara* employs, and weapons that he wields in his battle against us. What is the *yetzer hara's* most powerful weapon? When Pharaoh decreed that a more brutal workload be placed on the Jews in Mitzrayim, he declared, "תִּכְבַּד הָעֲבֹדָה — *Increase their workload.*" The *yetzer hara* uses this weapon as well. תִּכְבַּד הָעֲבֹדָה — the *yetzer hara's* strategy is to keep people busy, keep them working, keep them moving, and make sure that they do not have the time or energy to think.

The *Mesillas Yesharim* continues. If a person would stop and think, he would most likely motivate himself toward bettering himself. If a person would only pause to ponder, "Life is so short and precious. What am I doing with my life? Am I truly living up to my obligations in *avodas Hashem*? Am I learning enough Torah? Am I *davening* with enough focus? Am I spending enough time with my children? Am I being considerate enough to my wife? Am I creating a *kiddush Hashem* as I engage in business, or am I causing the opposite?

If a person would stop and think, he would likely change, so the *yetzer hara* keeps him too busy to think. He's always running and has no time to think. He could take advantage of the world's most awesome and inspiring machinery, but he doesn't press the button. Everything around him is crying out: "Become a better person. Pay more attention to those things in life that will endure forever. Look at what happened — another person died young. Listen to the message." But he is too busy to internalize the messages; he is too preoccupied to think.

The person who has a listening ear, and who lives with the guarantee of שְׁמְעוּ וּתְחִי נַפְשְׁכֶם, has an entire world of inspiration all around him, helping him to improve. But if a person is too busy to take things to heart, then what he sees around him will not motivate him at all. If a person does not take out a moment to ask himself, "What can I do with this?" then any potential inspiration that he may have felt will quickly dissipate. When the weapon of תִּכְבַּד הָעֲבֹדָה compromises the שְׁמְעוּ וּתְחִי נַפְשְׁכֶם in a person's life, so much opportunity is lost.

## Accepting *Mussar*

The *pasuk* (*Mishlei* 9:8) states: הוֹכַח לְחָכָם וְיֶאֱהָבֶךָ — *Give reproof to a wise person, and he will love you for it.*

Is there really someone who will love you if you tell him *mussar?* Who likes to hear *mussar?* We all want to hear compliments, not *mussar.*

The Vilna Gaon has an incredible insight on this *pasuk.*

Imagine a young woman as she prepares herself on her wedding day. She looks in the mirror and carefully examines her face to see if anything is amiss.

Someone watching might ask her, "Why are you looking for trouble? Why are you looking so carefully to find problems?"

But, of course, the question is foolish. The *kallah* is not looking to find problems; she is looking to bring out her beauty. If there is a blemish, she will locate it and remove it, in order to beautify herself.

Says the Vilna Gaon, this is what *tochachah* is. It is a call to remove a blemish and to bring about positive change. The most helpful thing a person can receive is *mussar,* and we should all have the willingness to hear it and to improve. .הוֹכַח לְחָכָם וְיֶאֱהָבֶךָ

Someone who ignores words of *mussar* is described in another *pasuk* (*Mishlei* 15:32): פּוֹרֵעַ מוּסָר מוֹאֵס נַפְשׁוֹ — *He who negates discipline despises his soul.*

There is an inspiring thought in *Maseches Tamid* (28a): אֵיזוֹ הִיא דֶרֶךְ יְשָׁרָה שֶׁיָּבוֹר לוֹ הָאָדָם — *What is the straight path that one should choose to travel in life?*

This is a very alluring Gemara; it is going to give us the secret to *gadlus* in one easy lesson. What is this *derech yesharah?*

יֶאֱהַב אֶת הַתּוֹכָחוֹת — *Listen and appreciate when someone gives you criticism* — whether directly, in a *drashah,* or in everyday conversation!

שֶׁכָּל זְמַן שֶׁתּוֹכָחוֹת בָּעוֹלָם — *for as long as there is critique in the world,*

נַחַת רוּחַ בָּאָה לָעוֹלָם — *satisfaction comes to the world,*

טוֹבָה וּבְרָכָה בָּאִין לָעוֹלָם — *goodness and blessing come to the world,*

וְרָעָה מִסְתַּלֶּקֶת מִן הָעוֹלָם — *and evil leaves the world.*

## ✑ Thanks for Your Help

Often, when a person receives criticism he naturally wants to defend himself, and excuse his behavior or his character. But a person who desires self-improvement is eager to hear what another person is telling him.

Imagine driving to the Catskill Mountains on Erev Shabbos with a car full of children. You left a bit late, and you have a long drive ahead of you. Suddenly, a car pulls up alongside you, and the driver frantically motions for you to pull over.

"I have been following you for the last few miles," he begins. "You have a leak in your gas tank. In a few minutes, you are not going to have any gas left, and you are going to be stuck. Shabbos is coming, and you have your whole family here. You better stop and fix this problem."

What would you say? Imagine responding this way:

"How dare you! What chutzpah! Who do you think you are to point out my problems and tell me what to do? I do not even know you!"

Could there be a more foolish response?

Now imagine that the concerned fellow motorist tells you that he happens to be a mechanic, with his tools in his car, and he can give you a quick fix that will stop the leak and enable you to make your trip safely. What would you say then?

"Did I ask you for your help? Do I need you? Don't tell me what to do, and don't fix my car."

That would be absurd.

The normal response in the above scenario is a sense of overwhelming gratitude. No words of thanks would be enough to convey your appreciation to this wonderful and caring person. If someone can help you with a problem, you should be thankful. That is הוֹכַח לְחָכָם וְיֶאֱהָבֶךָ. When someone points out something that can be corrected, he is helping you bring out your true beauty. Thank him for it.

## 🙠 The Call of Elul

If every day of the year is full of inspiration and opportunity, the days of Chodesh Elul are all the more so. אֱלוּל is the *roshei teivos* (an acronym) for: אֲנִי לְדוֹדִי וְדוֹדִי לִי — *I am to my Beloved and my Beloved is to me* (*Shir Hashirim* 6:3). During the days of Elul, Hashem is closer to us than the rest of the year. The *Mishnah Berurah* (*siman* 681) quotes early sources who teach us that during the days of Elul, it is easier for a person to do *teshuvah*, it is easier to finally change and improve oneself. In Elul the days themselves call out, "Come! Become a better person!" Someone who is already living with an *ozen shoma'as*, someone who does not ignore his messages, has even greater *siyata d'Shmaya* during these days.

We have to take the message of Elul personally. Elul cries out, "I mean you, and you, and *you*!" And we must respond, "כְּגוֹן אֲנָא! Yes, it's me!" Life is so precious, but life is so short; in the seventy, eighty, or ninety years that we are *zocheh* to live, there is so much to accomplish.

The *pasuk* (*Hoshe'a* 14:2) says: שׁוּבָה יִשְׂרָאֵל עַד ה' אֱלֹקֶיךָ — *Return, Yisrael, to Hashem, your G-d.*

The Gemara (*Yuma* 86a) points out: גְּדוֹלָה תְּשׁוּבָה שֶׁמַּגַּעַת עַד כִּסֵּא הַכָּבוֹד — *How great is teshuvah, for it reaches until the very Throne of Hashem.*

We can change until we reach the *Kisei Hakavod*. We can change and become great people.

I'll never forget when someone once told me, "To change is the hardest thing in the world to do. I want to change, believe me, but it is just too hard."

I told him that he is making a terrible mistake; what he said borders on *kefirah*. Regarding *teshuvah* the Torah (*Devarim* 30:14) says: כִּי קָרוֹב אֵלֶיךָ הַדָּבָר מְאֹד — *Rather, the matter is very near to you*, it's the *easiest* thing to do *teshuvah* (see *Ramban* ibid.).

Change is not the hardest thing. What is the hardest thing is to *want to change*. The challenge is to want to change, or, at least, to want to be a person that wants to change. Once you want to change, the change itself will eventually come.

## ❦ Make Commitments

The Chafetz Chaim used to ask if every Yid is inspired in Elul and wants to improve, why don't we see great waves of change in Elul? Why don't we see more people tapping into their potential and reaching great spiritual heights? Why are so many people inspired, harboring the purest thoughts of self-improvement, but then they fail to improve as the inspiration dissipates?

The Chafetz Chaim answers that this happens when the person hears the call of *Shuvah Yisrael*, but fails to follow through with the next *pasuk*:

קְחוּ עִמָּכֶם דְּבָרִים וְשׁוּבוּ אֶל ה' — *Take words with you and return to Hashem.*

Inspiration alone isn't sufficient. If a person doesn't follow the inspiration with concrete steps, it will dissipate. קְחוּ עִמָּכֶם דְּבָרִים — you have to sit down and think, "I'm inspired, I'm uplifted. Now what? Now I must take real action."

Sit down in a quiet moment, when the ears are listening, when the heart is feeling, when the mind is absorbing, and קְחוּ עִמָּכֶם דְּבָרִים. Think of something that you could improve upon. Each person knows himself. Think of some small, concrete practice that you can fulfill, and accept upon yourself to do it.

Rav Shach recommended to people to *bentch* with a *bentcher* during the entire month of Elul. "It will change your *bentching*," he said.

Make a stronger effort to come on time to *davening*; your whole *davening* will be different. Make a *seder* — two *halachos* a day — in *sefer Chafetz Chaim*; your speech will greatly improve.

Small steps lead to big changes. It is up to us to take those steps which bring us to our true greatness. Let us begin now.

# OPPORTUNITY'S HARD KNOCKS
## *Dealing with Challenges*

A Yid was traveling on Erev Shabbos when he got stuck in traffic and subsequently got lost. It was dangerously close to the *zman*, and he was far from where he needed to be for Shabbos. Frantically, he called his *rav*.

"Help me! What should I do? I'm lost!"

The *rav* answered him calmly. "We mustn't talk that way! A Yid is never lost; a Yid is *sent*. Get as close as you can to a shul, or to a Jewish community, and make the best last-minute arrangements that you can. And then remember, that is where you were sent for Shabbos."

Often, when confronted with a challenging situation or a difficulty, the main problem that people have is that they begin to feel despair. "Help! I'm lost! My life is falling apart!"

But our basic *emunah* tells us otherwise. A Yid is never lost; a Yid is *sent*.

### When Things Go Wrong

Someone once asked me, "Why is life like a yo-yo?"

I must admit I have heard many questions and problems, but this question was unique.

"What do you mean?" I asked my petitioner.

He explained: "I really want to do the right thing, but it's not easy. My life is so full of ups and downs, *aliyos* and *yeridos*, good days and then bad days. I feel like a yo-yo!"

Now I understood his question. And actually, I think that this is a question that we can all relate to. Of course, the "ups" aren't the problem. But how do we deal with the "downs," the "bad days"?

We all have rough moments in life. Maybe your boss yelled at you because you didn't do your job correctly. Or sometimes it's because you got into a quarrel with your spouse. It could be stress from your teenage children. It could be *parnassah* or health issues, *shidduch* problems, etc.

To *daven* and learn Torah is easy when things are going well, but what about when things aren't going well? How do we focus on our *avodas Hashem* when we are struggling? How does a person do mitzvos when he doesn't have *cheshek* (desire) to do them?

The answer to these questions lies in our *heilige Yiddishe emunah* — specifically *emunah* in one particular *pasuk* (*Yirmiyahu* 31:15): יֵשׁ שָׂכָר לִפְעֻלָּתֵךְ נְאֻם ה' — *there is reward for all your actions, said Hashem.*

## 🕮 *Mamma Rachel*

Rachel Imeinu, *Mamma Rachel*, has always been a wellspring of *chizuk* and encouragement for *Yidden* in *galus* — our beacon of light in the darkness. When Rachel passed away she was not buried in the Me'aras Hamachpelah, but rather in a roadside grave, on the road to Beis Lechem. Rashi (*Bereishis* 48:7) tells us why: so that she should be an inspiration for her children in *galus*, throughout the generations.

There is one very important point about Rachel's story that is sometimes overlooked. In reality, this significant concept should form the cornerstone of a Jew's attitude in *galus* and whenever things go wrong in his life.

The Midrash in *Eichah Rabbah* (*Pesikta* §24) recounts a very moving incident.

At the time of the *Churban*, Avraham, Yitzchak, and Yaakov implored Hashem to have mercy on Klal Yisrael in the merit of the various great things that they did, but their pleas were not accepted. Then, Rachel came forth and *davened*:

"Ribono Shel Olam, You know that Yaakov worked so hard for me, and at the end of his seven years of toil, when it was time for our wedding, my father intended to substitute Leah in my place. I became aware of this plan, וְהִקְשָׁה עָלַי הַדָּבָר עַד מְאֹד — *this was very difficult for me*; I could not bear the thought of such a thing happening! I could not imagine losing Yaakov as a husband. I was determined to stop this terrible trickery.

"So I told Yaakov about my father's plan, and I gave him *simanim* to differentiate between me and my sister, so my father wouldn't be able to switch us.

"But afterward, I had a change of heart. My pity for my sister won out, וְסָבַלְתִּי אֶת תַּאֲוָתִי — *I had to suffer the terrible pain of 'conquering' my desire* [for Yaakov], and of facing a doomed future as the wife of Eisav.

"Ribono Shel Olam! Look what I, a mere mortal did! Can't You also overlook what Klal Yisrael did wrong, and show them mercy?"

Says the Midrash: Immediately, Hashem's mercy was aroused and Hashem said, "In your merit, Rachel, Klal Yisrael will be returned to Eretz Yisrael!" This is as the *pasuk* (*Yirmiyahu* 31:15–16) states: מִנְעִי קוֹלֵךְ מִבֶּכִי וְעֵינַיִךְ מִדִּמְעָה כִּי יֵשׁ שָׂכָר לִפְעֻלָּתֵךְ נְאֻם ה' וְשָׁבוּ מֵאֶרֶץ אוֹיֵב וגו' וְשָׁבוּ בָנִים לִגְבוּלָם — *Stop crying, [Rachel,] hold back your tears; there is reward for all your actions, said Hashem, and they will return from the land of their enemies. Your children will return to their land.*

Rachel was told, "יֵשׁ שָׂכָר לִפְעֻלָּתֵךְ," your pain and your difficulties have been duly noted by Me, and rest assured, your *mesirus nefesh* to save your sister from embarrassment will bear tremendous fruit.

The question is obvious: Rachel's act was certainly very great, but was it greater than the actions of Avraham, Yitzchak, and Yaakov? They too invoked the merit of their accomplishments, including the *Akeidah*, and the many years of *chinuch* of the twelve *shevatim*! What was it about Rachel's action that succeeded in arousing Hashem's mercy more than the great deeds of the *Avos*?

Rachel's accomplishment was different because, in her own words, וְהִקְשָׁה עָלַי הַדָּבָר עַד מְאֹד. The mere thought of losing Yaakov was terribly difficult for her to bear. Yet she did what she felt was right.

Avraham, Yitzchak, and Yaakov perhaps did greater things, but, in a sense, their accomplishments came more easily to them. Certainly, it was a great *nisayon* for Avraham to slaughter his beloved son Yitzchak, but Avraham did not suffer from the trauma of not wanting to do the right thing. He knew it was the *ratzon* of Hashem, so he was able to act with *simchah* and *zerizus* to do it. The same is true regarding Yitzchak and Yaakov.

For Rachel, when the challenge presented itself, she was *not* equal to the challenge. At first, she was not able to do it. But then she rose to the occasion. She did something extraordinary. She drew strength from deep within herself to conquer all of her natural love, to drive back her fear, to do something that was terribly, terribly difficult for her, and give up her entire future to save her sister from being embarrassed.

## ℘ One Hundred Times the Value

Many years ago when long-distance travel was very difficult, a young American *bachur* traveled to faraway Radin to learn in the Chafetz Chaim's yeshivah. The Chafetz Chaim was very impressed with the *mesirus nefesh* this *bachur* displayed by leaving the comforts of America to come to learn in Europe.

One evening, the Chafetz Chaim met the *bachur*. He smiled and asked him, "Nu, what did you learn today?"

"*Ah blatt Gemara* — one page of Gemara..."

"*Nein, nein!* No, no...that is not what you learned today!"

The boy was puzzled, "Rebbi," he repeated, "I learned *ah blatt Gemara...*"

The Chafetz Chaim said, "*Nein, nein.* No, no. Your *chavrusa* learned *ah blatt.* But you learned one hundred *blatt Gemara!* You came from America with such great *mesirus nefesh!* Attending yeshivah here is so much more difficult for you. *Chazal* (*Avos D'Rabi Nosson* 3:6) say, טוֹב לוֹ לְאָדָם דָּבָר אֶחָד בְּצַעַר מִמֵּאָה בְּרֶיוַח — *one mitzvah done with suffering is worth one hundred mitzvos done without difficulty.*

## ℘ You Never Know

Let's take a look at the incredible words of the *Avos D'Rabi Nosson* (ibid.). (This *limud*, with slight variations, is found in *Yevamos* 62b as well.) אִם לָמַדְתָּ תּוֹרָה בְּנַעֲרוּתֶךָ — *if you learned Torah when you were young,*

אַל תֹּאמַר אֵינִי לוֹמֵד בְּזִקְנוּתִי — Don't say, "Well, I learned when I was young, and now it's too hard for me. Now I'm old and it's difficult; I don't have the same energy, or the same enthusiasm."

אֶלָּא לְמֹד תּוֹרָה — *Learn now as well!* Even though the Torah learning is not as fresh as when you were young, and you think that it is not as meaningful, you would be making a mistake not to learn,

כִּי אֵינְךָ יוֹדֵעַ אֵיזֶה יִכְשָׁר — *because you don't know which is more valuable.*

Of course, when you were young and vigorous your learning came easily. Now that you are old, you have to overcome your growing weakness and other challenges. The learning of your older years is perhaps more difficult, but you never know, this learning might be the truly valuable learning.

The *Avos D'Rabi Nosson* gives additional examples, as well: If you learned Torah when you were wealthy, learn now that you are poor. If you learned in a time of satiety, learn in hunger. If you learned in ease and comfort, learn with difficulties.

The *Avos D'Rabi Nosson* also applies this teaching to building a family, and to *chinuch habanim.* One must never give up.

שֶׁטּוֹב לוֹ לְאָדָם דָּבָר אֶחָד בְּצַעַר מִמֵּאָה בְּרֶיוַח — **because** *one mitzvah done with difficulty is worth more than one hundred mitzvos done when it is easy.*

These words have to ring in our ears and in our minds: אֵינְךָ יוֹדֵעַ אֵיזֶה יִכְשָׁר.

We think that we have "ups and downs." We think that those challenging days are downswings; they are signs that our life is falling apart, and that something is terribly wrong. But who knows which day's *avodah* is more valuable? They are really the "good" days!

This is the message of יֵשׁ שָׂכָר לִפְעֻלָּתֵךְ. Rachel thought that when she revealed the *simanim* to Leah she was sacrificing her entire future, that her life would fall apart. She would now be doomed to a life with Eisav. But, for overcoming her challenge in her most difficult moment, Hashem said, "*Mamma Rachel,* don't cry. יֵשׁ שָׂכָר לִפְעֻלָּתֵךְ." Your struggle is your *Akeidah.* And it is that very *avodah* that is going to give light to the *Yidden* in *galus.* It is you who has saved Klal Yisrael!

This is the eternal message, the *chizuk,* the inspiration, that we are supposed to be gleaning from *Mamma Rachel.*

Of course, we don't learn Torah in order to get *s'char*. But the *emunah* that we get one hundred times more *s'char* when it is difficult serves to highlight and accentuate the value of that mitzvah, and gives us more encouragement to do it. You have the ability to reach a higher plateau and a higher altitude, because now everything is worth one hundred times more.

On those days, when you think you are experiencing a "down," realize יֵשׁ שָׂכָר לִפְעֻלָּתֵךְ. *Der Ribono Shel Olam bleibt nisht shuldig* — Hashem sees each and every difficulty and Hashem always "pays His debts." And אֵינְךָ יוֹדֵעַ אֵיזֶה יִכְשָׁר. View every difficulty as an opportunity — an opportunity of טוֹב אֶחָד בְּצַעַר מִמֵּאָה בְּרֶיוַח. A mitzvah that requires you to struggle will be more meritorious in Hashem's eyes.

## ❦ True Value

Who is truly successful? One who must struggle to overcome his negative tendencies, or one who is naturally good? To the untrained eye, it may seem that the latter person is better. But that is not necessarily so.

When someone is able to give *ma'aser* generously because his *parnassah* is going well, that is very meaningful. But when a person has to struggle to give the same amount, isn't every dollar that he gives worth one hundred dollars in *Shamayim*?

When we have to give extra care and attention to the obnoxious child who needs it but doesn't deserve it, and we have to struggle to show the child love and affection, isn't that *chinuch habanim* so much more meaningful to Hakadosh Baruch Hu?

When you are so drained, but nevertheless push yourself to go to learn, that Torah is so precious. Yesterday was a great day, the learning flowed easily, but which day's learning is really more valuable, the easy day or the difficult day?

Which is a more precious *davening* — when you are in the mood to *daven* and your *davening* comes naturally, or when you have other things on your mind but you force yourself to concentrate anyway? Isn't the smile when you don't feel like grinning invaluable? When a person controls an uncontrollable anger welling up within him, isn't that *avodah* much more prized by Hashem than that of the calm of a person who naturally does not get angry?

## ❧ What Is My Role?

There is a beautiful *vort* on the Mishnah (*Avos* 2:5), אַל תֹּאמַר לִכְשֶׁאֶפָּנֶה אֶשְׁנֶה, שֶׁמָּא לֹא תִפָּנֶה. Literally, this means: *Do not say, "When I will be free, I will study," for perhaps you will never become free.*

Homiletically, the Mishnah can be understood to mean, "Don't say, 'When I will be free and at ease, I will study Torah and do mitzvos. But today is too difficult. I'll wait until tomorrow, when things will be easier.' שֶׁמָּא לֹא תִפָּנֶה — maybe your role right now is to be one who is 'לֹא תִפָּנֶה,' someone who must serve Hashem amid struggles and challenges."

When things are going well, we must thank Hashem for His benevolence. But when things go "wrong," we have to condition ourselves to function with these principles:

**The first principle** is this important idea of שֶׁמָּא לֹא תִפָּנֶה — this difficulty may actually be my new role. I am being sent on a new mission; now is the time for me to make a more cherished contribution. We *daven* for health, financial stability, success, and *nachas* from our children. But if we must serve Hashem with illness, or poverty, or family stress, we should not think that "My life has taken a wrong turn."

Rather, we must realize that "My life has taken a necessary turn into 'opportunity lane' where I was sent."

**The second principle** that we must bear in mind is that of אֵינְךָ יוֹדֵעַ אֵיזֶה יוּכְשָׁר — if I perform to the best of my abilities, my *avodah* in these circumstances may be even more cherished by Hashem than what I have been doing until now when things were easier. יֵשׁ שָׂכָר לִפְעֻלָּתֵךְ. Hashem is taking a careful accounting of everything that we are doing. Performing His *avodah* under challenging circumstances generates much more *s'char* for us. טוֹב לוֹ לְאָדָם דָּבָר אֶחָד בְּצַעַר מִמֵּאָה בְּרֶיוַח!

## ❧ Opportunity Knocks

Rav Boruch Ber Leibowitz would tell his students that he managed to successfully navigate a difficult situation in his life because of a story that he had heard about Rav Nosson Adler, the rebbi of the Chasam Sofer.

When Rav Boruch Ber arrived in the small town of Holosk to assume the position of *rav*, there was a surprise awaiting him. The housing committee had arranged living quarters for the new *rav* right across the street from a church!

Rav Boruch Ber's tremendous *kedushah* couldn't tolerate this. He couldn't decide whether or not to tell the townsfolk that the arrangement was unacceptable. But then he remembered a story about Rav Nosson Adler.

Rav Adler was once traveling by horse and buggy in a heavy blizzard, and the wagon became stuck in the snow. The lone horse was unable to pull the wagon out, so the wagon driver went off to find help. He returned a short while later.

"I couldn't find another horse, but my friend came with his ox!" he told the passengers.

Rav Adler jumped off the wagon into the freezing cold and driving snow. And he began to dance! The people stared after him. "Why are you standing in the snow? And what are you dancing about?"

Answered Rav Adler, "Look at this opportunity! It is forbidden to remain in a wagon while it is being pulled by a horse and an ox! When does a person come across this mitzvah of *kilei beheimah*, to be in a wagon drawn by two different animals? I never had the privilege to fulfill this mitzvah and I may not have another chance! Should I not dance?"

Rav Boruch Ber said, "I remembered that story, and I realized that living across the street from a church is a difficulty, but I can also view it as an opportunity! It is an opportunity for me to work on myself, to avoid looking there and to keep a distance from this place of *avodah zarah*, as set forth in the halachah."

When facing a challenging moment, or a challenging day, or a challenging week, instead of throwing your hands up in defeat, do a dance in your mind! "I have an opportunity to light up the darkness! I have an opportunity of יֵשׁ שָׂכָר לִפְעֻלָּתֵךְ!"

## ⚜ Easier, Not Better

A relative of mine was choosing between two potential jobs. One was a teaching job and the second was in a different field. He was more inclined to take the latter position, but he consulted with an *adam gadol* who advised him to accept the teaching position.

He said, "But the other job is a better one!"

"Why?" asked the *adam gadol*.

"*Vayl es ihz gringer*, because it's easier," responded my relative.

"Nu," said the *gadol*, "*vehr zogt ahz gringer ihz besser*, who says that easier is better? Teaching may be more difficult, but I feel that it is the better job for you."

"*Vehr zogt ahz gringer ihz besser?*" Who said that easier is better? A simple but penetrating statement. Sometimes, when we have a difficult moment let us remember those words — "*vehr zogt ahz gringer ihz besser?*" Maybe a more difficult day, a more difficult mitzvah is better? Not maybe, certainly, טוֹב אֶחָד בְּצַעַר מִמֵּאָה בְּרֶיוַח...אֵינָךְ יוֹדֵעַ אֵיזֶה יִכְשָׁר!

## ⚜ The Tzaddikim Cry

The Gemara in *Sukkah* (52a) says that in the times of Mashiach, Hashem will slaughter the *yetzer hara*. When He does so, both the tzaddikim and the *resha'im* are going to cry. Of course, the *resha'im* will cry when they realize that they could have accomplished so much in their lives and now it's too late. But why will the tzaddikim cry? Hashem has finally destroyed their archenemy, the ultimate evil!

The *Maharsha* has an incredible insight, based on the *pasuk* (*Bereishis* 1:31), וַיַּרְא אֱלֹקִים אֶת כָּל אֲשֶׁר עָשָׂה וְהִנֵּה טוֹב מְאֹד — *And G-d saw everything that He created and it was very good.*

The Midrash says, טוֹב מְאֹד — *it was very good* is referring to the *yetzer hara*. Evidently it is very good for the tzaddikim to have a *yetzer hara*, for this gives them an opportunity to struggle and overcome their temptations.

On that day, when the *yetzer hara* will be slaughtered, people will lose the opportunity of טוֹב מְאֹד. There will no longer be the temptation to *daven* quickly, and "move on" with the day. We will no longer be challenged to force ourselves to sit in a *shiur* or with a *chavrusa*, and concentrate on our learning. We will not have to struggle to hold our tongues in situations when silence is needed. (To the contrary, on that great day, we will see the *ohr haganuz* that one generates when he controls what he says.) Now that opportunity will no longer exist and this will cause the tzaddikim to cry. Tzaddikim understand that the bigger the *yetzer hara* to fail, the greater the reward when we succeed, and no *yetzer hara* at all is a reason to cry. So I ask you, isn't a challenging day really the good day — טוֹב מְאֹד?

## B'levavi Mishkan Evneh

In the era of the Beis Hamikdash, we merited continued opportunity for *kirvas Hashem*. In fact, the root of the word *korban* is *karov*, to come close. But what is left for the *galus* Jew?

When the Ramban debated the nonbelievers they asked him a spiteful question: "Of what value is your service to your G-d? You no longer have your glorious Temple. You are missing the *korbanos*, the basic element of *avodas Hashem*!"

The Ramban's response is so profound and uplifting.

"כְּשֶׁאֲנִי עוֹבֵד אֶת בּוֹרְאִי בְּגָלוּת" — *When I serve Hakadosh Baruch Hu in galus*, without a Beis Hamikdash, without the *korbanos*,

בְּעֵינוּי שִׁעְבּוּד וְחֶרְפַּת הָעַמִּים — *against the backdrop of the oppression and the ridicule of the nations*,

שְׂכָרִי מְרוּבָּה — *I have even more s'char* than from service in the Beis Hamikdash. Why?

אֲנִי עוֹשֶׂה עוֹלָה לֵאלֹקִים מֵגוּפִי — *because I become a korban!* I may not be able to bring a *korban* in the Beis Hamikdash, but I use my life as a *korban olah l'Hakadosh Baruch Hu*."

What a beautiful thought. In *galus* we don't bring *korbanos*, but we can make ourselves into *korbanos*. More so, as the Ramban concludes וּבָזֶה אֶזְכֶּה לְחַיֵּי עוה"ב יוֹתֵר וְיוֹתֵר, my *avodah* is much more significant since טוֹב אֶחָד בְּצַעַר!

In the moving words of the *Sefer Chareidim*:

בִּלְבָבִי מִשְׁכָּן אֶבְנֶה — *I will build a Mishkan in my heart,*

וּלְקָרְבָּן אַקְרִיב לוֹ אֶת נַפְשִׁי — *and I will sacrifice myself.*

And that is really the most meaningful *korban*. We are accustomed to think that *mesirus nefesh* means giving up your life. That's true, of course; giving one's life is the ultimate *mesirus nefesh*. But in the beginning of *Chayei Sarah* on the *pasuk* (*Bereishis* 23:8), אִם יֵשׁ אֶת נַפְשְׁכֶם, *Rashi* says *nafshechem* means *ratzonchem*, your desires and wants. *Mesirus nefesh*, then, can also mean giving up your desires, your wants, and your inclinations. When a person is tempted to do something but he does not do it because it is wrong, that is *mesirus nefesh* — he has given up his *ratzon*. That is also עוֹשֶׂה עוֹלֶה לֵאלֹקִים מִגּוּפִי!

## ❦ We Can Do It

The Midrash says that when the Beis Hamikdash was burning, some *kohanim* were so distraught and so broken from the scene, that they threw themselves into the flames; they simply could not bear to live without a Beis Hamikdash. Rav Chatzkel Levenstein commented that the actions of the *kohanim* who jumped into the fire is not the *chiddush*. The *chiddush* was those *kohanim* who did not do so! How did they have the strength to go on?

Perhaps, the words of the Ramban teach us the answer to that question. Those *kohanim* realized that there might be an *avodah* that is more cherished and more important in Hashem's eyes than the *avodah* in the Beis Hamikdash! That's a life of *galus*. It may be a life in darkness, but it is also a life of illuminating the darkness; it is an *avodah* of maintaining and strengthening our *emunah* in the darkness of the night.

One of the facets of *galus* is the gnawing fear that what we do is meaningless. Our service of Hashem often seems so pale when we compare ourselves to great people! But we must have *emunah* in ourselves and in our *avodah*.

Rabbi Tzadok Hakohen (*Tzidkas Hatzaddik* 154) writes words that must be repeated and repeated, until they are committed to memory:

כְּשֵׁם שֶׁצָּרִיךְ אָדָם לְהַאֲמִין בְּהַשֵּׁם יִתְבָּרַךְ — *Just as a person must have emunah in Hashem,*

כַּךְ צָרִיךְ אַחַר כַּךְ לְהַאֲמִין בְּעַצְמוֹ — *so, too, a person has to believe in himself.*

We have to believe in ourselves not only when the going is good, but perhaps more important, we have to believe in ourselves when things are difficult. That is our lot in *galus* — to be in frightening darkness, yet carry out our mission.

## ᏀᎦ *Oy! S'iz Guht Tzu Zein ah Yid*

Rabbi Shmuel Dishon told me the following story:

He spent a few weeks in a summer camp for Russian boys. Most of the boys had just started learning about *Yiddishkeit*, and were experiencing it for the first time. That summer, the camp's theme song was the Yiddish *niggun*, "Oy s'iz guht tzu zien ah Yid — Oh, it is good to be a Jew!" Throughout the summer, Rabbi Dishon was always moved when he would hear these sweet children, these not yet religious boys, heartily singing, "*Oy s'iz guht tzu zien ah Yid!*" But, he said, that was nothing compared to the amazing *kiddush Hashem* performed by one of the boys in camp.

During the summer, one of the campers, a seventeen-year-old boy, realized that he never had a *bris milah*. The boy was very upset about it and approached one of the *rabbanim* in the camp, who contacted a *mohel*. The *mohel* promised that he would come the very next day to perform the *bris*.

The next morning the *mohel* called the camp. He explained apologetically that he was unable to arrange for an anesthesiologist on such short notice. Of course, a teenage boy would need anesthesia to endure the pain of the *milah*, so he was calling to let them know that they would have to push off the *milah* for a day.

The boy would not hear of it. "I have missed having a *bris milah* all these years — I'm not waiting another day!"

"But how can we do it without anesthesia?" the *mohel* questioned.

"Don't worry," said the courageous boy. "We will take care of that..."

The *milah* took place that day. How? How did a seventeen-year-old boy endure the pain of *milah*? He had five of his friends pin down his arms and legs and head so that he couldn't move. And while the *milah* was taking place they were enthusiastically singing the camp song, "*Oy s'iz guht tzu zien ah Yid!*"

This boy literally experienced עוֹשֶׂה עוֹלָה לֵאלֹקִים מֵגוּפִי. He endured so much pain for the mitzvah of Hakadosh Baruch Hu, and he did it with such great *simchah*. I ask you, did the Ribono Shel Olam ever receive a *korban* as meaningful as this amazing sacrifice?

## ◎◯ Golden Opportunities

Let me close with the following story.

A diamond merchant traveled for many days to a jewelry fair, where he spotted the most beautiful diamond. The cost of the diamond was prohibitive, and he didn't have enough money to buy it. But this was the very diamond that he needed; this stone would bring him a handsome, and much needed, profit. He stayed at the fair for the entire week, and toward the fair's end, the diamond was still not sold.

He approached the seller.

"I'll give you all the money I have, every last penny — I am only withholding the money that I need to travel home." He put all of his money on the table.

"Not enough," said the seller. "Do just a little better…"

The merchant saw that he had a chance. He took out the money that he was keeping for his travel expenses and put that on the table as well. It swung the balance.

"For that amount, the diamond is yours," said the seller.

The merchant hesitated for just a moment. How would he get home? But he instantly decided that this was an offer that he could not give up. He bought the diamond. He had no choice but to walk home.

It was a freezing winter, and instead of several days in a coach, the journey home took many weeks. He endured the hardships of the road and slept at night in the shuls of the *shtetlach* that he passed through, keeping company with the poor and lost souls there. He was forced to rely on the kindness of strangers for a bit of food to eat.

When he came home, his family couldn't believe it. He had walked all the way home?

"How did you do it?" they cried. "How did you endure the constant exertion and weariness? And those freezing winter nights? And the humiliation of begging?"

"I had an instant source of *chizuk*," he replied. "Whenever my experiences seemed too hard to bear, I would open up my pack and take a peek at the most beautiful diamond within. The sparkling gem gave me the strength to move on."

That is the secret of living through *galus*. When it seems to be too difficult to bear, a Yid should stop for a moment and open up his "pack" to look at the diamonds that he is generating. He should look at the טוֹב אֶחָד בְּצַעַר מְמָאָה בְּרֶיַח, and have *emunah* in the טוֹב מְאֹד in what he is doing. He should remember אֵינְךָ יוֹדֵעַ אֵיזֶה יִכְשָׁר. He should realize that in *galus* he can bring a *korban* that may be even greater than the *korbanos* in the Beis Hamikdash — *ul'korban akriv lo es nafshi hayechida*. And then, he too can sing *Oy s'iz guht tzu zien ah Yid!*

# YOU'RE IN GOOD HANDS
### *Alleviating Worry*

Imagine someone was constantly at your side — and always making you miserable. Picture someone endlessly making you unhappy with horrible comments about the terrible state you are in, and with constant gloomy predictions about what will certainly go wrong in your life. He follows you wherever you go, his voice never stops: "How will you manage? How can you make ends meet? What if this happens? What if that goes wrong?" On a daily basis, he manages to turn you into a bundle of nerves. Before every *simchah* or Yom Tov, he ensures that you will be anything but joyful. In fact, he robs you of all the happiness from your life.

I am afraid to think how the average person would deal with such a scoundrel. Even a true *ba'al middos* would not tolerate it, and would certainly make every effort to rid himself of this unwanted companion.

Yet we all — each and every one of us — have an enemy within that does just that, plus much more. This enemy's name is *da'agah* — worry.

The human condition lends itself to worrying. At all stages of life, a person is worried. When young, a person worries about, "Whom will I marry?" Once married, people worry about having children. When the family grows, there are endless worries about raising the children. We're worried about their success in yeshivah, school, camp, etc. Then, we worry about marrying them off and supporting them. And then, we worry about the grandchildren. We are perpetual worriers.

Is there anything we can do to combat this enemy within?

## ☙ Man's Downfall

One of the *hoshanos* we recite on Sukkos is entitled *Adamah Mei'ered*. In this *hoshanah*, each individual line is a plea to Hashem to protect a specific part of creation from its particular downfall: save the earth from curse; save the animals from miscarriage; save the wheat from locusts.

Then there is a plea to save mankind. What is the one word that describes the human being's greatest threat?

הוֹשַׁע נָא נֶפֶשׁ מִבֶּהָלָה — *Save a person from behalah*, panic, from a confused state of worry and anxiety.

Our greatest enemy is the worries that constantly accompany us.

Worry is emotionally debilitating and robs us of our happiness, even at some of the most joyful moments in our lives. Often, people become terribly overwrought when they are making a wedding. It is as if they are dealing with a tragedy. How distressing it is to take a *simchah* that is meant to be a special time in one's life, and turn it into such a source of tension and anxiety. That is how deeply our worries can affect us.

Worry is also physically draining. The Gemara (*Brachos* 58b) comments: אֲנָחָה שׁוֹבֶרֶת חֲצִי גוּפוֹ שֶׁל אָדָם — *a worried groan breaks half of a person's body*. Another Gemara (*Gittin* 70a) teaches us that worry weakens a person.

There is a published medical study that details the physical dangers involved in worrying. A worrier, of course, has a higher stress level and is more prone to high blood pressure, heart attacks, and ulcers. Worry is a slow-motion suicide. But this study found that the negative effects of anxiety run deeper than that. When a person worries, it affects his facial expression, tone of voice, breathing rate, muscle tension, energy level, immune system, and even his brain waves.

To quote one of our past presidents, "We have nothing to fear but fear itself." Our greatest enemy is the *worry itself*, not the possible scenarios and potential problems that we agonize about.

## Forbidden to Worry

Aside from the detrimental effects of worrying, both emotional and physical, we have to understand that excessive worrying is wrong. A Yid is not allowed to worry. There are many sources in the Torah and *Chazal* that teach us about the *issur* of worrying:

* When the Jewish army goes out to war, there is a specific warning not to fear the enemy: לֹא תִירָא מֵהֶם — *Do not be frightened of them* (*Devarim* 7:18 and 20:21 and *Birkas Peretz* ibid.).

Rabbeinu Yonah (*Sha'arei Teshuvah* 3:32 with *Matnas Chelko*) deduces from this, that a person is not allowed to worry when he is faced with a difficulty.

\* The Gemara (*Brachos* 60a) relates: Rabbi Yishmael ben Rabbi Yosi saw that his *talmid* was frightened about something. He reprimanded his student: "חַטָאָה אַתְּ — *you are a sinner*. For the *pasuk* (*Yeshayahu* 33:14) says, פָּחֲדוּ בְצִיּוֹן חַטָאִים — *sinners were frightened in Zion.*"

\* וַיִּירָא יַעֲקֹב מְאֹד — *and Yaakov was frightened* (*Bereishis* 32:8). Before his encounter with Eisav, Yaakov was scared about what may happen to him and his family. The Midrash (75:3) views this as a misdeed and a shortcoming, because a *ba'al bitachon* should not worry (see *Sichos Mussar* p. 144).

## ⟨⟩ Your Choice

So the pressing question that we must address is: How can we avoid stumbling in this area? In life we must deal with problems. Things can go wrong — sometimes drastically — with our *shalom bayis*, our other relationships, our health, our *parnassah*, our children… There are endless crises and tragedies that can occur at any time. How can we avoid the tension and anxiety that come so naturally to us?

First and foremost, we have to understand — based on the timeless wisdom of *Chazal* — that a person *can* change. Many people do not fully believe or appreciate this. They say things like, "I'm a nervous wreck. I've been worrying for years and years. I can't stop it."

That is not true. If there is an *issur* to worry, then we all have the ability to overcome this tendency. Even a naturally nervous person, whose "middle name" is "Worry," and for whom anxiety is a constant companion, can conquer this counterproductive emotion.

When discussing the prohibition of jealousy, the *Sefer Hachinuch* (mitzvah 416) asks a compelling question: How can the Torah command us not to feel a certain emotion? How can we be told not to feel something that we feel?

The *Chinuch* answers with a very sharp comment: "*Only wicked fools and sinners*" think this way. In reality, *every person has within him the ability to be the master over his thoughts and feelings.* A person has control over his heart, and he *can* stop being envious. לִבּוֹ מָסוּר בְּיָדוֹ, עַל כָּל אֲשֶׁר יַחְפּוֹץ יַטֶּנּוּ — *His heart is given into his hand [is under his control], for all he desires he can direct it.*

I believe that the *Chinuch's* rule applies to any forbidden emotion or *middah*. Yes, we all can control our tendency to worry.

The Rambam (*Hilchos Teshuvah* 5:1–2) makes a very dramatic statement: *Each and every person has the ability to be a tzaddik or a rasha... Every person can be as great as Moshe Rabbeinu or as wicked as Yeravam ben Nevat.*

Sometimes we are quick to say, "I can't help it — I'm a jealous person, I'm a nervous person, I'm a quick-tempered person — that's just my nature." The *Chinuch* and the Rambam are both teaching us that even if it is your nature, nevertheless it is your choice to keep your nature. True, you may have a greater challenge, but you too can change.

If it is *assur* to worry, then we *can* change, and we *can* stop worrying.

## ⤷ Don't Be a Fool

Let's suggest some practical strategies that we can employ to help us remove worry from our lives.

Rav Yisrael Salanter used to say in jest that the very first obligation is "*zei nisht kein na'ar, zei nisht kein tipesh* — don't be a fool; don't act unintelligently." That would be an apt description of the person who worries.

The worrier is very foolish. After all, he gains nothing from worrying, yet loses so much. Being anxious is the ultimate exercise in futility, and only serves to make our lives miserable. Is there a more foolish way to act?

There is another aspect of foolishness involved in worrying: Imagine meeting your friend who looks deathly ill.

"What's the matter?" you cry. "You don't look good. Do you need me to call Hatzolah?"

"No, no. I'm just very, very worried about something."

"What are you worried about?"

"Well, it is something that might happen in a few months."

"What? You look like this because of what may be in a few months? Why don't you enjoy the next few months, and when the time comes, you can worry then. Why ruin all this extra time in your life because of something that might happen in the future?"

It is foolish to waste precious time of your life because of a possible eventuality.

The Gemara (*Yevamos* 63b) says: אַל תָּצַר צָרַת מָחָר — *Do not be distressed by tomorrow's troubles,*

כִּי לֹא תֵדַע מַה יֵּלֶד יוֹם — *for you do not know what a day may bring;*

שֶׁמָּא מָחָר בָּא וְאֵינֶנּוּ — *perhaps tomorrow will come and one will not be alive,*

נִמְצָא מִצְטַעֵר עַל עוֹלָם שֶׁאֵינוֹ שֶׁלּוֹ — *and it turns out that he was grieving over a world that was not his.*

Don't worry about tomorrow, because you don't know what tomorrow will bring.

Why are you losing happiness today because of a possible tomorrow? We have very limited vision of what's going to be. Hashem runs the world His way; things could completely change from one moment to the next.

The Steipler Gaon writes in a letter (1:55) that אַל תָּצַר צָרַת מָחָר is not a *gezeiras hakasuv*; it is a *metzius*, a reality. There is no sense at all in worrying about a tomorrow that may possibly not happen.

## ✆ Talk It Over

Another practical way to battle worry is found in the well-known *pasuk* in *Mishlei* (12:25): דְּאָגָה בְלֶב אִישׁ יַשְׁחֶנָּה — *when there is worry in a person's heart,* יַשְׁחֶנָּה.

The Gemara (*Yuma* 75a) explains this to mean: יְשִׂיחֶנָּה לַאֲחֵרִים — *discuss it with others.*

Sometimes we have a valid reason to be concerned about something serious, and we begin to become anxious and worried. Very often, a person gets carried away and he goes deeper and deeper into the murky depths of *behalah*. His worry overtakes him and gets completely out of control. Now what? Discuss the problem with others and you'll realize it's not so bad.

A child notices something insignificant — a pimple, or a blister, for example — and will become convinced that it is a dangerous growth and he has a dreaded disease. He can't bear the thought of causing his parents the terrible anguish of losing a child, so he keeps it to himself. He walks around for a few days with the terror of death in his little heart, until he can no longer take it and finally shows his parent the "growth."

"It's just a pimple," says his mother. "It's nothing."

Sometimes, even as adults, we get carried away with a problem. If we keep it to ourselves it can get out of hand as it grows and intensifies. The worry can be alleviated by discussing your problem with someone with a clear-minded perspective.

Rav Yaakov Kamenetsky used to suggest discussing problems with an older person. People who have traveled a long way on the road of life have surely experienced those moments when their world was caving in, but they lived happily ever after, and are here to tell the tale. They are living testimony to the fact that our problems can be resolved.

It is also particularly helpful to speak with someone who has once navigated the same experience that you are dealing with. If you are making a wedding, and have much anxiety from it, discuss it with someone who has already made a wedding — or two or three. That person will probably tell you, "Don't forget — this is a wedding, not a *levayah*. Why ruin your *simchah* with worry?"

Alleviate your fear of the unknown by talking to people who have worked through the same challenge that you are facing and can offer you practical advice.

## It's Only a Moment

Rav Shraga Feivel Mendlowitz suffered indescribable *yissurim* in the last years of his life. Someone once had the courage to ask him, "How do you absorb so much suffering daily?"

His reply was noteworthy: "The *yissurim* that are past no longer affect me. What I'm going to suffer in a moment is not yet here. The only really challenging part of *yissurim* is the pain of this very moment. Nu, I can deal with one moment of suffering."

That is an incredible insight, and another great strategy: Take your problem and divide it; reduce it. This is the depth of the well-known quote (*Yosef Ometz* 295 and *Pele Yoetz: da'agah*).

הֶעָבַר אַיִן — *The past is gone,*

וְהָעָתִיד עֲדַיִן — *the future is not here yet,*

הַהֹוֶה כְּהֶרֶף עַיִן — *the present is only a fleeting moment,*

דְּאָגָה מִנַּיִן — *so why worry?*

## 🕭 In Good Hands

Beyond these few strategies, the most important *eitzah*, the most practical bit of advice, is the solution to so many of our problems: *emunah* and *bitachon*.

כָּךְ הִיא דַּרְכּוֹ שֶׁל עוֹלָם — *This is the way of the world.* Life is not easy. There are always things to worry about, and we are only human. But the solution to any and every problem is our *emunah* and our *bitachon*.

I once saw a very wise sign that someone had hanging on his refrigerator. The first line was in big, bold letters:

**DON'T WORRY! EVERYTHING IS UNDER CONTROL**

Underneath that, in smaller print, was the punch line:
*Not Yours.*

This is actually the true definition of *bitachon*, which is often misunderstood. People think, "I have *bitachon* that I am going to find a job, that I will find a *shidduch*, that my relative will get better… I will have *bitachon*, and it is going to happen."

The Chazon Ish (*Emunah U'bitachon* 2:1) writes that this is not *bitachon*. We do not know what the future will bring. *Bitachon* means that we believe that everything is *b'yad Hashem* and that everything follows His plan. Everything is under control, *but not yours.* Someone who lives with this mindset will find no need to worry, even in difficult situations.

Rav Aharon Kotler was suffering from his final illness. His *rebbetzin* noticed his suffering and said, "*Zorg zich nisht* — don't worry, *es veht zein guht* — it will be good."

Rav Aharon protested, and said, "*Nein, nein* — no, no; *es ihz shoin guht* — it's already good, *veil ich bin in Guhte Hent* — because I am in Good Hands."

That is the true definition of *bitachon*. Rav Aharon was not living in denial. He knew that his days may be numbered, but he had the *emunah* that he was in the best hands.

## ⟨♫⟩ Sweet Singer of Israel

Dovid Hamelech is known as *Na'im Zemiros Yisrael*, he composed so many beautiful songs — *shiros v'sishbachos* — to Hashem. However, Dovid Hamelech did not spend his life in a plush meadow, with a harp in his hand. His life was not worry-free, just singing praises to the Ribono Shel Olam for the wonderful life that he was experiencing. Anybody familiar with Tanach knows that Dovid's life was extremely difficult, full of terrible trials and *tzaros*.

Dovid Hamelech always had adversaries. In his own words (*Tehillim* 69:5): רַבּוּ מִשַּׂעֲרוֹת רֹאשִׁי שֹׂנְאַי חִנָּם — *More than hairs on my head, I have enemies that hate me for no reason.* Among these adversaries were Dovid's own brothers, sons, father-in-law, etc. But nevertheless Dovid was able to be the *Na'im Zemiros Yisrael* because his *shiras hachaim*, his life's song, was כִּי לְעוֹלָם חַסְדּוֹ, which he repeated twenty-six times.

The Navi (*Yeshayahu* 12:2) says: הִנֵּה קֵל יְשׁוּעָתִי אֶבְטַח וְלֹא אֶפְחָד — *Behold, G-d is my salvation, I shall trust and not fear.*

I will have *bitachon*, וְלֹא אֶפְחָד, and I will not have fear; **I will not worry.** Yeshayahu is teaching us the formula to a life of serenity: אֶבְטַח וְלֹא אֶפְחָד — *bitachon* is the antidote to *pachad*, to worry. *Bitachon* relieves a person of worry because *bitachon* gives the person the ability to see that "*ich bin in Guhte Hent* — I am in Good Hands"

In life there are things that we cannot control, but we cannot let them control *us*. That is the crux of *bitachon*. Even if things are not going the way we want, even if things are out of *our* control, nothing is out of the control of the *Yad Hashem*. If so, we are in *Guhte Hent* and there is no need to worry.

There is a remarkable Midrash (*Bereishis Rabbah* 65:22):

Rav Yosi ben Yo'ezer was being led to his execution by the Greeks. His nephew, Yakum, a renegade Jew, joined the execution procession riding a fine horse.

He taunted his uncle, "Look at my horse, and look at your 'horse!'" referring to the pole that the Greeks were carrying, on which they were going to hang Rav Yosi ben Yo'ezer.

Rav Yosi responded: "If this is what awaits those who please Hashem, imagine what awaits those who anger Him!"

Those words cut into Yakum like a serpent's poison. Right then Yakum performed on himself all four *misos beis din*.

At that moment, Rav Yosi dozed off and saw a vision of Yakum's *aron* (bier). "Look!" he cried. "In one brief moment, Yakum has preceded me to Gan Eden!"

This Midrash is often quoted to highlight the greatness of *ba'alei teshuvah*, and the reward that awaits them in *Olam Haba*. But Rav Chaim Shmulevitz, with his uncanny ability and very sensitive heart, saw another tremendous lesson in this Midrash. Just think: Rav Yosi is being led to his execution — and he dozed off!

There are people who cannot sleep the night before a doctor's appointment or a visit to the dentist. And here Rav Yosi falls asleep while being led to his own execution, while staring the Malach Hamaves in the face. That is true *menuchas hanefesh*. And that is the difference between a life of *menuchas hanefesh*, and a life of *behalah*, of panic. The secret is אֶבְטַח וְלֹא אֶפְחָד.

Rav Pam once became very emotional when he told us about a woman who had called him with a *she'eilah*. She had the dreaded illness and wanted to know if she should *daven* for a *refuah*.

Rav Pam asked her, "Why not?"

The woman answered, with all sincerity, that if Hashem gave her this illness then this is what is best for her. And if so, why should she want to change what Hashem knows is best?

Now the answer is, of course, that we still have to *daven*. Hashem wants us to use our *ko'ach* of *tefillah*. He wants us to petition Him to change a *gezeirah ra'ah*. But look at the level of *bitachon* that this "simple" woman reached. אֶבְטַח וְלֹא אֶפְחָד! She was staring the Malach Hamaves in the face but she was able to say, "This is the *yad Hashem*. *Ich bin in Guhte Hent!*"

Internalizing this concept is the greatest strategy for removing worry.

The Steipler writes in a letter to an individual who was worried: *you cannot run away from yourself.*

I think that his message was this: Hashem has a plan for each and every one of us, and we cannot run away from His plan. More so, we don't *want* to run away from His plan. To us it might seem terrible, but Hashem knows better. We are in *Guhte Hent;* Hashem is watching us and is there for us.

Imagine someone who never practiced walking on a tightrope and now must traverse a mighty canyon over a thin wire. He is petrified. Who can blame him? One slight misstep and he's doomed. But then someone tells him, "Don't worry. Way down below, across the entire area, there is a huge safety net. If you fall, you'll be caught by the net." All of a sudden, the tightrope becomes a pleasure walk. That's *bitachon*. *Bitachon* is the safety net under all of the challenging times in our lives.

כָּל הָעוֹלָם כּוּלוֹ גֶּשֶׁר צַר מְאֹד — *The entire world is a very thin, narrow bridge.* You look down to your left, you look down to your right, and there is so much to worry about.

וְהָעִיקָּר שֶׁלֹא לְפַחֵד כְּלָל — *but the main thing is not to worry.*

Not to worry? You just told me that I am on a tightrope. Yes, the world is a tightrope, but there's a safety net underneath.

When Rav Pam was diagnosed with the dreaded illness that eventually claimed his life, his reaction was, and I quote, "*Hashem, hatov be'einav ya'aseh* — Hashem will do what is good in His eyes. The Ribono Shel Olam, the Good G-d, will do as He sees fit. I am filled with great *hakaras hatov.*" That is *bitachon*. That is אֶבְטַח וְלֹא אֶפְחָד. There was a very bleak reality that faced him, but instead of filling his heart with worry, he filled his mind with the feeling that "I'm in good hands."

At the end of *Parshas Beshalach*, the Torah relates that Klal Yisrael was attacked by Amalek. Why were they attacked? Rashi (*Shemos* 17:8) quotes the Midrash that gives a *mashal*:

A father was carrying his son on his shoulders, taking care of him, and seeing to all of his needs. Suddenly the son asked a passerby, "Have you seen my father?"

The father was very hurt. "I'm carrying him on my shoulders, and he doesn't know where I am? I know how to make sure he sees me."

The father lowered the boy, and a dog came and bit him.

Klal Yisrael was privileged to the protection of Hashem, yet they asked, "הֲיֵשׁ ה' בְּקִרְבֵּנוּ — *Is Hashem among us?*" Where is Hashem? Is He with us?

"*Chayeichem*," responded Hashem, "I will send Amalek to remind you of My loving devotion to you — of My protection."

Hashem was upset with Klal Yisrael for not recognizing His constant *hashgachah*, His loving supervision. Rashi quotes this *lashon*:

תָּמִיד אֲנִי בֵּינֵיכֶם — *I am always with you,*

וּמְזוּמָן לְכָל צָרְכֵיכֶם — *and I'm ready to give you what you need,*

וְאַתֶּם אוֹמְרִים הֲיֵשׁ ה' בְּקִרְבֵּנוּ — *and you ask, "Is Hashem in our midst?"*

That is the formula for *bitachon*: תָּמִיד אֲנִי בֵּינֵיכֶם. Hashem is always with us, even in our challenging moments. Sometimes I catch myself beginning to worry, and I remind myself of this Midrash. How dare I worry? I could almost hear the disappointment that Hashem has when we worry. "I give you so much and you worry? Don't you know that I'm carrying you on My shoulders, that תָּמִיד אֲנִי בֵּינֵיכֶם?"

I know someone who reached a practical understanding of "תָּמִיד אֲנִי בֵּינֵיכֶם." When his first child began the process of *shidduchim*, he was worried, but the child married a wonderful person. When his second child's turn came to marry, he was worried again. This child, as well, found a perfect *shidduch*. At that point, he already realized the unmistakable *yad Hashem* that he was experiencing and he began to feel that it is simply a chutzpah for him to worry. And since then he no longer worries about *shidduchim*. Of course, the *shidduchim parshah* is a very difficult one, but the solution is not worrying, the solution is *bitachon.*

## ༄ *Im Yirtzeh Hashem*

There is a wonderful Jewish *minhag* to append the words "*im yirtzeh Hashem* — if Hashem so desires" whenever we discuss things that we are planning to do. "I'm going to the store, *im yirtzeh Hashem*…"

Why do we say this? Going to the store takes all of three minutes. The store is right down the block; what could happen? But we have an ingrained *emunah* that nothing can happen without "*im yirtzeh Hashem.*"

I think that it would be a good idea to start appending another phrase when we talk about things that have *already* happened: "*kach ratzah Hashem* — so was the will of Hashem.*"

When we see something that isn't the way we want it, we should say "*kach ratzah Hashem* — this was the will of Hashem.*" Maybe I don't want it that way, but that is what Hashem wants. When we see something that worries us, we should remember תָּמִיד אֲנִי בֵּינֵיכֶם, and *ich bin in Guhte Hent.* This should prompt us to say, "*kach ratzah Hashem.*" That's a wonderful way to train ourselves, and to train those around us who hear our reactions to life's events.

This is why we make a *brachah* when we see lightning or hear thunder. A person is naturally frightened by lightning and thunder, so we say, *Baruch Atah Hashem Elokeinu Melech Ha'olam* — this comes from You, Hashem. We connect the problem with the solution. We remind ourselves that it is Hashem Who is making this happen, so why should we worry or be frightened?

## ༄ I Envy You

Rav Moshe Tuvia Lieff told an incredible story about a young *bachur* from Eretz Yisrael who had the dreaded illness. The doctors were unsure of how far the disease had spread in his body. They told the family that they were going to operate. Possibly, they would be able to save the boy's life by amputating his leg. If, however, they saw that the disease had spread further, then it would be pointless to remove the leg and there would be nothing to do but wait for the unfortunate eventuality.

Here was a young boy, facing such a difficult trial. He went into the surgery understanding that he would either be losing his leg, or his life.

Rav Lieff came to the hospital after the surgery and met with the doctor. The doctor was an irreligious Israeli, yet he told the rabbi, "I am envious of you religious people and your *emunah*. I'll tell you what I saw with my own eyes.

"As we performed the surgery we saw that we were able to remove the boy's leg, and the boy would survive. After the surgery, while still heavily sedated, the patient woke up a bit, and felt for his leg. Nothing was there. Immediately he made a *brachah, Baruch Dayan Ha'emes*. I was told that this means that he was accepting his loss by blessing G-d.

"Then, a few moments later, he again woke up a bit, and again felt for his leg, whereupon he made another blessing, *Baruch Hatov V'hameitiv*. This blessing is for good news. Right after accepting such a difficult loss, this young boy was able to bless G-d for granting him life.

"I am envious of his *emunah*, of the strong faith of religious people!"

In *Parshas Vayigash*, the Shevatim were being harassed by the evil viceroy of Mitzrayim. He was constantly antagonizing them. The Shevatim were, understandably, worried and upset. Then, suddenly, Yosef revealed himself. "*Ani Yosef!*" he cried. In a flash, all of the worries vanished; all of the strange behavior and all of the questions were answered. This is not an evil monarch; it is their brother who was designated to save them, spiritually and physically.

With just two words — "*Ani Yosef*" — everything was resolved.

The Chafetz Chaim would say: In *galus* we have difficulties, we have one *tza'ar* after the other, but we, too, wait anxiously for two words. When Mashiach arrives, Hashem Himself will call out, "*Ani Hashem!*" Those two words will be the answer to all of our problems as well.

### ❧ Wake Up!

Let me conclude with a story told by Rav Yaakov Galinsky.

Rav Yaakov once met the Ponevezher Rav who asked him, "Reb Yankel, tell me, what would you do if you were dreaming one night, and you found yourself on the tenth floor of a burning building? The fire is raging out of control but you cannot jump from the building because you are too high up. The flames are coming ever closer, and you are choking on the smoke. The heat is unbearable, the fire is overtaking you. What would you do?"

"The Ponevezher Rav's description of the scene was so vivid," said Rav Galinsky. "Listening to him, I broke out in a cold sweat. My heart was racing. What should I do? I can't jump. The fire is upon me! I couldn't answer the Rav. Help me! What should I do?"

The Ponevezher Rav looked at him and smiled. "Reb Yankel, I'll tell you what to do. Wake up! It's only a dream!"

I don't remember what message Rav Galinsky drew from the story, but for me it encapsulates all that we have discussed. A person in life has problems. He's worried about his health, about *parnassah*, about *shidduchim*, about raising children…and he breaks out in a cold sweat. He is overtaken by the darkness of *nefesh m'behalah* and he cries out, "Help me! What can I do?"

Do you know what the *eitzah* is? Wake up! It's only a dream. The life of *nefesh me'behalah* is only a bad dream, because you are a Yid; you can live in the magnificent reality of *bitachon*, in a world of אֶבְטַח וְלֹא אֶפְחָד. That is the real world. תָּמִיד אֲנִי בֵּינֵיכֶם; you are in *Guhte Hent*. That is the answer to all of your problems.

The next time we are faced with a challenge, let us remember that if we worry, it is our decision to do so, and a very poor decision at that. We give up everything for nothing. We must always remember a Yid is never hopeless, and a Yid is never helpless. A Yid is forever in good hands. He can always sing כִּי לְעוֹלָם חַסְדּוֹ.

I recently spoke to someone whose home was burglarized in the middle of the night. Besides the financial loss that he incurred, he was also suffering from the emotional trauma of the burglary: a sense of helplessness and anger, and, above all, the feeling of having been terribly violated.

"Someone took what is rightfully mine!" he told me.

I deeply empathized with him. After all, a burglar does not only take money; he takes away some of our emotional balance, some of our peace of mind.

Now imagine that you were the very one who allowed the burglar access to your home! Imagine if you were the one who allowed the burglar to come in and rob you of your most valuable possession — your happiness.

Sometimes we ourselves allow the world's most ruthless *ganev* into our lives, and we allow him to deprive us of what is rightfully ours. This *ganev* is not a person, it is an attitude — specifically, a negative attitude. How can we keep him out? And if he came in once or twice, how can we reclaim all of the *simchas hachaim* that he has stolen? How can we enjoy that which is rightfully ours?

### A *Tov Lev*

Shlomo Hamelech writes (*Mishlei* 15:15): כָּל יְמֵי עָנִי רָעִים — *All the days of a poor person are bad*; וְטוֹב לֵב מִשְׁתֶּה תָמִיד — *but a tov lev is always feasting.* A *tov lev* has a happy life, a life that is one long Yom Tov, one long expression of *simchah*.

We read this *pasuk* and we pity the poor person. If only he would have money, he would be as happy as his friend! But the *mefarshim* explain, Shlomo Hamelech is actually talking about two people with the same financial situation. They may both be rich or they may both be poor. Their financial status is irrelevant; the *pasuk* is contrasting their attitudes.

One person lives his life with his share of problems and challenges, and he is always happy. He is living a life of a מִשְׁתֶּה תָמִיד; he is in a constant state of *simchah*. And his colleague, who has basically the same life situation, is experiencing the misery of כָּל יְמֵי עָנִי רָעִים — an endless feeling of sadness and depression. Why is that? They have the exact same background in life, yet one is always happy and one is always sad.

Take a look at the world around us, at all of the unhappiness, all of the people who are upset and complaining. You look at them and you wonder: Is this all you have in life? Problems and setbacks? Isn't there any good in your life? Why are you not happy with what you have? Why are you grappling with, and focusing on, what you do not have? Why do you see a cup that is half empty if you could be like your friend who sees a cup that is half full? Why do you allow a *ganev* into your life to rob you of the happiness that is rightfully yours?

Life is all about attitude. It is our decision to choose whether we live a life of טוֹב לֵב מִשְׁתֶּה תָמִיד or whether we subject ourselves to a life of misery, of כָּל יְמֵי עָנִי רָעִים.

### Dayeinu!

I know someone whose wife did something which he thought was wrong, and he could not move past the experience. I told him the following Gemara. If we would successfully internalize this Gemara's message it could have a tremendous impact on our *simchas hachaim*, and it could change our lives.

The Gemara (*Yevamos* 63a) says that Rav Chiya had a wicked wife. Not just a wife who was constantly complaining, or who was careless and neglectful. Rav Chiya's wife was out to make his life miserable. In fact, the Gemara says about her (*Koheles* 7:26): וּמוֹצֵא אֲנִי מַר מִמָּוֶת אֶת הָאִשָּׁה — *And I have found that which is more miserable than death, the woman.* A wicked wife is worse than death.

How did Rav Chiya deal with his wife? I'm afraid to think what we would do. The Gemara says that when he saw something nice for sale, he bought it for her — and he gift-wrapped it!

One of his *talmidim* asked him, "How can you buy her gifts? She is determined to make your life miserable!"

Rav Chiya's response is the important message that we should all try to remember. "דַּיֵּנוּ שֶׁמְּגַדְּלוֹת בָּנֵינוּ לַתּוֹרָה וּמַצִּילוֹת אוֹתָנוּ מִן הַחֵטְא — *It is enough that she raises our children and that she saves me from sinning* [saving me from the evil thoughts that an unmarried man may have]."

It is mind-boggling. Why didn't he say, "I bought her a gift because she washes my laundry and makes me supper?" The answer is, obviously, she did *not* wash his laundry and she did *not* make him supper! The only thing she did for him was to cause him pain and misery. She was a living example of a wife who is worse than death. But Rav Chiya looked and searched, and he penetrated all of the levels of evil and found something positive. "There is evil, but I am going to look at the good and I am going to be happy with the good. *Dayeinu!*"

I told this Gemara to the unhappy husband, and then I added: "Your situation is obviously so much easier; there's so much apparent good that your wife does for you. So why choose to focus on the one incident that was wrong? Why do you choose the misery of כָּל יְמֵי עָנִי רָעִים if you could experience the delight of טוֹב לֵב מִשְׁתֶּה תָמִיד? You can also sing the *niggun* of *Dayeinu!*" I told him to sit down and instead of thinking about this negative incident, think about all of the good that his wife does for him. Wouldn't this make a difference?

### The City of Happiness

Rav Pam once said that in his youth he read a statement that left an indelible impression upon him:

**"The City of Happiness is in the State of Mind."**

People in this world are all pursuing that elusive goal — happiness. Do you want to find the city of happiness? The city of happiness is in your state of mind. How true. If a person's life attitude is *dayeinu*, if he always sees the good, then he will always be happy. But if he focuses on the negative...unfortunately, there will always be something negative to make him miserable. We live in a very imperfect world, and people make mistakes. What should we do when a mistake is made? We have to look at the positive.

I know of two people who were best friends, closer than the closest brothers. I used to marvel at the extent of their friendship. From their yeshivah days, and for literally forty years thereafter, they were living examples of גַם יָחַד. הִנֵּה מַה טּוֹב וּמַה נָּעִים שֶׁבֶת אַחִים גַּם יָחַד. And then their relationship soured to the extent that it was described as אַחַת דָּתוֹ לְהָמִית — they would have wanted to see the other dead! Imagine, for forty years they've lived together in bliss, and now — אַחַת דָּתוֹ לְהָמִית!

When I heard this I thought, "This is what Shlomo Hamelech meant. If these two individuals would focus on all of the years of good then they would still be happy now. Instead, by focusing on one wrong and unfortunate incident, they allowed that ruthless *ganev*, the negative attitude, to rob them of their friendship."

### ⮞ *U'vacharta Ba'chaim!*

I recall that when I heard about this tragedy, that two close friends became אַחַת דָּתוֹ לְהָמִית, I understood the meaning of a *pasuk* at the end of *Parshas Nitzavim*.

The Torah (*Devarim* 30:15) says: רְאֵה נָתַתִּי לְפָנֶיךָ הַיּוֹם אֶת הַחַיִּים וְאֶת הַטּוֹב וְאֶת הַמָּוֶת וְאֶת הָרָע — *Look, I have placed before you a choice of life and good, or death and evil.*

The Torah continues (v. 19): הַחַיִּים וְהַמָּוֶת נָתַתִּי לְפָנֶיךָ הַבְּרָכָה וְהַקְּלָלָה — *I have placed before you a choice of life and death, blessings on the one hand, and curses on the other,*

וּבָחַרְתָּ בַּחַיִּים — *and you should choose life!*

Isn't the choice so obvious? And yet the Torah enjoins us, וּבָחַרְתָּ בַּחַיִּים. Choose life! Why does the Torah have to implore us, to beg us, to choose life? Who wouldn't choose life?

But look at this story. That is who the Torah is crying out to, to those two friends: "וּבָחַרְתָּ בַּחַיִּים!" Why do you choose to harp on one incident? Yes, there was something that went wrong in your relationship. But does that negate forty years of brotherly love?

This applies to any *machlokes* — in a family, with neighbors, in a shul. A person makes a choice — "I am going to be upset." If only he would have the הִנֵּה מַה טּוֹב וּמַה טוֹב לֵב מִשְׁתֶּה תָמִיד attitude, he could have a life of נָּעִים, instead of the misery of כָּל יְמֵי עָנִי רָעִים. A person is so consumed with that one incident that he loses the ability to think and to remember all of the good. Shouldn't all of the good overwhelm that little bit of evil? Isn't it true that the most ruthless *ganev* that robs us of so much happiness is a negative attitude? It is this terrible *ganev* who urges us to see the cup that is half empty when instead we could delight in the sight of a cup that is half full.

I once attended a very beautiful, joyous wedding. A few days later, I approached the *ba'al simchah* to compliment him on the beautiful wedding. Before I had a chance to say a word, he told me, "I'm still very upset that so-and-so didn't come to my wedding…"

I was amazed. He had such a magnificent wedding. Yet for the past few days, all he could think about is that so-and-so didn't come! One has to be deaf not to hear the Torah crying out to that individual: "וּבָחַרְתָּ בַּחַיִּים! Don't be a victim of כָּל יְמֵי עָנִי רָעִים." You're choosing to negate all the good and to fill your heart with so-and-so didn't come to the wedding?

You are giving up the city of happiness because of your state of mind, of focusing on what was lacking instead of what was there.

## ᗣᔓ Happiness Training

The Alter from Kelm (in *sefer Chachmah U'mussar* 2:347) teaches that the Torah's mission statement is to make us happier people, and to train us to live happier lives. I'll give you a wonderful example of this.

A kosher animal, such as a cow, that was killed by wild animals is a *treifah*. The meat of the dead cow is not kosher and may not be eaten. What do you do with this *treif* animal? I would have suggested that the farmer should take it to a *treif* butcher shop, sell it, and recoup most of his losses. However, the *pasuk* (*Shemos* 22:30) instructs us, לַכֶּלֶב תַּשְׁלִכוּן אֹתוֹ — *throw the dead cow to a dog*. Why give it to the dog? That is quite expensive dog food!

The *Da'as Zekeinim* (ibid.) provides a penetrating insight: What happened here? Why was the cow attacked? Didn't the farmer set up a watchdog to protect his animals? He did, but last night the dog evidently fell asleep on the job, allowing the wild animal to enter and kill the cow. The farmer must be very angry at the dog that caused him to sustain a significant loss.

The Torah responds, "But what about all the good the dog did? What about all the days and nights that the dog served you faithfully and protected your herd? Indeed, last night the dog was negligent, but why are you looking at the bad when there is so much good to appreciate?"

The Torah then instructs us that instead of being upset and punishing the dog, we are to reward the dog for all the good it had done previously. Amazing! The Torah trains us to see the good, to live *dayeinu*, thereby enabling us to overlook the negative.

## ᎶᏨ All the Good

The *pasuk* (*Devarim* 26:11) says: וְשָׂמַחְתָּ בְכָל הַטּוֹב אֲשֶׁר נָתַן לְךָ ה' אֱלֹקֶיךָ — *You should rejoice with all the good that Hashem, your G-d, has given you.* The Torah is not addressing someone who has it "pretty good" or "basically good." The Torah is talking to someone who has "*all* the good." Yet the Torah must tell that person to rejoice with his good!

Unfortunately, there are so many people who answer this question. They have so much good in this world, but they're focused on one problem they have. They have to be told וְשָׂמַחְתָּ בְכָל הַטּוֹב over their wedding or friendship of forty years!

I recall an incident that took place after the summer months in the camp that I attend. Overall, it was an unusually successful summer. One group of campers, however, was challenged by the fact that their *rebbi* had been dealing with a family crisis and had to leave camp several times, which disrupted the boys' learning and the rhythm of their day.

At the end of the summer, the boys came to me to say goodbye. One boy told me, "This was not a good summer — my *rebbi* kept leaving. Well, I hope that next summer will be better." A few minutes later another boy came over to say goodbye and said, "This was the most wonderful summer, it was such a great season. True, our *rebbi* had to miss a lot, but we had a good substitute, and things worked out. It was such a beautiful and uplifting summer." I was amazed. Two people experienced the same summer, in the same location, under the same circumstances. Yet one is unhappy and one is full of happiness. One is the embodiment of כָּל יְמֵי עָנִי רָעִים, and the other is living testimony of טוֹב לֵב מִשְׁתֶּה תָמִיד. One is groping in the darkness of what didn't happen, and one is living וְשָׂמַחְתָּ בְכָל הַטּוֹב. It is all about the *dayeinu* attitude.

## ◌ Taking Good for Granted

If we are not careful, human nature conditions us to feel negativity when things go wrong. This is because a person gets used to all the good he has and expects it to continue forever. Then, if something goes wrong it fills our heart and mind with negative feelings. It can destroy *shalom bayis* or a relation *bein adam l'chaveiro*. It can ruin someone's *chasunah* or someone's summer. When we take the good for granted, we lose sight of the good, and our ability to maintain a positive attitude is compromised.

Rabbi Yosef Karo, author of the *Beis Yosef* and the *Shulchan Aruch*, was privileged to learn with a *malach* — an angel. He recorded much of the conversations that he had with his heavenly *chavrusa*. Once, the *malach* told him, "I want to tell you the greatness of your wife." And the *malach* went on to tell him that he has to cherish her, and respect her, and treat her properly (*sefer Maggid Meisharim*, beg. *Parshas Va'eira*). This is very strange. The Gemara (*Bava Metzia* 59a) requires a person to treat his wife properly. Why did the Beis Yosef need a *malach* to tell him that? It seems that even the Beis Yosef could take the good for granted and he needed to be reminded of the greatness of his spouse.

One certainly should not take a spouse — or parents, or friends — for granted. The *malach* was reminding all of us וּבָחַרְתָּ and וְשָׂמַחְתָּ בְּכָל הַטּוֹב בַּחַיִּים. Sit down and think of the goodness that you have in your life, think of the spouse that you have, the children that you have. Don't just focus on the empty half of the cup.

Someone who was very upset once told me: "I have complaints against my parents." I stopped him, saying: "Don't continue; I don't want to hear. If you lived for a hundred years it would not be long enough to thank your parents for all that they did for you! How can you have complaints against them?" This is another example of כָּל יְמֵי עָנִי רָעִים. Imagine what parents invest into a child! And yet that child has complaints...

## ◌ The Golden Years

We were *zocheh* to see the Steipler at the end of his life. He was the perfect picture of *simchas hachaim*, always happy, always *freilich*. Yet in the last decade of his life, the Steipler once said, "From head to toe, there isn't a bone that doesn't ache me constantly. I live with constant suffering. But, יְמֵי שְׁנוֹתֵינוּ בָהֶם שִׁבְעִים שָׁנָה. The average lifespan is seventy years. Once I reached seventy, every subsequent day I am given is a gift! When someone receives a gift he accepts it and appreciates it no matter what it is."

That is a shining example of טוֹב לֵב מִשְׁתֶּה תָמִיד. Life held so much suffering for the Steipler, but he chose to live in the city of happiness, to fill his mind with the happiness of the gift of life.

Rav Pam expressed a similar statement at the end of his life, while suffering from his final illness. His doctor, who was so devoted to him, realized that Rav Pam must be suffering, but he was not complaining. It is hard to treat a patient who does not complain. So the doctor told Rav Pam's grandson, "Tell your grandfather that whenever he is suffering he should complain about it and I'll help him." The grandson agreed and mentioned this to Rav Pam. Rav Pam was aghast. "I should complain? You know I'm eighty-eight years old. Some people don't live until sixty; some people don't live till seventy. At eighty-eight I should complain?" Obviously, he was living in the city of happiness.

## ❧ Transforming Suffering into *Simchah*

That is the wisdom of *Mishlei* in all its practicality. How many people tragically live their golden years complaining, kvetching, *krechtzing*, about this and about that? Another victim of that most ruthless *ganev*, the negative attitude. Day in and day out that *ganev* robs them of the gift of life because they have aches and pains, and things are not like they used to be; life is no longer like "the good old days."

But the wise among us see the gift of life, the blessing of every single day. They live a life of *dayeinu*, of heeding the cry of וְשָׂמַחְתָּ בְּכָל הַטּוֹב.

Rav Nosson Tzvi Finkel, the beloved *rosh yeshivah* of the Mirrer Yeshivah, was one of the greatest *ba'alei yissurim* in our generation. For over twenty years, he lived with unfathomable suffering due to an extreme form of Parkinson's disease. Yet a smile never left his face. Someone once asked him how he manages to maintain his schedule of constant learning amid such suffering.

"How can the Rosh Yeshivah learn with such suffering — מִתּוֹךְ יִסוּרִים?"

Rav Nosson Tzvi smiled and said, "I don't learn with suffering, I learn with *simchah*!"

That is an attitude of טוֹב לֵב מִשְׁתֶּה תָמִיד, an attitude that empowers a person with the ability to transform unfathomable suffering into *simchah*.

Of course, life sometimes brings some bitterness, the bitter taste of *maror*. One of the types of *maror* listed in the Mishnah (*Pesachim* 39a) is the תַּמְכָא. Our tzaddikim point out that the word תַּמְכָא can be viewed as an acronym; it is the initials of תָּמִיד מְסַפְּרִים כְּבוֹד אֵ-ל — *constantly relating the glory of Hashem*. A proper attitude can enable a person to change תַּמְכָא into תָּמִיד מְסַפְּרִים כְּבוֹד קֵל and can enable him to see the good in every situation.

## ◌ Focus on the Positive

Rabbeinu Yonah in *Sha'arei Teshuvah* (3:217) tells a seemingly strange story.

A wise person was walking with a *talmid* and they came across a dead carcass in the street. It emitted an unpleasant odor, and the *talmid* reacted, "How terrible is its stench!" The wise person corrected him and said, "Look how white are its teeth."

What was the *chacham* trying to tell his *talmid* as he focused his attention on the white teeth of a dead animal? Is there really a mitzvah to see the positive in a dead animal's carcass? *Oy*, was he a *chacham*, teaching him a lesson for life. "You are so unhappy, you feel so unpleasant, from the stench. But I see the good in it and I'm happy." He was teaching him to look at the good. Be a positive person. Be a טוֹב לֵב מִשְׁתֶּה תָמִיד person.

The Gemara (*Chagigah* 27a) quotes a *pasuk* in *Shir Hashirim* (4:3): כְּפֶלַח הָרִמּוֹן רַקָּתֵךְ, which literally means: *your cheeks are like a slice of pomegranate*. The Gemara interprets this *pasuk* to mean that even the *poshei Yisrael* — the sinners among the Jewish People — are *melei'im mitzvos k'rimon*. Just as a pomegranate contains within it a multitude of seeds, so, too, Jewish sinners are full of mitzvos.

Now I ask you, when we see someone who is from the *poshei Yisrael* today, do we see a *malei mitzvos k'rimon*? Or do we see *malei aveiros k'rimon*? Were the *poshei Yisrael* in those days different from nowadays?

Certainly not! They did not have different *poshei Yisrael* — they had different eyes. They had eyes that focused on the good, on the aspect of the person that was *malei mitzvos*. They had eyes that were able to see through the layers of evil and discern the good. They were able to project a positive feeling toward others, and to thereby open the possibility of establishing a positive relationship. They were able to avoid causing a feeling of alienation among *Yidden* who were estranged from them. They were able to extend an expression of "I see and appreciate the good that you do. I hope that you will do more of the same, and strive to avoid sin." This is the secret of success in *kiruv rechokim* — to see what these *Yidden* are doing right, not what they are doing wrong.

Isn't it amazing how much a positive attitude affects a person's life? *Shalom bayis* is all about living *dayeinu*, appreciating what we *do* have. *Bein adam l'chaveiro* is all about focusing on the good. The *simchos* that we make are all about attitude. Our "golden years" are defined by whether or not we truly view them as "golden." How we deal with suffering, our success in raising our children, in *kiruv rechokim* — it's all about seeing the white teeth of every situation, seeing the cup half full.

### Keili, Keili…

I remember many years ago, a friend of mine was going through a very, very difficult situation. I was sitting with him in the *beis midrash*, and he started singing a well-known *niggun*, "*Keili, Keili, lamah azavtani.* Ribono Shel Olam, why have You forsaken me?" And I could feel that he was not just singing the *niggun*, he was living it, experiencing it, feeling pain with the *niggun*…because he felt *lamah azavtani*. I wanted to strengthen him and I did not know what to do or say. But the *Eibishter* gave me a good idea.

I told this *bachur*, "You know, I like you and I'm telling you this out of love. I know you're going through a very challenging situation. But tell me about the good that you're experiencing in your life at this time. Let's try and make a list together."

Suddenly, his face began to shine. "What do you mean, I have plenty of good! I have this and this and this…" Together we made a pretty long list.

Then I said, "You certainly have the right to sing *Keili, Keili, lamah azavtani*. But why don't you change the words a bit and sing *Keili, Keili lamah ahavtani?* Hashem, why do You love me so much, why do You give me so much good? Look at all the good that I have!"

As I was speaking to him, I was inspired myself. Life is all about attitude. One could see what he is missing or see what he has. A person's life-song could be *dayeinu* and neutralize suffering that is worse than death, rejoicing *lamah ahavtani,* or one can cry *lamah azavtani*.

During the last decade of his life, Rav Shimon Schwab was confined to a wheelchair. Rav Schwab had always been a very energetic person, and it was very difficult for him to be disabled. Despite this very challenging situation of life, he was always happy. His grandchild once asked him frankly, "How do you do it?"

Rav Schwab said, "I want to ask you a question. Imagine that someone entrusts you with a large fortune of money and tells you that it's yours to invest, to use for business, or to use however else you please. He tells you that he will eventually come to reclaim whatever money is left, but until that time, the money is, for all practical purposes, yours to use freely.

"Now imagine that you use it for years and years, for decades! One day, the phone rings and your benefactor informs you that he is coming to take back the money. Would you be upset when you return the money, or would you be grateful for the decades that you enjoyed all his money unconditionally?

"I look at life just that way. For years and years, for decades, the *Eibishter* gave me optimum health. Now He took back some of it. Why should I be unhappy? I'm so grateful for all of the years that I *did* have health."

That is a person with an amazing ability to transform *lamah azavtani* into *lamah ahavtani*. To transform תַּמְכָא into תָּמִיד מְסַפְּרִים כְּבוֹד אֵ-ל. To take an unfortunate situation and sing *dayeinu*.

I want to share another important story.

A friend of mine who is a *rav* had a tragedy in his community. A young lady was in an accident and she lost one of her arms. He felt that he had a responsibility to talk to her and to be *mechazek*, to strengthen her. She was a single girl, and now she was in this terrible situation of having only one arm.

The *rav* invited this young lady for Shabbos and set aside time to talk to her. Before he could say a word, she said, "You know, people look at me and they pity me for what I don't have, but I rejoice for what I do have."

When I heard this story I realized that we *all* have the ability to live a life of *dayeinu*, and enjoy the *brachah* of טוֹב לֵב מִשְׁתֶּה תָמִיד. You don't have to be the Steipler, or Rav Pam, or Rav Schwab. In any situation, it is *our choice* if we see the white teeth or the negative. It is up to us, and it is what Shlomo Hamelech — what the Torah itself! — is imploring us to do: Live a life of וְשָׂמַחְתָּ בְּכָל הַטּוֹב.

## Peanut Butter

Imagine: Every day at work, your co-worker pulls out his lunch bag, and takes out a sandwich. And every day, he looks at the sandwich and says, "Peanut butter again! Ugh! I *hate* peanut butter!" And he eats his lunch very grudgingly. This goes on day in, day out, week after week. Finally, you can't take it anymore. This cannot go on! Your co-worker must be suffering from a serious *shalom bayis* problem! You decide to try and help.

You approach him, and begin diplomatically, "I know it's not my business, but I noticed that you don't like peanut butter. Why don't you communicate to your wife that you prefer tuna fish? You don't have to be negative, you can be positive and say something like, 'I really like tuna fish.'"

His response? He looks at you incredulously, and says, "My *wife*?! I'm not married! I pack my own lunches!"

Well, that person does not have a *shalom bayis* problem — he has a much more serious problem. He makes his own sandwich every day and then endures the misery of complaining that he does not like peanut butter! He is a victim of his own doing.

The story, of course, is just a *mashal*. But all too often we are the *nimshal*. We take a day that has so much potential and we choose to make a peanut butter sandwich. We choose to allow negative feelings to dominate our minds and our hearts and we focus on the bad that happened and miss all the good. It is to us that the Torah calls out וְשָׂמַחְתָּ בְכָל הַטּוֹב. Hashem tells us, "I put you in a world of so much *simchah*, with the potential for so much happiness…"

When we come home from work and trip on a toy that a child left on the floor, we may feel an automatic anger surfacing. "Why does this house have to be so topsy-turvy?" But stop for a moment and visualize your friend who does not trip on toys because he doesn't have any toys! And then thank Hashem for the mess. וְשָׂמַחְתָּ בְכָל הַטּוֹב!

Your friend made a mistake? *Baruch Hashem*, last time he did it correctly. Say *dayeinu*! And the same is true of a spouse, or a parent, or an employee. The next time we are upset about something that someone close to us did, instead of lashing out over the bad, thank that person for all of the good that he or she invariably does. It may seem like a surprising reaction on our part, but it is good training; it trains us to see the good. This world is very imperfect, but remember the formula: The city of happiness is in the state of mind. טוֹב לֵב מִשְׁתֶּה תָמִיד is the formula for *simchas hachaim*.

Let me conclude with the following exchange, as related to me by a friend of mine.

My friend Yaakov once observed that Moshe had taken to *davening* a very long *Shemoneh Esrei*. Now, Yaakov knew that Moshe read Hebrew fluently, and he also knew that Moshe was not an overly pious type of person. Such a lengthy *tefillah* seemed unusual for him. The two were very close, and Yaakov felt comfortable approaching Moshe and asking him, frankly, what was taking him so long to *daven*.

Moshe answered, "I am getting older and life is getting challenging. So, when I get to *Modim*, I think about all the good in my life. I made a list of things to thank Hashem for, and I think of each one of them during *Modim*. I think of my health and my family and my friends… and my '*Modim anachnu lach*' takes on so much meaning for me. Since I think along these lines, well, it just takes me a long time to say *Modim*.

What a simple, but profound, practice. And what a practical lesson, an example for us to follow. I am envious of Moshe's beautiful attitude

I am envious of such a person who is living a life of *modeh ani,* who is surrounded by happiness.

\* \* \*

Let us learn the lesson of Shlomo Hamelech, the *chacham m'kol adam.* Let us remember that the city of happiness is in the state of mind. Let us focus on all the good. Let us live a life of *modeh ani.* And may we experience the true *brachah* of טוֹב לֵב מִשְׁתֶּה תָמִיד.

# LITTLE, OLD ME
*Believing in Ourselves*

Rav Shraga Feivel Mendlowitz was once sitting with a group of *talmidim* on the lawn of Beis Midrash Elyon, in Monsey. He turned to one of the *bachurim*, pointed to the ground, and said, "Do you see that large, flat stone there? Turn it over, please." The *bachur* complied.

"Look!" said Rav Shraga Feivel. "What do you see?" he asked the *talmidim*.

The boys looked down, but did not see anything of particular interest, just some ants scurrying about after suddenly losing the protective cover of the stone.

"What do you see?" he repeated. The boys looked down again, but didn't notice anything.

"I will tell you what you see," said Rav Shraga Feivel. "Thirty seconds ago those ants under the rock were living in a world of total darkness. Some of those ants have never left their underground colony. Those ants never saw a sunrise. They never saw a bird; they never saw a tree. When you picked up that stone, you revealed to them a whole new world — you thrust them into a world of brilliant light, a world of so much life!"

Sometimes we hear a *vort* that opens up a whole new world, that thrusts upon us a *lichtigkeit*, a clarity, granting us a new perspective on life. I would like to share with you a thought that I believe does just that, that offers us a new appreciation of the potential built into our lives.

## ⌘ Believing in Yourself

Rav Tzadok Hacohen was one of the great thinkers who lived at the end of the 19th century. He writes (*Tzidkas Hatzaddik* 154) an important point which we must always keep in mind:

כְּשֵׁם שֶׁצָּרִיךְ אָדָם לְהַאֲמִין בְּהַשֵּׁם יִתְבָּרַךְ — *Just as a person must have emunah in Hashem,*

כַּךְ צָרִיךְ אַחַר כַּךְ לְהַאֲמִין בְּעַצְמוֹ — *so, too, a person has to believe in **himself**.*

Rav Tzadok teaches us that there are two parts to *emunah* — believing in Hashem, and believing in oneself. At first glance, this seems shocking. *Emunah* in Hashem, of course, is the cornerstone of *Yiddishkeit*. But to believe in *myself?*

Rav Hutner once made a similar point. In ancient times, he recounted, people were foolish enough to serve idols. The challenge of those times was to resist the lure of investing one's faith in powerless objects. Today we no longer believe in idols, but we face an opposite challenge: We *don't* put value into what *is* a very powerful force. We don't believe in ourselves.

You may be wondering: Why should I believe in myself? What should I believe about myself? I am not a *rosh yeshivah* or a *rav*, I am not a famous personality, I am not a well-known *rebbetzin* — I am just plain, old me. What does it mean that I should believe in myself? And isn't that *ga'avah?*

## ⟋ Holy Bread

What should a person believe about himself? Rav Tzadok explains: הַשֵּׁם יִתְבָּרֵךְ מִתְעַנֵּג וּמִשְׁתַּעֲשֵׁעַ בּוֹ כְּשֶׁעוֹשֶׂה רְצוֹנוֹ — *That Hashem appreciates him, and cherishes his avodah.*

The following moving story, told by Rav Yeruchem Levovitz (*Da'as Torah, Bamidbar* p. 153), can help us begin to appreciate how much Hashem values our service. This story took place during the times of the Arizal, and was recorded by the Maharam Chagiz (*sefer Mishnas Chachamim* §220).

There was a very simple Yid, who we will call Yehudah, who once heard his *rav* speak about the *Lechem Hapanim*. These were the special loaves of bread that were baked weekly in the Beis Hamikdash, and were placed on the golden *Shulchan*, the Table, in the *Kodesh*. The *rav* described this special *avodah*, and how much we are missing by not having it in our times. In his innocent, and perhaps foolish, way, Yehudah thought to himself, *I will bring the missing Lechem Hapanim!*

Now, of course, this is impossible. We have no Beis Hamikdash, and no *Kodesh*, and no *Shulchan*. But this simple Yid decided that every Friday he would bake challos, and place them into the shul's *aron hakodesh*, and that will be the *Lechem Hapanim*.

The next Friday he did just that. He waited until late in the afternoon, when he knew that everyone was busy at home preparing for Shabbos. Then he entered the shul, placed the two freshly baked challos in the *aron*, and tearfully *davened* to Hashem to accept his *Lechem Hapanim*.

When Yehudah returned after Shabbos, the challos were gone. Yehudah believed that Hashem had accepted his offering. With even more excitement, he placed his challos in the shul the next Friday as well. And the same thing happened — on Motza'ei Shabbos, the challos were gone. Every Friday Yehudah brought his "*Lechem Hapanim*," and *davened* that Hashem accept them. And every Motza'ei Shabbos they were gone.

One Friday afternoon, the *rav* was in the shul as Yehudah brought his challos, and he asked Yehudah what he was doing.

Upon hearing the explanation, the *rav* told Yehudah that this can't be true. "But, Rebbe," said Yehudah, "every Friday I bring my *Lechem Hapanim*, and after Shabbos they are gone."

"Nonsense!" said the *rav*. "If the challos are removed every week, it must be that the *shamash*, who comes to clean the shul, finds them and eats them. Let's wait and see."

Just then the *shamash* entered the shul. Sure enough, the *shamash* went to the *aron hakodesh* and took his weekly treat.

Yehudah was crushed. How silly he had been! He thought he was offering *Lechem Hapanim*, and look what was really happening.

Shortly after this incident, the holy Arizal had a dream. In the dream, it was revealed to him that there were great indictments on the *rav* because he stopped this Jew from bringing his *Lechem Hapanim*.

And here I quote the words of the Arizal, as recorded by Maharam Chagiz: מִיּוֹם שֶׁחָרַב הַבַּיִת לֹא הָיָה נַחַת רוּחַ לְהקב"ה כְּמוֹ בְּאוֹתָה שָׁעָה שֶׁהָיָה זֶה מֵבִיא שְׁתֵּי הַלֶּחֶם בִּתְמִימוּת לִבּוֹ — *Since the destruction of the Beis Hamikdash, Hashem had not experienced such a nachas ruach, as when this person brought his Lechem Hapanim with such a pure heart.*

If we do not relate to this story, it is because we do not believe in ourselves, or in the greatness we can achieve. We do not understand the importance of what we do. The Maharam Chagiz recorded this occurrence to teach us the ultimate truth in *avodas Hashem*: Greatness is not measured by titles, popularity, or fame — greatness is defined by a person doing all that he is capable of doing. Yehudah was, obviously, a simple Jew; he was not able to reach a high level of Torah knowledge or *avodah*. But with his devotion and sincerity, his *temimus*, and his simple love for Hashem — and even with his expression of those feelings in a fashion that could rightfully be called wrong and foolish — he performed an exalted *avodah*, an *avodah* whose *chashivus* in the eyes of Hashem was unparalleled for almost 1,500 years!

Yehudah attained greatness because he was doing everything that he was capable of doing.

## All That You Can Be

Rabbeinu Yonah wrote a classic *sefer Sha'arei Ha'avodah*, which is a veritable guide for every Jew. His opening remarks are: A person must realize his self-worth.

He then adds: Each and every one of us is required to strive to attain the greatness of the tzaddikim and *chassidim*. And we can do it.

But, asks Rabbeinu Yonah, how can we do that? How do we dare compare ourselves to the great *gedolim*? Rabbeinu Yonah answers that all one is expected to do is to fully utilize his *kochos*:

כַּאֲשֶׁר יַעֲבוֹד כְּמוֹתָם כָּל יְמֵי חַיָּיו כְּפִי כֹחוֹ וְהַשָּׂגָתוֹ — *He must serve [Hashem] as they did, all the days of his life, according to his capability and capacity...*

כִּי הָקֵל יִתְבָּרַךְ אֵינוֹ מְבַקֵּשׁ מִבְּנֵי אָדָם כִּי אִם לְפִי כֹּחָם — *for Hashem only asks and expects from a person a service that is commensurate with his abilities.*

The true definition of a great person is someone who is using all of his abilities. Certainly, the greater one's capabilities, the greater is his mission. More is expected of a brilliant *rosh yeshivah*, a *chashuve rav*, or a great *tzaddekes*. But the rest of Klal Yisrael, each and every member of it, can also reach greatness if they take full advantage of their potential and capabilities.

In truth, this is really the depth of the famous words of the Ramchal in his classic *sefer Mesillas Yesharim*. He begins the *sefer* with the statement that the first step in a person's journey toward *shleimus* (spiritual completion) in his *avodas Hashem* is to clarify for himself: מַה חוֹבָתוֹ בְּעוֹלָמוֹ.

Look at those words, how accurate and meaningful they are.

What is חוֹבָתוֹ — *your* obligation, בְּעוֹלָמוֹ — in *your* world?

This is a fully subjective exercise — *your* mission in *your* world. There are so many variables to consider: your health, intelligence, financial status, difficulties, strengths and weaknesses… But in the final analysis, your greatness will be measured by how well you lived up to חוֹבָתוֹ בְּעוֹלָמוֹ — *your obligation in your world*.

This thought is echoed in our *tefillos* on Rosh Hashanah when we say that Hashem "זוֹכֵר מַעֲשֵׂה אִישׁ וּפְקוּדָתוֹ." Simply translated this means Hashem remembers "the actions of man and his remembrance." But the *mussar sefarim* explain that the word וּפְקוּדָתוֹ also derives from the word *pikadon*, something entrusted to someone. This is a reference to a person's unique mission in the life which has been entrusted to him.

Not everybody can be a *gadol hador* or a *rosh yeshivah*. But if one is true to his own mission, if he is doing the best he can, then his greatness is comparable to the greatness of the *gedolei olam*. This is what both Rabbeinu Yonah and the Ramchal meant to convey to us in their opening statements.

Individuals, especially young people, are often unhappy with themselves. When I hear someone complaining that he wishes that he were someone else, I tell him, "You're not happy with what you are, but you can't be someone else. Why not become yourself? Become the real you with your full potential realized."

## No Mistakes

Every good writer ends his written work with his strongest message, the idea that he wants the reader to internalize and hopefully eternalize. We have seen the opening remark of the *Mesillas Yesharim*; now let us look at the end of that remarkable work. What is the grand finale — the closing comment of the *Mesillas Yesharim*?

יָכוֹל לִהְיוֹת חָסִיד גָּמוּר אִישׁ אֲשֶׁר לֹא יִפְסוֹק מִפִּיו הַלִּמּוּד כְּמוֹ מִי שֶׁמִּפְּנֵי צָרְכּוֹ הוּא בַּעַל מְלָאכָה פְּחוּתָה — *It is possible for a "blue-collar worker," engaged in menial work, to be a chassid, a completely righteous person, comparable to the talmid chacham that does not stop learning.*

How can that be? Even though the blue-collar worker is occupied with work all day, if every spare moment is devoted to learning he is considered as having attained the greatness of *gedolim*. He is compared to the *talmid chacham* because they both spend all of their available time learning.

What a profound thought. Hashem gives every person a fair chance; each individual has his own "חוֹבָתוֹ בְּעוֹלָמוֹ."

The *sefer Pele Yo'etz* (*Ahavah*) makes a remarkable statement: A person's biggest enemy is the feeling of a lack of self-worth.

This is so very true, because life is a self-fulfilling prophecy. If you believe that your actions are important, you will strive to succeed. If you are convinced that you're a nothing, then you will accomplish nothing. And eventually you will be just that — a nothing.

One may think, *Who says I have an important mission to fulfill... I'm just "little, old me." I'm not a great person.* That is a grave error. A lack of self-respect is not *anavah*, it is not humility — it is a lack of *emunah*. One who thinks this way obviously does not believe that Hashem has given him a fair chance to be a true success. He is weak in his belief that there are no mistakes in Hashem's world. He has failed to fully internalize the truth that Hashem created him the way he is, and that He only expects from him that which he is entirely capable of.

A person must believe in himself and in the important role that he plays in this world. This is not *ga'avah*. *Ga'avah* is when a person feels haughty about past accomplishments; this is an improper feeling. But *ga'avah* for the future is very necessary. וַיִּגְבַּהּ לִבּוֹ בְּדַרְכֵי ה׳. — *His heart was elevated in the ways of Hashem* (*II Divrei Hayamim* 17:6). This is a feeling called *ga'avah d'kedushah* — a burning desire to be all we can be.

The Rambam on the Mishnah in *Avos* (2:13) that says that one should not consider himself a *rasha*, explains that one won't refrain from sinning if he feels that his actions don't make a difference. One must believe in himself. This double *emunah* — *emunah* in Hashem and *emunah* in oneself — is essential for life.

## ⚜ Raise Your Hand

Rav Shach related the following story, which is recorded in the *pinkas* (the chronicles) of the Vilna community.

The Vilna Gaon's *rebbetzin* had a friend with whom she used to collect money to distribute to needy families. Once, they made an agreement, that whoever dies first would return to the survivor in a dream and relate what is taking place in the *Olam Ha'emes*. The *rebbetzin's* friend died first, and, shortly after her demise, she appeared in a dream to the Vilna Gaon's wife and told her, "You cannot fathom the *s'char* (reward) in the *Olam Ha'emes*. But let me give you an inkling…" And she went on to remind her of an episode that had occurred years earlier:

"Do you remember the time that we went to the home of a wealthy woman to ask for a donation but she was not in? A while later as we were walking, you spotted her across the street. So you raised your hand to point to her. We then both crossed the street, and asked her for *tzedakah*, which she happily gave us.

"We are both receiving *s'char* for going to her home. We are both receiving *s'char* for crossing the street, to solicit her donation. But for that particular solicitation, you will receive a greater reward than me! Do you know why? It is because you lifted your hand to point to her whereas I did not do so."

We can't imagine the merit that awaits us just for lifting a hand in *avodas Hashem*. Believing in oneself is the conviction that my every action is truly significant. It doesn't just make a difference. It makes all the difference.

## ⚜ Who Am I?

The *Mesillas Yesharim* (ch. 19) discusses an incredible insight regarding *davening*:

וְאִם יֹאמַר אָדָם מִי אֲנִי וּמָה אֲנִי סָפוּן שֶׁאֶתְפַּלֵּל עַל הַגָּלוּת וְעַל יְרוּשָׁלַיִם הֲמִפְּנֵי תְּפִלָּתִי יְכָנְסוּ הַגָּלִיּוֹת וְתִצְמַח הַיְשׁוּעָה — *And if a man will say, "Who am I that I should daven that the galus should end and that Yerushalayim should be rebuilt? Will my tefillah* make a difference? Will my *tefillah* cause the exiles to be gathered in, and the redemption to occur?"

The *Mesillas Yesharim* continues:

תְּשׁוּבָתוֹ בְּצִדּוֹ, כְּאוֹתָהּ שֶׁשָּׁנִינוּ (סנהדרין לז, א) לְפִיכָךְ נִבְרָא אָדָם יְחִידִי כְּדֵי שֶׁכָּל אֶחָד יֹאמַר בִּשְׁבִילִי נִבְרָא הָעוֹלָם — *The answer is to be found in the Mishnah (Sanhedrin 37a): humankind was brought forth through one individual man, Adam Harishon, in order to teach us that every person in required to say, "The world was created just for me!"*

This magnificent world was created just for me. My *davening* is important, my *chessed* is important, my refraining from sin is important.

In the *sefer Nefesh Hachaim* (1:3), Rav Chaim Volozhiner describes the cosmic effect that our actions have. When we do a good deed, we build *olamos* (spiritual worlds); and when, *chas v'shalom*, we sin, our improper actions wreak havoc and destruction in the *olamos*.

He then presents a very striking explanation on the exhortation of the Mishnah in *Avos* (2:1) דַּע מַה לְמַעְלָה מִמָּךְ — *Know that which is above you.*

Says Rav Chaim Volozhiner:

דַּע מַה לְמַעְלָה — *know that what is going on in the other world, in the Upper Spheres,*

מִמָּךְ — *is from* **you!**

Your actions have an enormous effect. With your good deeds, you are building worlds, and a person's sins are destroying worlds.

YES! Little, old me can build worlds.

When Rav Hutner taught this piece in the *Nefesh Hachaim* he became very emotional.

"We have the ability to create worlds with our actions. *Bachurim!*" he cried out, "*Ihr zen doch borei olamos* — you are builders of worlds!"

He was making a play on words, conveying the message that we all have the capacity to resemble the *Borei Olam*. That is *emunah* in oneself.

When a person chances upon an immodest scene on the street, and he turns his eyes from viewing those immodest images, he is building worlds. When a person travels on a train or plane and he takes out a *sefer* to learn, he is building worlds. When one is tempted to say *lashon hara*, or something nasty, but controls himself, he will merit, in the words of the Midrash (quoted in *Iggeres Ha'Gra*), לָאוֹר הַגָּנוּז שֶׁאֵין כָּל מַלְאָךְ וּבְרִיָּה יְכוֹלִים לְשַׁעֵר — *the "hidden light" that even angels cannot fathom.*

That is *emunah b'atzmo*. "Little, old me" is not so little, after all.

The *pasuk* (*Bereishis* 1:31) says: וַיַּרְא אֱלֹקִים אֶת כָּל אֲשֶׁר עָשָׂה וְהִנֵּה טוֹב מְאֹד — *And Hashem saw all that He created and, behold, it was very good.*

What is *tov me'od*, the quintessential good? Says the Midrash (*Bereishis Rabbah* 9): טוֹב מְאֹד, זֶה אָדָם — *"it was very good," this refers to Man.*

The Midrash continues: How is it that טוֹב מְאֹד refers to man? Because the letters of אָדָם — *aleph, daled, mem* — are the same as the letters of the word מְאֹד.

This Midrash is difficult to understand. We define אָדָם as מְאֹד just because the two words have the same letters? What does this mean?

Rav Hutner explained this as follows: Everything in Creation is limited. Food lasts a certain amount of days; clothing lasts longer; a house lasts even longer. But everything decays and eventually falls apart; everything is limited. There is only one aspect in Creation whose essence is unlimited — a human being. אָדָם is the essence of מְאֹד, of more and more and more. An individual can keep climbing higher; he can be as successful as he dreams of becoming. אָדָם is מְאֹד; our potential and our capabilities are limitless.

## ❦ A World of Opportunities

Look at the world around us — by doing a small *chessed*, we build *olamos*. By withholding a sharp or negative comment, we merit the *ohr haganuz*. This world is one of unlimited opportunities, and a person, by his nature, by his very essence, has unlimited potential.

It is well known that before the Vilna Gaon passed on, he started crying. Those at his bedside asked him, "Why is Rebbi crying?"

The Gaon answered, "I am crying because I am leaving this world — a world where, for a few small coins (here the Gaon picked up the strings of his *tzitzis*), you can have a mitzvah!"

The Gaon saw this world as a world of unlimited opportunity.

People often say, "*Ach. Ah meshugene velt!* A crazy world!" This outlook is not the way we should approach life. It is not a crazy world; it is a wonderful world of unlimited opportunity. And I, in my very essence, have unlimited potential to transform אָדָם into מְאֹד. I am certain the Gaon would never say it is a *meshugene velt*.

We are familiar with the *pasuk*: צַדִּיק יְסוֹד עוֹלָם (*Mishlei* 10:25). What does this mean? On a simple level, it means that a great tzaddik is a foundation of the world. That is true, but there is more to it. The Chazon Ish once commented that there exists a concept of a momentary צַדִּיק יְסוֹד עוֹלָם. We are all faced at times with the sudden temptation to do something wrong. When one has such a *nisayon* — whether it is in maintaining *kedushah*, in his financial dealings, or in any area of *avodah* — and is struggling mightily to overcome it and no one will ever know if he succeeded or failed, yet he musters all of his strength and he overcomes the desire to sin, **at that moment he is the** צַדִּיק יְסוֹד עוֹלָם. That triumph, that victory in achieving the almost impossible, earns him that most exalted title.

Perhaps, that is the message of the Arizal mentioned previously. "Yehudah" in the story, with his *Lechem Hapanim*, was a צַדִּיק יְסוֹד עוֹלָם.

## ❧ *Ana, Ana, Ana...*

The secular society espouses the insane theory of "evolution." Why would any human being want to believe that his grandfather was a monkey?! It is madness! But they actually claim to believe this, and the reason they do so is because they do not want to feel any obligations or restrictions. They reason, "What am I, anyway? I come from a monkey." That is why they can act and dress any way they desire. If a person feels he is worth nothing, he acts like a "nothing." A "*bas melech*" must dress properly. A "*bas* monkey" doesn't have to.

A boy once showed me a gaudy T-shirt, with a very funny design. "What is wrong with wearing this?" he asked me.

I countered with my own question: "Would you put this on a *sefer Torah*? Would you use this *schmatteh* as the *mantel*? So why do you put it on yourself? Are you any less *heilig*? Aren't you a living *sefer Torah*?" (see *Shabbos* 105b). That is the principle of *emunah b'atzmo* at work.

Did you ever watch someone walking to shul to *daven*? All too often one is sluggish, lethargic; he is going so slow he is almost going backward. Do you know what the root of the problem is? He doesn't believe in himself; he doesn't believe in the importance and potential of his *davening*. If he believed in the words of the *Mesillas Yesharim* that his *davening* can make all the difference, he would run to shul to *daven*. This is *emunah b'atzmo*, and it has to be our attitude as we go about our daily lives.

Rav Yeruchem Levovitz used to say, "Woe to the person that does not know his shortcomings. But even worse, woe to someone who does not know his capabilities and his *ma'alos*!"

דַּע מַה לְמַעְלָה — מִמְּךָ!

The *pasuk* (*Amos* 4:13) says: וּמַגִּיד לְאָדָם מַה שֵּׂחוֹ. Simply, this is referring to the Day of Judgment when Hashem will tell a person the words that he has said throughout his lifetime. However, the *Nefesh Hachaim* (*sha'ar aleph*, ch. 13) gives a unique interpretation of the *pasuk*. A person has to be told now, מַה שֵּׂחוֹ, *the value of his words*. He needs to deeply comprehend the importance of each word of his Torah study. He must understand how essential his *davening* is. He has to appreciate how important every word that he utters is. All of this is part of *emunah b'atzmo*.

During the *hakafos* on Simchas Torah, one of the popular songs is אֲנָא עַבְדָּא דְקוּדְשָׁא בְּרִיךְ הוּא — *I am a servant of Hashem*. Typically, the first word, *ana*, is repeated several times: "*Ana, ana, ana, avda d'Kudashah Brich Hu*..." Someone once asked me, "Why do we have to stress *ana, ana, ana*? We should sing *Ana **avda, avda, avda** d'Kudashah Brich Hu*... Wouldn't that be more appropriate?" I answered, "You are right, but I think our generation has to sing it this way; we have to put an emphasis on **ana, ana, ana** — me, little, old me. I am important, I count, I am part of the Master Plan. I, too, am *borei olamos*."

In order to be successful, an individual must feel good about himself. One should go to sleep with a sense of accomplishment, with a feeling that he did something worthwhile over the course of his day. A person who ends his day that way will rise with a renewed sense of purpose, and a burning sense of mission to accomplish. If a person lives with the fire of *Ana, ana, ana avda d'Kudashah Brich Hu* then he is living *ga'avah d'kedushah*. He thereby *davens* differently, learns Torah differently, and speaks and acts differently.

The Mishnah (*Sanhedrin* 4:5) requires every person to say, "בִּשְׁבִילִי נִבְרָא הָעוֹלָם," the world in all of its magnificence and all its glory was created just for me! The *ko'ach* of one individual can make all the difference.

## ❧ Safety Seals and Power Balls

Sometimes it is hard to relate to this idea. Can one person really make a difference? Consider this example:

I remember the time when food and medicine were sold in jars without the plastic seal that is commonly used today. Nowadays, most products are packaged with a seal. The reason for this change was because, quite a few years ago, a madman put poison into Tylenol capsules, and several people died when they bought and ingested the pills. The country was in uproar, and laws were passed requiring safety seals to prevent recurrences of this crime.

Think about it — millions, or probably billions — of dollars have been spent in the food and medicine industry to create and produce various types of seals and protective wrappings, and to incorporate them into the packaging process. All because of one individual. One man — albeit an insane person, a murderer — changed the world. And we know *middah tovah merubah* — good has more potential than evil. So we must consider what one person could do in the realm of good: how he could be *borei olamos*, how his *tefillah* could bring the *Geulah*. We have to believe in the *ko'ach* of a *yachid* — little, old me.

Let me conclude with something that Rav Yeruchem Levovitz said. This passage should be required reading; it is printed in Rav Yeruchem's *sefer Da'as Torah* (*Bamidbar* p. 146):

We all anticipate Mashiach, we all eagerly await Mashiach. Who will Mashiach be? We think he will probably be Avraham Avinu, or maybe Rabbi Akiva — someone of that stature. But, no, that is not true; Mashiach will be from our own generation. How can that be?

Moshe Rabbeinu could not be a Mashiach, Rabbi Akiva could not be a Mashiach — can our generation of such darkness produce a Mashiach? Rav Yeruchem reveals the secret:

*Ohr*, light, is an outgrowth of darkness. The more darkness there is, the more *ohr* can be produced. An individual who overcomes greater difficulties, greater struggles, and more challenges in life, has the ability to create an even more brilliant *ohr*, an even more glorious *lichtigkeit*, than someone who lived in a generation of higher spiritual attunement. The generations of Moshe Rabbeinu and Rabbi Akiva, in all of their greatness, did not have our *nisyonos*. Specifically our generation, with all of its darkness, has the ability to produce the *ohr* that we call *yemos haMashiach*.

What a powerful lesson. We live in a generation of so much darkness, and of unprecedented *nisyonos*. Part of *emunah b'atzmo* is to believe that we — and only we — have the opportunity to create an unparalleled *lichtigkeit* with our actions. We can create this *lichtigkeit* **because** of our *nisyonos*, not in spite of them. One is tempted to think, "How can we compare our paltry *avodas Hashem*, or our mitzvos, to the generation of the Arizal, the Vilna Gaon, or the Chafetz Chaim?" Such a thought is lacking in *emunah*. We have to believe that *because* of our generation's unprecedented darkness, we have the opportunity to create a *lichtigkeit* that no previous generation was able to produce.

We live in a world that is in a perpetual frenzy over big lottery winnings. You can win millions of dollars in one moment. I believe that there is a very profound and practical message that we must learn from this.

How much is the actual lottery ticket (cardboard) worth? Not even a penny. But if that ticket is drawn, suddenly this little slip of cardboard is worth millions of dollars.

When Mashiach comes, all of our mitzvos, which we thought were worth so little, and which we thought to be so insignificant, will be like those lottery tickets. At that time, we will look back in awe; we were in a generation of such darkness, yet we still performed all of those mitzvos. And every one of those mitzvos will be a Powerball ticket that will suddenly be transformed into an item of unfathomable value.

These mitzvos contributed to the long awaited *lichtigkeit* of Melech haMashiach. This is what we have to believe about ourselves, and our contribution to the world's Master Plan. If we work hard, if we each do the best we can, our contribution will be astounding. And we will once again be privileged to see the *Lechem Hapanim* in the Beis Hamikdash.

Little, old me is not so little after all.

# "DO I HAVE TO?"

*Harnessing the Power of Ratzon*

---

The great *Amora* Rava was sitting and studying Torah. He was so absorbed in his learning that he did not realize that he was crushing his thumbs, and bleeding.

A *Tzeduki* (a heretical Sadducee) was witnessing the scene.

"*Ama peziza!*" he cried. "You reckless nation. You hasty and impulsive people. You are the same nation that said '*Na'aseh v'nishma*' and accepted the Torah before finding out what it entails. And you're still reckless and impulsive! Look at you, Rava! You are drawing your own blood and you don't even notice it!"

Hakadosh Baruch Hu had a different reaction when He heard the *Yidden's* declaration of *Na'aseh v'nishma*:

"Who taught My children this secret — the secret of *Na'aseh v'nishma*? That is something for the *giborei ko'ach* — the very angels in heaven! Where did they learn this from (*Shabbos* 86a)?"

Given the high praise that the *Yidden* received from Hashem, the *Tzeduki's* accusation is all the more startling. Are we a reckless nation? Was this *apikores* right?

He was, and he wasn't…

## ◈ In the Valley of Death

A while ago I came across an incredible *sefer* called *M'ma'amakim*. This is a five-volume set of *She'eilos U'teshuvos*, questions that were asked to the author, Rabbi Ephraim Oshry, the unofficial *rav* of the Kovno Ghetto during the Holocaust. In the author's words, these were questions that were asked "in the valley of death" — in the gehinnom of Nazi occupation.

If you want to feel really proud to be part of the Jewish nation, I advise you to look into this incredible work. There you will see the truly remarkable greatness of Klal Yisrael.

A young boy, clearly no older than twelve years old, came to the *rav* and asked, "May I begin to put on *tefillin?*"

"Surely you know that we only begin to put on *tefillin* right before the age of thirteen," said the *rav*. "Why do you think you should begin so early?"

"Well," replied the boy, "usually we do not put on *tefillin* when we are twelve years old because we will put them on at our bar mitzvah. But I'm afraid I won't live until my bar mitzvah! And I also want to put on *tefillin!*"

This story is heartrending, but so inspiring. A twelve-year-old boy staring the Malach Hamaves straight in the face and all he is worried about is doing the mitzvah of *tefillin!*

There is another story in that *sefer* about a Yid named Moshe Goldkorn. Reb Moshe came to Rabbi Oshry right after Chanukah and said, "*Rebbi!* It's almost Pesach!"

"Almost Pesach?" wondered the *rav*. "It's just after Chanukah!"

"*Rebbi!* We have to begin now to make sure that we have matzah for Pesach!"

Rabbi Oshry looked at him. "Matzah in the ghetto? *Oneis rachmana patrei* — in our circumstances we are exempt!"

"But I have a plan!" said Reb Moshe. "I am part of a work detail that is stationed outside the ghetto. If I smuggle in a little bit of flour every day I could probably make matzah. But you understand, I am escorted back and forth under Nazi guard, and if they detect this they will kill me."

"What is your question?" asked the *rav*.

"*Rebbi*, I will be endangering myself, but I want to do this. Is it halachically permissible?"

Rabbi Oshry ruled that he was permitted to do so.

Reb Moshe went through with it. Incredibly, when Pesach arrived he had baked — in the ghetto! — almost one hundred matzos! Day in and day out for almost four months he lived in fear of being apprehended, yet he smuggled in enough flour for almost one hundred matzos! Mostly for others!

One day, right before Pesach, as he entered the ghetto he was caught with some flour. The Nazi guards didn't realize that he was using it to bake matzah, and therefore they didn't shoot him on the spot. They thought he was simply being "greedy" and stealing some food. They beat him mercilessly and they knocked out all of his teeth. They told him sarcastically: "You want more to eat? Now try to eat! Don't ever smuggle food again!"

Reb Moshe came back to Rabbi Oshry crying like a baby. His tears did not flow as a complaint against Hashem. He did not cry over the tragedy of *tzaddik v'ra lo*, because something so terrible happened to him. He was crying because he was worried about his next question for the *rav*:

"How can I eat matzah now? I have no teeth! Other people could soak the matzah in water and swallow it. But *rebbi!*" wailed Reb Moshe, "my *minhag* is not to eat *gebrokts*. Am I allowed to disregard my *minhag* in these extenuating circumstances?"

*Mi k'amcha Yisrael.*

The above stories are examples of simple people doing things that don't seem to make sense, and that even seem to border on the impossible. How did they manage to do the impossible? By living *Na'aseh v'nishma!* By rising to the challenge like a lion.

Imagine telling this story to a non-Jew. "He risked his life for matzos? And then bewailed his fate only because he could not eat them for his mitzvah? You impulsive, reckless nation!"

## ☙ Like Lions

Do you know what is the very first halachah of the four sections of *Shulchan Aruch*? The *Shulchan Aruch* quotes the words of the Tur:

יִתְגַּבֵּר כַּאֲרִי — *Rise up like a lion,*

לַעֲמֹד בַּבֹּקֶר לַעֲבוֹדַת בּוֹרְאוֹ — *to arise in the morning for the service of your Creator.*

This first halachah, which prefaces the entire *daled chelkei Shulchan Aruch*, is a golden rule which must be at the forefront of a Jew's consciousness as he journeys through life: יִתְגַּבֵּר כַּאֲרִי.

Why a lion? The lion is not the strongest animal, nor the biggest animal.

The Taz seems to be bothered by this question: Why the analogy to a lion? The Taz explains, a lion may not be the strongest animal, but a lion is the most *fearless* animal. It is not the biggest or mightiest, but it rises up and roars! And that is the lion's *gevurah* — its courage and defiance.

## ✿ True *Ratzon*

The greatest strength of the Jewish nation is called *ratzon*. אֵין דָּבָר הָעוֹמֵד בִּפְנֵי הָרָצוֹן — *nothing stands in the way of ratzon*; when a Jew taps into this inner *ratzon* he is unstoppable.

What does *ratzon* mean?

*Ratzon* is not a superficial, spontaneous "desire" to do what is right. *Ratzon* means a commitment and a **determination** to do right, based on an appreciation of the value and the **privilege** of doing right.

There are difficulties involved in doing good; this world is a world of challenges and *nisyonos*. But when someone looks at a challenge and says: "This is a small price to pay for such a big mitzvah"; if someone understands, as the *Sefer Chareidim* says, that every mitzvah is a *doron*, a gift, he is able to harness the power of *ratzon*. And when he does so, he experiences the unlimited *brachah* of אֵין דָּבָר הָעוֹמֵד בִּפְנֵי הָרָצוֹן.

That is יִתְגַּבֵּר כַּאֲרִי. That is a nation of lions who stands proudly, defiantly, and courageously and who does what is right no matter what the consequences may be. That is a nation that is unstoppable and unconquerable.

Try telling a non-Jew that thousands of men, women, and children live lives free of *lashon hara*. He won't believe it, especially in America where character assassination is a constitutional right. But we are doing it!

In the Gemara in *Maseches Shabbos* (cited above), Rava responded to the *Tzeduki*, "We go with *temimus*, with a simple and sincere faith in Hashem."

Rashi explains Rava's reply: We have faith in Hashem that He won't ask us to do the impossible.

If Hashem gave us the Torah, He expects us to follow it. And that means that we *can* do it. And if we *can* do it, we *will* do it. That is *ratzon*.

The Alter from Novaradok once said something that is so practical and helpful in all aspects of daily living:

"When I come to a challenging or difficult situation, I never ask, 'Can I do this?' Instead I ask, 'Must I do this?' If I am required to do it, then I *can* do it, and then I *will* do it!"

That's the secret of *Na'aseh v'nishma*. יִתְגַּבֵּר כַּאֲרִי means to look at a situation and to say: If I have to do it I will do it! It means to stand proudly and courageously, to declare fearlessly and defiantly, "If I have to, I *will*!"

We are not a reckless nation; we are a very sensible nation. But we are also a very committed, devoted, and determined nation. We feel the privilege in every word of Torah that we are connected to, and we fulfill the entire Torah because we have the *ratzon*, and are empowered with that unstoppable force of אֵין דָּבָר הָעוֹמֵד בִּפְנֵי הָרָצוֹן.

But you can't explain that to a *Tzeduki*. You can't explain *Na'aseh v'nishma* to an *apikores* because it doesn't make sense. From a realistic and practical perspective, the *Tzeduki* was right. But in reality he was totally wrong. We are not an *ama peziza*, we are *giborei ko'ach*. In Hashem's eyes, we are like angels, like His *malachim*.

The Jewish People accepted the Torah, and said *Na'aseh v'nishma*. They accepted what they did not know because they had the *emunah* that Hashem does not ask the impossible. If we have to do it, we will do it. This is the secret of Klal Yisrael, the secret of *netzach Yisrael*, the indestructible existence of Klal Yisrael.

## Does It Make Sense?

A number of years ago I received a phone call from a woman whom I did not know. She told me her history; she was a single mother raising a large family who basically survived on welfare. And then she asked me a question that took me by surprise.

"How do I take off *ma'aser*, the required tenth, from my welfare check?"

I told her, "I don't think you have to give *ma'aser* in your situation."

She told me politely but very firmly, "I didn't ask you if I have to or not. I *want* to. What I am asking you is *how* do I calculate how much I have to give?"

Does it make sense? A single mother, raising a large family, and subsisting on government programs, who wants to give *ma'aser*? A woman who is barely surviving, yet she is willing to give a tenth of the food out of her mouth, and the mouths of her children, to *tzedakah*? If a non-Jew would see this, he would exclaim: "You *ama peziza*! You don't have what to live on and you're giving to others?" But he doesn't realize that we are a nation of lions. We appreciate and cherish every mitzvah — especially the mitzvah of *ma'aser kesafim*. This woman simply did not want to lose the opportunity for this lofty mitzvah.

And some people have so much but "can't afford" to give *ma'aser*. They have a plentiful income, but they have to put away for this and for that, which leaves them with nothing left for *tzedakah*. Is it because they lack the money? Or it is because they lack the *ratzon*? They do not appreciate the sacred mitzvah of *ma'aser*, a mitzvah that makes the giver a partner with Hashem.

## Sacrificing for Torah

Does it make sense to see men with full-time jobs devoting many hours of their day to learning Torah?

Not from a practical point of view. But that is *Na'aseh v'nishma* at work.

Perhaps a more compelling question is this: Does it make sense that a woman who has not seen her husband all day willingly sends him out to learn in the evening? He has been at work all day, and comes home for a few minutes to eat supper. In truth, his wife needs him, she needs his help around the house, and his help with the children, but she encourages him with *simchah* to go out and learn! Does that make sense? Imagine the reaction of a non-Jew who would see this: "He comes home, and a few minutes later he's out the door? You're an *ama peziza*, a rash nation!"

The non-Jew can't understand it because he doesn't know what we know. He does not know that חַיֵּי עוֹלָם נָטַע בְּתוֹכֵנוּ. He doesn't realize that כִּי הֵם חַיֵּינוּ וְאֹרֶךְ יָמֵינוּ. He cannot fathom that when we learn Torah we are making an "eternal living."

The root of true *ratzon* is the appreciation of the value of what we do and how privileged we are to do it.

* Two women once met at a family *simchah* — one was wealthy, and the other was poor. The poor relative complimented her cousin on her new magnificent ring. "It was a gift from my husband," explained the wealthy woman. The other woman smiled and said, "My husband also recently gave me a beautiful gift!"

"What was it?" asked her curious cousin.

"He gave me the gift of *Maseches Shabbos*. I send him out to learn, and he just finished learning *Maseches Shabbos*!"

* A young man who had recently left yeshivah to go to work made a lot of money very quickly. An old friend of his asked him, "Nu, how's it going?" He replied, "Today I made a nice few thousand dollars, but believe me, it doesn't come close to the *simchah* that I had from a full day's learning in yeshivah!"

This is why the *Am haTorah* is flourishing today — because there are people like these. In a world that is in pursuit of unbridled pleasure, we have *giborei ko'ach* who realize that the most beautiful gem is a *blatt Gemara*! People who are actually living טוֹב לִי תוֹרַת פִּיךָ מֵאַלְפֵי זָהָב וָכָסֶף.

## ⌒ The Privilege of *Tefillah*

I once observed an individual who *davens* the way a person is supposed to *daven*. He always arrived early and stayed beyond the conclusion of *davening*. I was envious of his *davening*. He must have noticed that I was observing him and he turned to me and said, "If you give me a *heter* to *daven* again, I'll give you a hundred dollars cash on the spot!"

He said it as a joke, of course. But he meant it. His comment spoke volumes of his appreciation for *davening*. He understood the privilege of *tefillah*, and he took great pleasure from *tefillah*. He was running to work like the rest of the *minyan*. But he would *daven* a careful and proper Shacharis, and a meaningful *Shemoneh Esrei*.

And then there are people who cannot find the time to learn, or to stay in shul until the conclusion of *davening*. Is it because they don't have time or because they don't have the *ratzon*?

If one starts from a pragmatic point of view, he might become discouraged. If I ask myself, "Can I do it?" my answer might be, "No, I can't! I can't find time to learn, or to stay in shul. I can't commit to things that are beyond me!" But I don't do that. I ask, "Do I *have* to do it? If I have to do it, then I *can* do it, and I *will* do it!"

## Overcoming the Obstacles

I was recently inspired by one of my family members who was struggling with a certain *tznius* issue. She was undergoing that oldest of challenges: She knew what the right thing to do was, but so many of her contemporaries did not do it. "Why do I have to be different?" she asked.

It certainly is very difficult to be different and to stick out. But do you know what this brave young woman did? She said, "*Na'aseh v'nishma!* — if this is the right thing to do then I have to do it. And if I have to do it, who cares what everybody else does?"

It was hard, and it meant going against the tide, but she fulfilled the injunction of יִתְגַּבֵּר כַּאֲרִי! She rose proudly and did it, and continues to do it, and continues to inspire me because she successfully tapped into the unstoppable force of *Na'aseh v'nishma*.

## A Nation of Lions

At the bar mitzvah of one of my sons, which took place on Sukkos, a well-known *rav* recounted the following incident. A member of his shul visited his grandchildren's sukkah which was beautifully decorated. With great emotion, he told them, "My *zeidy's* sukkah wasn't as decorated; all it had were pink slips. But it was more beautiful." And then he explained: Finding a job during the depression years was so difficult, because maintaining it was conditional with working on Shabbos. When his *zeidy* came to work the next week, he was fired because of his absence on Shabbos and was handed a "pink slip." When he came home, he would wave the pink slip ecstatically. "Look what I got because of the *heilige Shabbos!*"

And he kept these "medals of honor" for a special occasion. When Sukkos arrived, he used them to decorate the sukkah! Believe me, there were days we went hungry, but we had a beautiful sukkah!

*Mi k'amcha Yisrael!* A nation of lions!

Have we forgotten that a mere seventy years ago Klal Yisrael was almost annihilated? That we were almost able to say Kaddish on Torah in the world? The Nazis annihilated six million of our people and made a special target of the "*Talmud lehrers*," the Gemara learners, whom they hated so much and whom they wanted to wipe off the face of the map. From a realistic point of view, Klal Yisrael was doomed. The Germans went so far as to make a museum to chronicle the soon to be extinct Jewish nation! And seventy years later Torah and *kedushah* are flourishing! How did this happen? By courageous Jews rising up and roaring. "*Na'aseh v'nishma* — we are going to start building anew!"

The Vilna Gaon used to say "*akshan yatzliach*, an *akshan* will be successful." *Akshan* could mean an obstinate and obnoxious person. That is a usually a very bad *middah*. What the Gaon was calling an "*akshan*" is a person who is determined, and stubbornly committed to doing what is right; a person who embodies the essence of יִתְגַּבֵּר כָּאֲרִי.

## ◎◎ Dreaming at the *Siyum HaShas*

At the recent *Siyum HaShas*, I was tempted to do something that would be very helpful to many people. I would ask all those thousands of people who finished *Shas* to write down all of the challenges, obstacles, disappointments, setbacks, and failures that they had encountered in the past seven years. I would offer each one as much paper as he needed, and I would tell him: Whether you are a *Daf Yomi maggid shiur* or an attendee, write down how many times you felt, "I just can't do this," "I can't go on like this," "I don't have it in me," "I don't have the patience," "I don't have the time," or "I don't have the ability."

How many thousands upon thousands of magnificent stories would there be of how people almost gave up — with very justifiable reasons! I would take all these thousands of papers and put them into a multivolume book which would be called אֵין דָּבָר הָעוֹמֵד בִּפְנֵי הָרָצוֹן. Look at what a human being is capable of doing if he's committed to do it. Look at these *giborei ko'ach* that have done the impossible! That is Klal Yisrael. That is *Na'aseh v'nishma*.

I had a second dream. I'd give out papers to the thousands of *neshei chayil* who raised a family of *ehrliche kinder*, of *frum, Torahdige* children. I would ask them to write down all the difficulties, challenges, obstacles, disappointments, setbacks, and failures that they experienced while raising their families in a world that is so, so far from *frum* and *ehrlich* and *heilig*. I would give that book a similar title, *The Book of Giborei Ko'ach*, or *The Book of Na'aseh V'nishma*. It would be the book of *Yidden* doing the impossible, which becomes reality — when we have *ratzon*.

There is no easy path in *Yiddishkeit*. But there is one thing that is perhaps the closest to the easy path that gets us through all difficulties, and that is the *ko'ach* of *ratzon*. The *ko'ach* of roaring proudly, "*Na'aseh v'nishma!*" Of rising defiantly and saying, "I will do what's right even if no one else is doing it!" It is the *ko'ach* of commitment, of making the decision that I'm going to do what is right no matter what.

## A Moment That Changed History

On the second day of Shavuos, we read *Megillas Rus*. One reason that we do so is because Rus was the grandmother of Dovid Hamelech whose *yahrtzeit* is on Shavuos. But, of course, the connection between Rus and the day of *Mattan Torah* runs much deeper than that. There is a very practical lesson that we have to take from Shavuos for the rest of the year.

When you think about it, the story is amazing. These two sisters, Rus and Orpah, had the same royal background and upbringing. They exhibited the same *mesirus nefesh* to marry into the family of Avimelech, and they shared the same fate. Their husbands died, their father-in-law died, and they were left as *almanos*, together with their mother-in-law, Naomi. But then Rus and Orpah part ways. Rus goes on to become the grandmother of Dovid Hamelech, and Orpah becomes the grandmother of Golias Harasha. What happened? How did two sisters end up in totally different worlds?

It was one crucial moment when Naomi told her two daughters-in-law, "I have nothing for you; go back home." Naomi was right. There was nothing that she could do for them. By all counts, both princesses should have returned to their homeland. Orpah must have asked herself, "Can I do this now?" And she looked at the situation with a practical eye. Realistically, Naomi had nothing for her. So she went back home.

But Rus persevered. וְרוּת דָּבְקָה בָּהּ — *and Rus clung to her* (*Rus* 1:14). Rus did not ask herself, "Can I do this?" She asked herself, "Do I have to do this? Is this the path that I must take in order to attain the personal greatness that I seek?" And she responded to her own question with great courage: *Na'aseh v'nishma!* She roared defiantly, "I will do it!" It was a moment of determination, a moment of decision, a moment of commitment: I will do what I have to do, no matter what is going on around me. And she became the forebear of Melech haMashiach. That is the message that we have to hear before Shavuos, on Shavuos, and every day of the year: the greatness of *Na'aseh v'nishma* and how it impacts our daily living.

## ✿ Brick Walls

The *Chovos Halevavos* (*Cheshbon Hanefesh*, *oifen* 21) writes that as part of a person's *cheshbon hanefesh*, his personal accounting, he must ask himself, "Am I becoming as great as I can become?" And he goes on to say that a person has to have aspirations and goals to do the impossible.

To do the impossible?

Yes, because the impossible is really possible. We have to try to discover the full potential that sometimes lies dormant within each one of us. To do so is to tap into the endless strength of אֵין דָּבָר הָעוֹמֵד בִּפְנֵי הָרָצוֹן.

Imagine a person who is thrown into jail. The day before his incarceration, he was unrestricted — he could live a full, active life. But now his life is reduced to staring at the four walls of the prison. He is thinking, "There's a world with so much to offer, just beyond these walls! I'm denied everything because a brick wall separates me from everything that is so precious to me." Every day that he sits in jail, he thinks, "If only I could penetrate this wall! This wall is separating me from all the *brachos* of this world!"

We should all think like that once in a while. There is so much that this world has to offer, and so much that a person can accomplish. But every person has his or her own struggles. For some it may be in learning or in *davening*, for others it may be in *tzedakah*, in *shemiras halashon*, in *tznius*. And the list goes on. And when people feel that they "cannot do it," they erect their very own brick wall blocking them from all of their potential greatness.

A person should think, "If only I could penetrate that wall, I could accomplish so much more!"

How do you chip away at that wall? How do you destroy that wall? The chisel is called *ratzon*. If there is a Klal Yisrael today it is because brave *Yidden* never let those brick walls stand for long.

How tragic it is when good people who mean well, and who struggle with issues, hear words of inspiration but make the fatal mistake of looking at their situation practically. "I can't do it, I can't change." And then all the words of inspiration are just nice words, easy listening, but lack any meaningful relevance.

This is when *Na'aseh v'nishma* becomes so crucial, when יִתְגַּבֵּר כַּאֲרִי becomes so important.

Many people have things that they really want to change, but they are convinced that they cannot. Let's use this as inspiration, these wonderful words of *Chazal*, to finally take that step to stand proudly, courageously and fearlessly, and to say *Na'aseh v'nishma* — "I will change; I will do this. I will begin to be more faithful in giving *tzedakah*, more involved in *tefillah*. I will start attending the *shiur* that I know I should be attending. I will show more excitement when my husband goes to learn because then he'll learn more and we will both earn more חַיֵּי עוֹלָם."

Let me conclude with this inspiring story.

The Vilna Gaon once met an old friend of his, whom he went to *cheder* with. The Vilna Gaon was at that time the *gadol hador*, the great Vilna Gaon. This friend was a far simpler person, but was personally close enough to the Gaon to ask this question:

"We both went to the same *cheder* and had the same upbringing. But look at me and look at you; how do you explain the difference?" The Gaon, who rarely spoke and certainly didn't make jokes, responded:

Do you remember when *rebbi* taught us the famous Gemara (*Chagigah* 9b):

אֵינוֹ דוֹמֶה מִי שֶׁשּׁוֹנֶה פִּרְקוֹ מֵאָה פְּעָמִים, לְמִי שֶׁשּׁוֹנֶה אוֹתוֹ מֵאָה וְאֶחָד — *It isn't the same when one learns something 100 times as when he learns it 101 times.*

The friend said, "Yes, of course I remember learning that Gemara as a young child…"

"Did you believe the Gemara?" asked the Gaon.

A bit taken aback, the friend replied, "But of course…!"

Said the Vilna Gaon with a twinkle in his eye, "Well, I didn't just believe the Gemara. I wanted to see for myself and tried it!"

There's so much practicality to that statement. We all believe that הַבָּא לְטָהֵר, מְסַיְּעִין לוֹ — *one who comes to purify himself [i.e., to improve] is granted Heavenly assistance.* We all know that אֵין דָּבָר הָעוֹמֵד בִּפְנֵי הָרָצוֹן. But the great person doesn't just believe it; he doesn't leave these statements of *Chazal* in the realm of the academic, he puts them into practice. He lives these lessons, he tries them out, and he sees how much *brachah* there is in uttering *Na'aseh v'nishma* in every situation.

לזכר ולעילוי נשמות

ר' פינחס וליבא סמיט ע"ה

———

ר' יצחק ומאטיל זעלענגוט ע"ה

———

ר' אפרים בן ציון וקילא וואלפין ע"ה

———

ר' ישראל מענדל וצירל גלאסמן ע"ה

———

גיטל ע"ה בת ר' יצחק נ"י

תנצב"ה

בס"ד

מוקדש לז"ן מורי ורבי הרה"ג הצדיק

**רבי חיים ברוך וואלפין זצ"ל**

שזכיתי ללמוד אצלו בשיעורי ערב יותר מעשרים
שנה, וזכיתי להתקרב אליו מאוד ולהנות מעצתו
בכל מקצועות החיים, עד שנעשתה נפשי קשורה
בנפשו. נועם מדותיו ואהבתו לכל אחד ומדת
הענוה שלו היו לנו למופת.

ואני תפילה שנזכה אני וב"ב לילך בדרכיו הנפלאים

הונצח ע"י תלמידו **פרץ חיים הלוי לעווין**

זכות הספר

יעמוד לזכות ולכבוד

**אדוני אבי מורי שיחי' ואמי מורתי תחי'**

אשר משחר נעוריהם העמידו ביתם

באור התורה והיראה סמוך ונראה לישיבות הק'

והנחילו לנו הדרך להיות תמיד דבקים בתלמידי חכמים

ושתולים בבית ה' בישיבות הק'

יתן השי"ת שיזכו ל'עוד ינובון בשיבה'

אורך ימים ושנים טובות

לראות דורות ישרים

בנים ובני בנים עוסקים בתורה וביראה

כברכת הבן

**פרץ חיים הלוי לעווין**

לזכר ולעילוי נשמת

ר' חיים צבי בן ר' שלמה ז"ל
רוזא בת ר' גדליה הלוי ע"ה
למשפחת וויינבערגער

ר' בנימין בן ר' יחיאל הלוי
רבקה העֶנא בת הרב ר' מנחם מעֶנדל ע"ה
למשפחת שֶאכנעֶר

הונצח ע"י שלמה אברהם וויינבערגער ומשפחתו

# לזכר ולעילוי נשמת

אבי מורי

הרה"ג רבי אורי שרגא הכהן הלמן זצ"ל

בן הר"ר ראובן ז"ל

תלמיד ישיבת מיר בפולין ובשנחאי, איש אשר רוח בו,

מסר נפשו למען חינוך בנות ישראל ברוח ישראל סבא

במשך למעלה מששים שנה

נלב"ע ביום כ"ז בניסן ה'תשס"ה

ואימי מורתי

הרבנית מרת חיה בלומה הלמן ע"ה

בת הגאון רבי נחום זצוק"ל הי"ד

נפש יקרה ואצילה, אהבת התורה נר לרגלה, יראת ה' היא אוצרה

שפכה ליבה כמים בתפילה, כל ימיה חסד וצדקה

נלב"ע ביום ט' באדר א' ה'תשע"ו

ת. נ. צ. ב. ה.

הונצח ע"י בנם

משה ורחל הכהן הלמן ומשפחתם

לזכר ולעילוי נשמת

האדם היקר באנשים
ר' אברהם זאב בן ר' יששכר ז"ל
למשפחת פרנס

הונצח ע"י משפחתו

לזכר ולעילוי נשמות
הרב דוד בן הרב צבי זצ"ל
ואשתו חנה בת רבי יוסף ע"ה
למשפחת צוקער
הונצח ע"י משפחתם

לזכר ולעילוי נשמת
רבי צבי בן רבי דוב הלוי זצ"ל פראנק
הונצח ע"י משפחתו